WOMEN IN AGRICULTURE

WOMEN IN AGRICULTURE

Strategy for Socio-Economic Empowerment

Dr. K. P. Wasnik

Publications

KALPAZ PUBLICATIONS
DELHI-110 052

Women in Agriculture
Strategy of their Socio-Economic Empowerment

Rs.750

ISBN: 81-7835-427-6

Published in 2006 in India by
Kalpaz Publications,
C-30, Satyawati Nagar,
Delhi-110 052
E-mail : kalpaz@hotmail.com

Contents

डॉ० भालचंद्र मुणगेकर
सदस्य
Dr. BHALCHANDRA MUNGEKAR
MEMBER

योजना आयोग
योजना भवन
नई दिल्ली–११०००१
PLANNING COMMISSION
YOJANA BHAWAN
NEW DELHI-110 001

Foreword

Women represent a crucial development force in the world economy and society. Despite significant contributions of women in the crop production, animal husbandry, fisheries and forestry, and post-harvest operations, those engaged in the formulation of policies have often tended to neglect the productive role of women. Similarly, rural development policies too rarely have taken into account women's needs and problems.

Women in the farm sector stand to benefit from new agricultural technologies and other innovations only if they have some control over household income from land, labour and other income-generating assets. Today, women in the farm sector do not seem to have meaningful access to the new farm technologies as agricultural extension services are favourably exposed to men. Further, farm women have little access to non-formal education, rural institution and extension services. Unless both women and men get an equal opportunity to contribute to various activities, their human capabilities cannot be equally and optimally utilized for productive purposes, which is conceived to be the crux of holistic human development, particularly, gender development.

Rural women's problems are further accentuated due to underemployment, unemloyment and poverty. To create a general awareness about the role played by women in agriculture and to increase their access and involvement in the overall farm economy with a view to increasing efficiency in agricultural sector, the Ministry of Agriculture, Government of India had formulated a scheme called 'Women in Agriculture'. In view of this, the research study conducted by Dr. K.P. Wasnik could be considered one of the good efforts of assessing the impact of this scheme on the decision-making, having a bearing on the socio-economic status of the women, resource use in agriculture, employment and income and constraints faced by the women in the farm sector, and ultimately sharing the benefits of the development programmes.

I am confident that the book would get wider acceptance by all concerned who are engaged in the welfare of farm women in particular and the women empowerment in general. Since the book provides new information about rural women, I am sure, it may help to stimulate further research on the socio-economic issues concerning the farm women.

New Delhi
17th November 2005

(Bhalchandra Mungekar)

Preface

The basic realities of development are not to be seen through a tremendous visible growth in the cities and increment of purchasing power of urban dwellers, but the social, economic and personal living constraints in the rural areas and particularly with the women folk. The important contribution of the farm women in agriculture production in India is being realized and their importance in decision making is now been taken care of. No doubt, women specific and women related policies and programmes have brought a perceptible improvement in the socio-economic status of the farm women in the country. Farm women's participation in income is believed to increase their socio-economic status and decision making power. With empowerment, women do not remain as 'object' of social change but become 'agent' of it.

In the present book, the scientific evaluation of the programme 'Women in Agriculture' for the farm women implemented so far have conclusively proved that when farm women given access to improved information and resources could increase agricultural production significantly. Their access to credit and employment opportunities have also been improved. Thus, access to modern agricultural technology and support services are the vital for the socio-economic empowerment for farm women.

It is matter of great privilege to express my deep sense of gratitude and feeling of indebtness to Dr. D.V. Kasar, my Ph.D. research guide and chairman of the advisory committee and Head of the Department of Agricultural Economics, Mahatma Phule Agricultural University, Rahuri, Maharashtra (India) for this scholastic guidance and constant encouragement throughout the course of this investigation and in preparation of this manuscript.

I avail this opportunity to express my deep sense of gratitude and indebtness to Dr. V. V. Sadamate, Additional Commissioner (Extension), Ministry of Agriculture, Govt. of India for continuous encouragement during the course of investigation. I also extend my thanks to my colleagues Dr. Balasaheb Pawar, Assisitance Professor MPKV Rahuri, Mr. A.G. Karande, Librarian MPKV, Mr. Ravidra Ingle, Chief Catalogour, MPKV and Mr, Pramod Jiwane for their valuable suggestions and inspiration to bring this book. My thanks are also due to Dr. Anil Surya for conceptulising the cover page of this book.

During the field work phase of the study, I was very fortunate to have a cooperation of Shri. Ashok Lokhande, District Superintending Agricultural Officer (DASO), Thane district and all his colleagues.

Heartiest thanks are also due to all beneficiary and non-beneficiary farm women and their family members of the selected villages among whom I had an opportunity to live and work who so gorgeously shared their work experiences, their worries and aspirations with me while collection of data for the present investigation.

I should not forrget to acknowledge the patience displayed moral support and encouragement given by my mother Smt. Puspa, wife Jyotsna and daughters Aishwarya and Avantika, my younger brothers Dayakar and Sunil which made this endeavourer possible.

Finally, Kalpaz Publications, Delhi deserved my special thanks in bringing out this work in the book form in a short period of time. Views expressed here are of mine not of the Government.

New Delhi
Nov. 2005.

(Krupakar Pralhad Wasnik)

1
Introduction

Women represent one of the crucial development forces in the world. As per the world economic profile, they form 50 per cent of the world population, contribute 60 per cent of working force, making up to 30 per cent of the official labour force and contribute 50 per cent in the food production. At the home front, nearly 84 per cent of all economically active women in India are engaged in agriculture and allied activities (Anonymous, 2002 a).

Agriculture, the single largest production endeavour in India, contributing 25 per cent of GDP is increasingly becoming a female activity. Agriculture sector employs 80 per cent of all economically active women in the country as compared to 63 per cent of men. It is estimated that there are 75 million women in dairying as against 15 million men and 20 million in other livestock activities as compared to 1.5 million men (Anonymous, 2002 b).

Status and role of Indian women and their problems are linked to the history and social system of the country. Women constitute half of the population. Yet, they are not treated on par with men in many aspects of life. Though five decades have passed since independence, women are yet in the grip of the traditional role resulted into the economic dependence, social neglect and political ignorance, eventually preventing them to attain their due place in society.

During 1990's, five decades after independence, women were travelling the long road towards freedom. For many, women development means increase in hardships and marginalization. Given India changed position vis-à-vis the global capitalist economy, there is increasing polarization within all manner of groups (Roy and Basu, 1999).

Women's status in society can be measured in terms of educational level, income, employment as well as the role played by them in the family, society and the community. Education affects employment opportunities and the decision-making role. Economic viability and education contribute either singly or jointly to women's emancipation. In fact, education and employment of women (Sarma, 1991) are the first prerequisite not only for improving the status of women but also for moving towards gender equality.

Regarding farm labour, female workers contribute significantly to household income across all farm sizes and their earnings are found crucial for landless and small farm households. The status of female agricultural workers in decision-making is very poor. Female workers belonging to big farm households have a better say as compared to others. The ownership of land is almost nonexistent for female workers from small and landless households. They usually surrender their earned income to the family pool and they have no freedom to spend their earned money. Female agricultural workers contribute significantly to households but they lack education, health and other support services and often do not have access to economic resources. Moreover, they are not integrated into the mainstream of the development process. As revealed by Tuteja (2000), in the rural areas despite being backbone of the village economy, the strategy adopted by the government to increase women welfare during the past decade has not yielded adequate results.

1.1 Socio-Economic Issues of the 'Farm Women'

Gender inequalities have the largest impact on women and it has wider detrimental impact on development. When the creative abilities and personal contributions of half of the population are subjected to constant subjugation, economic progress is bound to be adversely affected. Within the household, women have less entitlement to household goods and poorer command over a range of other productive resources including education, land, information and financial resources and the labour to help them to undertake economically gainful activities. This in turn prevents women from building up their skills and resources. Beyond the direct effect on their ability to generate income, these factors adversely affect the decision-making capacity within the family. Women play a crucial role in all societies. However, their low socio-economic status in a historical perspective is largely based on the myth that women are inferior agents of production. Much of the labour contributed in the domestic chore and outside is not usually considered as productive, even though their work is equally essential for the smooth functioning of the economy whether at the community, farm or at household level. In the recent past, the World Women Conference was held at Nairobi (1985) has drawn attention to the productive nature of domestic work done by women and demanded that proper valuation should be made of such work. If the domestic work is paid, it would account for as of national income.

Empowerment of the women with resource support and information is crucial to ensuring sustainability in food production and consumption. Women occupy a central role in food production, food processing and consumption. They often participate in the cultivation of food crops and are active managers and users of resources in the most cases. However, they do not own land and therefore lack collateral assets, which could give them access to credit thus imploring to take the decision on what should be produced. Various studies have revealed that when women control the household income, they generally spend on entire household, while men spend more on items for themselves. One of the studies in Jamaica showed that compared with male-headed households, female-headed households consume food of higher nutritional quality. Women make food choice to nurture the family and, therefore, empowering them with resources to make decision in food production is essential (Gopalan, 2001).

1.2 Farm Women and Modern Technology

In the words of Merton (1973) "technology is good not because of the intrinsic character of the advancing technology, but because of its human implications. As large number of diversely placed men have the occasion to regard it as such, and this in turn depends upon the structure of society which determines which group and individual gain from this increased bounty and which suffer social dislocation and human cost entailed by the new technology". In accordance with this line of thinking, the impact of new farm technology on women would be different from men as women occupy different positions in the social system. There is growing evidence from several countries that opening up of international trade in commodities and farm products tends to marginalize women in the formal production system. The latest census leads further evidence of this with a sharp rise in female work participation in rural areas from 22.3 per cent in 1991 to 25.7 per cent in 2001. In fact, there are enough indicators that morale, structural, institutional and organizational changes underway push women further to the fringes of the formal economy. Studies of green revolution economies have shown that introduction of technology which was traditionally considered women's domain pushes farm women out of jobs.

The women farmers have multi-dimensional roles as mothers, housewives, producers and entrepreneurs. Therefore, it is essential to adopt a multidimensional technology approach for women covering essentially four spaces namely, psycho-space related to her mental makeup and attitude, socio-space attached to her house and society, techno-space related to her productive aspects and eco-space related to credit aspects. Because of the responsibility of the households and children, women prefer to have home-based enterprises. Agribusiness is considered to be a sub-sector governed by women, however, credit gap and quality control are the major problems faced by the women entrepreneurs (Rao, 2002).

Modernization and advancement of technology have not benefited women. In fact, in many areas women have been displaced from their traditional jobs because the technology necessitates training, upgradation of knowledge and skill which are out of their reach. Improved agricultural technology accompanied by partial mechanization had affected women from all socio-economic background positively, either by relieving the women cultivators who were from higher socio-economic strata having large land holding or by increasing employment of women who were from lower socio-economic strata. Full mechanization of agriculture had to relieve the women of high socio-economic strata and it had negatively affected the women from lower caste and lowest income groups by reducing the demand for employment in peak season (Kaur, 1988).

Farm women in Japan account for just over 60 per cent of total agricultural labour force and provide about 40 per cent of labour in rice cultivation. They operate and maintain farm machinery and play an important role in farm decision-making. Fifty per cent of women have access to machinery, which implies that women are no longer mercy to labourers, sub-ordinate to patriarch but are independent workers capable of using machineries on their own judgment. In China too, women farmers perform all type of operations, which are done by their male counterparts.

Thus, when Japanese farm women can perform such heavy and arduous farm activities, then why the Indian farm women cannot do so. It clearly shows that technology is not sex-biased, it is gender-neutral. There is no defect in technologies generated, rather it is the socio-economic barriers which prevent Indian farm women to adopt such modern technologies. In India, very few or no efforts have been made to ensure that farm women are also exposed to new technologies in agriculture. (Ohki, 1983)

1.3 Involvement of Farm Women in Decision Making Process

Decision-making is the process of consciously choosing courses of action from available alternatives and integrating them for achieving the desired goal. It involves deciding on what goals are to be achieved, what means and methods are to be adopted in reaching them, based on what facts are available and how they are integrated. The decision-making is generally influences by the level of knowledge, cost involved and time available in taking and implementing the decisions. Women participate in decision making related to farming and household service, despite their access to production resources and extension services had so far been very limited. Though there are rapid advances in new technologies, their transfer to the rural women has largely been neglected. It is being increasingly felt that the technical knowledge of the farm women acquired over the generation is not being updated. However, during the recent years, farm women are being viewed as an important source of diffusion of technology and thereby strengthening the process of decision making in agriculture. Though decision-making is a complex process, nevertheless, farm women knowingly or unknowingly participate in the decision- making process regarding the farming enterprise which is based on their long standing field experience.

1.4 Economic Empowerment of Farm Women

The issue of women empowerment is very complex and multidimensional. Besides, providing rights and creating awareness does not solve the problem of women. The development programmes and policies, which aim at women empowerment, should categorize women based on their age, caste, class, region, education, etc as they are not a homogeneous group which aims at empowerment.

For more than a decade in India, the term 'empowerment' has been widely used in relation to women. The Eighth Five-Year plan gave greater emphasis on women as equal partners and participants in the development process and thereby conceptual thinking shifted from development to empowerment of farm women. Obviously, empowerment is about power and about changing the balance of power. Power itself can be simply described as control over resources and ideology. This means that women in general and poor women in particular are powerless because they do not have any of these controls.

Any intervention for improving the condition of women involved in agricultural activities should begin with an understanding of their role profile in terms of various agricultural and related activities. Analysis of their role, both traditional and current will enable one to identify the areas of intervention. This becomes the input for designing programmes of development by way of opening up of new avenues of income generation and matching technologies to the specific tasks However, in carrying out the programmes, appropriate research and extension, input supply and policy backup is of supreme importance. Once the programme of women's development in agriculture is launched fulfilling all these necessary conditions, it facilitates better performance of the role by the women, thereby enabling them to increase income, reduce drudgery and enhance their status in the society.

In ordor to improve upon socio-economic status of women, areas of possible interventions are:

1. Providing more assured wage labour market,
2. Identification of land based employment avenues, and
3. Non-farm employment.

All development programmes designed for women empowerment can broadly be categorized into:

1. Income generation through land based activities coupled with non-farm activities based on dissemination and adoption of modern farm technologies, and
2. Exclusively non-farm activities with least focused on adoption of latest agricultural technologies.

The basic objectives of India's agricultural and rural development programmes through state intervention were:

1. Increase in agricultural productivity and diversification of rural economy,
2. Reduction of poverty, inequality, and unemployment to achieve the growth with social justice,
3. Promoting people's participation for stimulating growth and expanding democratic base, and
4. Improving the quality of life in rural areas.

The major instruments designed to achieve these objectives were

(a) Agrarian reforms,

(b) Modernization of agriculture,

(c) Development of rural infrastructure and delivery system especially communication, education, primary health centre and other basic services,

(d) Development of irrigation, extension services and institutional credit to reduce poor farmers dependence on traditional exploitative credit system,

(e) Promotion of rural growth and diversification with the programmes of employment generation, and

(f) Democratic decentralization through the Panchayat Raj Institution.

At the time when strategies to increase the food production were viewed as crucial, farm women's role was viewed as food producers, processors and distributors, apart from the stray reference to women's role in the post-harvest operations and their role as consumers.

1.5 Development Projects based on Non-Farm Activities

The need for tackling women's problems through organized institutional mechanism was first recognised in the Community Development Programme initiated in 1952. In this programme, the economic component for women was missing as they were primarily seen as housewives with major focus on their physical welfare with slant on social education. The programme for rural women followed this course until the sixth plan where there was a major shift in the government policies and programmes for women in India by recognizing them as an important economic agent. The Sixth Plan introduced some major changes in the programme for women's empowerment primarily through promoting economic independence. It was stipulated that women were to form at least one-third of the beneficiaries of the scheme of Training of Rural Youth for Self-Employment (TRYSEM). Credit from bank and subsidies to the beneficiaries below poverty line were provided for self- employment and income generating activities in a variety of sectors like animal husbandry and other land-based activities such as weaving and handicraft. The Seventh Plan document acknowledged that during the first three years of the Sixth Plan, benefits were not flowing to women adequately. The new scheme for the Development of Women and Children in Rural Areas (DWCRA) was launched on pilot basis. This programme aimed at enabling women to take up income generating activities. Simultaneously, the National Rural Employment Programme (NREP) and Rural Landless Employment Guarantee Programme (RLEGP) were introduced during the Sixth Plan. (Sen, 1993). During the Ninth Plan period, IRDP, DWCRA, TRYSEM, Million Well Scheme merged into single programme called Swarna Jayanti Gram Swa Rojgar Yojana (SGSRY) in April, 1999. It aimed at promoting micro enterprise and helping the rural poor into self helps group (Economic Survey, 2001). In this programme, the major focus has been given on empowerment of rural and farm women.

1.6 Development of Farm Women through Agriculture based Projects

The Government of India have started various planned programmes for farm women which aim at creating desirable productive assets and income generating capacities of farm women. These programmes lay emphasis on the economic upliftment and empowerment of farm women.

It was for the first time in the Fourth Five Year Plan that efforts were made by the Ministry of Agriculture to address the training and extension needs of women farmers with new and improved technology through "Farmers Training and Education Programme" in which a network of 150 Farmers Training Centres (FTCs) were established to seal the invisible gap between the recommended package of practices and farm women's knowledge and skill. In this programme, linkage of the supply of production inputs with improved technical training supported by farm radio broadcast and functional literacy was provided The unique feature of this programme was that for the first time, a cognisance of women's participation in agriculture was taken.

During the Fifth Five Year Plan, the transfer of technology approach through Training and Visit System (T&V) of extension was launched on pilot basis in the mid 1970's in Rajasthan and Madhya Pradesh. This programme was subsequently expanded to other parts of the country. The Training and Visit System of extension was not able to reach to farm women because it was based on the assumption that information given to family head would automatically be disseminated to other family members. So, the technical advice regarding activities performed by women farmers was channelized by male extension workers to the male family members. Moreover, the concentration of the system was only on important crops rather than diversified agriculture in which women are generally involved. Thus, the system failed to address itself to information needs of women farmers.

The intervention of planning mechanism for the development of women, in fact, started in the Sixth Five-Year Plan (1980-1985). The earlier FiveYear Plans (1950-1979) treated the issues of women development as subject of 'welfare' and clubbed these with other categories of welfare, such as, the old, the disabled and the destitute. On the line with the facts of the sixth plan, Ministry of Agriculture, Government of India had launched a special project viz; 'Women in Agriculture' with the assistance of DANIDA, aid agency of Danish Government. The project was launched in eleven districts of Karnataka State. Institutional training to farm women followed up with the village-based pre-seasonal training was the main training component of the programme. Mobilization of women into groups for channelizing other support services to women farmers was another feature of the programme. The programme is currently being implemented in all the districts of the Karnataka State except Bidar district.

Seventh Five Year Plan (1985-1990) stressed the need for paying special attention to improve the existing skills of women by imparting new skills under various programmes like farmers training, fodder production, post-harvest technology, training in horticulture, etc. Two more women specific projects in agriculture sector were launched in Tamil Nadu and Orissa (1987) and Gujarat (1989) with the assistance of DANIDA.

The strategy of the Eighth Five Year Plan (1990-95) was to increase participation of women in economic activities by getting them organized, to expand their access and control over resources. During this plan, two more projects with DUTCH assistance were launched i.e. one in six districts of Andhra Pradesh and another in eight districts of Madhya Pradesh. Both these projects aimed at providing training and extension support to women farmers through Farmers' Training Centres.

The central sector scheme viz, 'Women in Agriculture' was launched during the Eighth Plan on the pilot basis fully supported by Extension Division of the Ministry of Agriculture, Goverment of India. This programme was launched in Himachal Pradesh, Haryana, Kerala, Maharashtra, Punjab, Rajasthan and Uttar Pradesh which was aimed at to motivate and mobilise the farm women through Self Help Groups (SHGs) so that agricultural support services, technology, extension services, credit and marketing intervention were channelized through these SHGs. Besides regular technical training in agriculture and allied areas, managerial, organizational and entrepreneurial skill development trainings were provided to farm women to help them to develop into 'self help viable groups' which can orchestrate their own activities. Most of the women groups have become activity groups and are making efforts to consolidate these activities by linking them with the markets. During the Ninth Plan period, it was extended to fifteen states with an estimated cost of Rs. 4.67 crore.

Special sub-programmes on the 'empowerment of women farmers' were launched during the Ninth Plan period with assistance under UNDP Food Security Programme in Orissa, Andhra Pradesh and Uttar Pradesh. Addressing the gender concern was one of the priority areas under Innovations in Technology Dissemination (ITD) component of National Agricultural Technology Programme (NATP), which was implemented in the seven major States of the country.

The National Agriculture Policy announced in July 2000, seeks to mainstream gender concerns in agriculture. It promises to initiate appropriate structural, functional and institutional measures to empower women, build their capabilities and improve their access to inputs, technology and other farming resources. Reforms in agricultural extension have already been initiated and proposed on wider scale, which envisage mainstreaming of women in agriculture as one of the key areas of reforms during the Tenth Five Year Plan period. In the Tenth Five Year Plan, the activities of the central sector scheme of 'Women in Agriculture' have been successfully subsumed and 30 per cent of the total resources have been allocated for gender purposes and benefit in proportion have to essentially flow to women farmers to them to ease their day-to-day problems and requirements in agriculture and allied sectors.

The Extension Division of the Agriculture Ministry has been implementing farm women specific programmes in agriculture with central and bilateral assistance since 1982. The experiences of working with women programme has highlighted a series of critical gap which needs to be addressed along two path namely through 'Strategy of Mainstreaming' and through 'Strategy of Agenda Setting'. Agenda setting essentially aims at providing women farmers with structural, legislative and material resource so that they can participate and benefit at par with male farmers by setting their own development agenda. The setting up of the Gender Resources Centre in the Ministry of Agriculture is step towards initiating action on the said two paths. The gender resource centre is a focal point for convergence of all issues related to gender in agriculture and would serve as a watchdog to identify and address gender related issues and ensure that policies in agriculture reflect the national commitment to empowerment of farm women. It is also rendering advisory services to the state in implementing the extension reforms by adequately incorporating gender in their state extension work plan. A Gender Budgeting Cell has also been constituted in the Ministry of Agriculture, which is located in the Directorate of Extension, Pusa, New Delhi. Gender budgeting cell looks into the budgetary commitments of various schemes / programmes of the Ministry of Agriculture, Goverment of India and the proportionate flow of benefits of the programmes to women farmers.

The Central Sector Scheme 'Women in Agriculture' was implemented in 15 states in the country since 1994-95. This was the first extension scheme of its type which exclusively targeted on farm women to mobilize them for adoption of improved agricultural technology, creation of off-farm employment and empowering farm women to assert their rights in family and society. This programme was being regularly monitored to assess the status of project implementation through the implementing agencies. To assess the socio-economic impact of this scheme, a few studies have been undertaken in the state of Haryana by Rai *et al* (1999) and Anita *et al* (2000), in Andhra Pradesh by Chandravati *et al* (1999) and in Tamil Nadu by Jayasree (1997). Gitanjali and Kathy (2001) had evaluated impact of the scheme in Karnataka, Madhya Pradesh, Orissa and Tamil Nadu. Ramkrishnan and Reddy (2002) undertook a study to find out the impact of Tamil Nadu Women in Agriculture (TANWA) in Tamil Nadu. All these studies highlighted the impact of the scheme on farm women in respect of their technical knowledge, operational skill, attitude toward agriculture, participation of farming activities, involvement in decision-making and other socio-economic impacts. However, not a single study was targeted to assess the scheme impact in respect of socio-economic development and empowerment of farm women, involvement of farm women in decision making, increased use of resources, gaps in technology adoption, cost and return structure of beneficiary farms, income and employment generated because of the implementation of this scheme and constraints in availing the benefits of scheme.

Hence, it was felt necessary to take up an economic study for scientific assessment of this scheme in terms of its socio-economic impact on the sample households.

1.7 'Women in Agriculture'–The Scheme under Study

A central sector scheme 'Women in Agriculture' had been formulated and implemented by Extension Division, Ministry of Agriculture, Goverement of India during the Eighth Five Year

Plan on pilot basis covering one district each of the seven States in the country.

In Maharashtra, the central sector scheme 'Women in Agriculture' was in operation since 1994-95 in three blocks of Thane district viz. Dahanu, Palghar and Wada. The present study, therefore, has been conducted in Thane district of Maharashtra State.

1.7.1 The Broad Objectives of the Scheme

1. To motivate, mobilize and organize farm women into small groups in order to channelize agricultural developmental programmes and extension support system through network of women groups,
2. To co-ordinate group activities for agricultural and income generating activities,
3. To assess the need of women farmers in terms of agriculture support such as input, technology and extension support, and
4. To provide adequate organizational and financial support to the women's groups to organize them into self-help thrift groups.

1.7.2 The Major Components of the Scheme

There are six major components of the scheme, which are stated below:

- *Identification of facilitators*—One women facilitator in block preferably Agriculture or Home Science graduate to liaison between the Department of Agriculture and groups of farm women within taluka.
- *Identification of link workers*—A forward looking women from the group is identified as a link worker to keep the liaison among women group, facilitator and Agricultural Department.
- *Organization of women*—In a block, 10 women groups each consisting of 25 farm women to promote thrift habit,

acquiring agricultural technology and to undertake economic activities.

- *Result demonstrations*—Technology dissemination through result demonstrations.
- *Mahila Gosthi*—Once in a year inviting all women's groups in district.
- *Village level training and Study tour*—Study tours are organized within and outside of state and frequent training at village for group members.

1.7.3 Implementation of the Scheme

The scheme was implemented and executed by the State Agriculture Department, Maharashtra State through District Superintending Agricultural Officer (DSAO) of Thane district. At the field level, Taluka Agricultural Officer (TAO) was an executing officer. This scheme was monitored regularly by the Secretary, Agriculture through Commissionorate of Agriculture Pune, Divisional Joint Director Thane, DSAO Thane and TAOs Dahanu, Palghar and Wada. The implementation performance was periodically reviewed by the senior officials of the Directorate of Extension, Government of India, Ministry of Agriculture, New Delhi, Commisionorate of Agriculture, Maharashtra State Pune and District Superintending Agricultural Officer (DSAO), Thane, Maharashtra. To facilitate coordination of the scheme, the District Coordination Committee and State Coordination Committee were set up. These committees were to review the progress and sort out constraints, if any, in the implementation and to ensure the flow of benefits of other developmental programmes to the farm women of the scheme.

The Directorate of Extension, New Delhi, was responsible for providing financial assistance and advise to the State governments at all stages of implementation of the scheme including planning and implementation of the training programmes for the facilitators.

1.7.4 Organizational Set-up for Implementation of the Scheme

1. At the National Level	Directorate of Extension Ministry of Agriculture Govt. of India, New Delhi
2. At the State Level	The Secretary of Agriculture, Dept. of Agriculture, Govt. of Maharashtra, Mumbai
Commissioner of Agriculture Pune, Maharashtra State	
3. At District Level	District Superintending Agricultural Officer, Thane, Maharashtra State
4. At Sub-Divisional Level	Sub-Divisional Agricultural Officer, Deptt. of Agriculture (Wada and Palghar)
5. Taluka Level	Taluka Agriculture Officer (Dahanu, Palghar and Wada)
	Facilitator (One)
6. Village Level	One Link Worker for group of 25 farm women

The State Agriculture Department was responsible for the implementation of the scheme in the State through the Director (Extension and Training). The District Agency was accountable for the motivation, and mobilization of farm women for formulation of women's groups to channelize technical, managerial and entrepreneurial trainings.

1.7.5 Progress of the Implementation of the Scheme under Study

1.7.5.1 Progress of the Scheme in the Country (1994-95 to 2001-02)

The scheme of Women in Agriculture was approved for implementation and extended in one district of 15 States in India during the Ninth Plan under which, about 415 viable groups of women farmers were constituted. About 7200 farm women were trained through 1603 village-base training camps. The link workers were also trained through 78 training camps. The extension support was provided to the enrolled farm women through 497 result demonstrations and 66 study tours. A supplementary credit delivery system in the form of Self–Help Groups (SHGs) to addresses the problems and aspirations of the poor women.

1.7.5.2 Progress of the Scheme in Maharashtra State

The scheme was launched in the Thane district of Maharashtra State in the year 1994-95 and Rs. 53. 35 lakh was spent on different activities till 2001-02. During this period of scheme implementation, 14 study tours were organised through which 337 farm women were benefited. The facilitators and the link workers were trained by organising 8 and 14 training programmes respectively, and beneficiary farm women were trained through 469 three days refreshment trainings in their villages. To demonstrate the latest technology on their farms, result demonstrations were conducted on various aspects such as paddy, vegetables, mushroom production, bee keeping, vermi-compost and hybrid rice. The group activities were promoted through 30 Self Help Groups (SHGs) of beneficiary farm women.

The interactions of beneficiary farm women from three tahsils of Thane district were promoted by organising six one day Mahila Gosthis i.e. seminar at the district level.

1.8 Objectives of the Study

The following objectives were set for this study:

1. To study the impact of the scheme on level of decision making by farm women and their socio-economic empowerment,
2. To study the impact of scheme on the farm business economy and resource use productivity of major inputs in crop production on sample households.
3. To examine the differentials in employment and income of sample households as a result of implementation of the scheme,
4. To identify the factors influencing employment and income of sample households, and
5. To study the problems faced by the beneficiaries while availing the benefits of the scheme.

1.9 Hypotheses

The study had the following hypotheses:

1. The continuous training, result demonstration, exchange visits and mahila gosthies have helped to enhance the knowledge of beneficiary women and these have resulted in greater involvement in decision making and family management.
2. The scheme has benefited the farm women beneficiaries in terms of higher input use, productivity and returns besides relatively efficient farm resource use,
3. The assistance received by sample beneficiaries helped in increasing the employment and income of their family, and
4. The problems being faced by the beneficiaries of the scheme are redressed regularly.

1.10 Utility of the Study

On realizing the involvement of farm women in technology dissemination and adoption process through the scheme under study many State governments are diverting the resources for expanding this project in the respective States. The detailed outcome of the study on employment, income, rise in productivity and resources use, constraint analysis would certainly facilitate planners, extension managers, Agricultural Universities and NGO's working for farm women in designing the effective projects which will have bearing on the empowerment of farm women. The result of the study would facilitate for effective interventions in the following areas.

- To design the farm women empowerment strategies through the agricultural development programmes.
- To design the programmes for rural areas to generate the employment and income.
- To formulate the strategy for convergence of agricultural and rural development programmes at various levels.
- To design the proper farm media strategies.
- To develop the redressal system on the basis of constraints analysis, and
- To formulate the strategies for technology dissemination through the farm women.

This study will able to provide the insight to the researchers engaged in social sciences on the issues of development of farm women in general and their decision making, socio-economic empowerment and different strategies for gainful employment in rural area in particular.

2

Review of Literature

This chapter is devoted to review in brief some of the relevant empirical studies related to the topic under study. Scanning of relevant literature is immensely important while undertaking any systematic research study. It helps the researcher in many ways. Firstly, it helps to formulate the theoretical framework. Secondly, it tells what has been done in the past and what remains to be attended and thirdly, it helps to build up the confidence of researcher in conducting and interpreting the results. In a way, it forms an integral part of any systematic research work.

In India, women in general and farm women in particular were neglected before and for long time even after independence. On realizing the need of welfare of farm women by providing all sorts of assistance, the government had started some programmes on pilot basis throughout the country. A few research scholars had attempted to study the impact of rural development projects on farm productivity, employment, income and the different facets of farm women's contribution to the household economy. Therefore, an attempt is made in this chapter to review some of the relevant studies conducted earlier, which have direct or indirect bearing on the objectives of the present investigation. The same have been presented under the following sub-headings.

2.1: Decision Making and Socio-economic Empowerment of Farm Women,

2.2: Impact of Development Programme on Farm Business Economy,

2.2.1: Resource use in Crop Production,

2.2.2: Labour Utilization Pattern in Crop Production,

2.2.3: Gaps in Technology Adoption,

2.2.4: Costs and Returns Analysis in Farm Business,

2.2.5: Resource Use Efficiency in Corp Production,

2.3: Differentials in Employment and Income because of Schemes/ Programmes, and

2.4: Constraints observed by Beneficiaries while Availing the Benefits of Projects/Schemes.

2.1 Decision-Making and Socio-Economic Empowerment of Farm Women

As regards to participation of farm women in decision making process at the household as well as beyond the household level, the separate spare of responsibilities between women and men tend to support the fact that women and men have different access of influence. Men, most commonly run the family farm and exercise the control over the family activities. Both spouses take joint decisions related to family matters such as the allocation of money for the household needs, children's education, health problems and assistance to the elderly persons. However, rural women's ability to make independent decisions on education, employment and in agricultural production activities is still considerably smaller than men. Studies undertaken by several researchers in the past related to the extent of decision making by farm women and factors which influence the decision making behaviour of farm women have been reviewed and presented below.

Alcober and Parrilla (1989) based on their study on gender role in sweet potato production, processing and utilisation in eastern Visayas of Philippines indicated that joint farming and decision-making were carried out by males and females in sweet potato production, processing and utilization. Generally, women (housewives and daughters) tended to concentrate on certain farm practices such as planting, weeding, harvesting, marketing, and processing. Men were charged with land clearing, ploughing and transporting the produce. Except in processing, decisions related to sweet potato production were mostly made by the husbands. However, the wives, sons and daughters were always supportive. Apparently, the urgency to increase the overall production and the very limited farm resources were the reasons for the housewives and daughters' high level of involvement in sweet potato farming. Majority of the root crop farmers could not afford to finance farm activities. Thus, most family members worked together in the various agricultural tasks to operate their small farm.

Punia *et al* (1991) conducted a study in three districts of Haryana and observed that involvement of women in decision making was found to be more in age group of 36-45 years as compared to younger women who were considered inexperienced and did not have the status as the middle aged mother had. About 60 per cent of the farm women were engaged in the activities related to agriculture, but their participation in decisions regarding farm affair was much less as only 18. 75 per cent.

Ghose (1993) conducted a study in Birbhum District of West Bengal which revealed that 20 per cent women beneficiaries of IRDP could exercise their options at the time of spending, while 65.42 per cent women were not at all consulted by male members though the IRDP assistance was given to female members. This indicated that women had to accept the male supremacy within the households with nil or low entitlements of income.

Shirolkar (1993) conducted a study of 97 farm women engaged in dairy occupation from Pune district of Maharashtra state regarding extent of participation of farm women in decision making about the important aspects of dairy occupation. She concluded that out of eleven socio-economic parameters, six parameters namely age of farm women, size of family, social rank, experience, knowledge and participation in work were positively and significantly influenced the decision making of farm women. The farm women of 30 years age, belonged to small family size (up to 5 members), more the experience in dairy occupation (21 years and above), higher knowledge in dairy occupation (score above 35), higher participation in work (score 91 and above) had highly and statistically significant influence on decision making. The another five parameters namely higher education of farm women, higher size of holding (5 ha. and above), exposure to more sources of information, extension contacts and size of livestock had no bearing on decision making of farm women. The farm women had participated in decision-making irrespective of source of information, either more or less extension contacts and irrespective of size of livestock maintained by them.

Kadlag (1994) conducted a study on role of farm women in decision-making in farming in Ahmednagar district of Maharashtra. She concluded that a majority of farm women had actively participated in decision making belonging to major age group (35 years and above), small size of family, low economic status and low annual gross income. The study further revealed that there was positive impact of participation of farm women in the decision-making process on productivity of crops. Major reasons for low participation of farm women in decision making were dominance of men in the family, illiteracy of farm women, less exposure to the outside world, lack of confidence, shyness, lack of knowledge regarding improved agricultural technologies.

Nand *et al* (1994) conducted a study of 98 farm women belonging to the families participating in the Central Potato Research Institute's Technology Transfer Programme in Bhojpur district of Bihar. The study revealed that women provided the high level of consultancy in decision making with regard to marketing of produce and storage, a medium level of consultancy on sale and purchase of land, purchase of farm machineries, sale and purchase of animals, purchase of fertilizers, sowing time, method of sowing and intercultural operations. Farm women were less consulted while taking decisions on adoption of new technology, crop protection, fertilization, use of chemicals for spraying and time of irrigation which indicated that the final decisions on all these matters were taken by men only.

Chakravarty and Chakravarty (1996) conducted a comparative study of Dutch and Indian farm women and concluded that the respondents regarded themselves as helpers on the farms, not workers. However, an increasingly business-like attitude was observed among the women. It was further observed that women from both the countries had greater involvement in decision making if the farms were of small size. However, decision-making was the responsibility of the men in large holdings. It was also concluded that very few differences exist in the status of farm women from the Netherlands and India.

Thakor (1996) conducted a study in Kheda district of Gujarat state which revealed that more than 50 per cent of farm women having small farm holding never participated in decision making regarding choice of crop, type of weeding to be adopted, type of labour to be taken to field and distribution of work to labour. More than 60 per cent of farm women who belonged to medium categories of farms could take a decision about time of sowing, transplanting and type of weeding to be adopted. In case of large farm's women, it was observed that, majority of women (60 per cent) always took decisions regarding storage of produce, number of animals to be maintained and type of feed to be given to animals. In the absence of male partner of her family, she sometimes took a decision related to distribution of work to the hired labour. Women who belong to the large families because of their socio-economic status in the society felt that doing work with hired labour in the farm was a way to lose their dignity. Therefore, their direct involvement in various agricultural operations such as sowing, weeding, working with labourers and the extent of their decision making on such issues was very low.

Khatik and Pandey (1997) conducted a study of 100 farm women to assess the extent of their involvement in decision making and the effect of various socio-economic variables on their participation in sugarcane cultivation in Uttar Pradesh. The results indicated that 57 per cent of farm women had a medium level of decision-making ability and 43 per cent had a high level of involvement in decision making related to sugarcane cultivation. Education was found to be significantly correlated with women's participation in sugarcanc cultivation and the decision making process.

Talukdar and Karmarkar (1997) identified the problems faced in decision making in agriculture through personal interviews of 100 randomly selected farm women in Golaghat district of Assam, India. The major problems faced by farm women in decision making were lack of economic resources under their command (90 per cent), lack of contact with information sources (87 per cent) and lack of pertinent facts or knowledge about agriculture (81 per cent). The other important problems identified were lack of support from extension agencies, lack of command in implementation of decisions, low educational status and low mobility.

Rimawi (1998) investigated an impact of the selected socio-economic characteristics on the contribution of Jordanian women farmers in plant production activities and participation in decision-making process using a sample of 152 farm women. The degrees of farm women involvement in farming activities and participation in decision-making were 84 per cent and 70 per cent, respectively. The findings indicated that less educated women whose husbands had off-farm employment and smallholdings in the irrigated areas were likely to contribute more in farming activities and decision-making. Women who were married to illiterate husbands or unmarried who had smaller households, whose farms had a source of irrigation and who contribute more to farming activities were likely to participate in decision making. Regional differences were observed between women farmers in contributing to farming activities, but not in participation in decision-making. The study recommended for training, extension and development programmes targeted at women farmers to address their needs. Efforts need to be made to train farm women to simplify their work and to promote the use of intermediate technologies which would make women's work more effective, productive and less tedious.

Alagumani (1999) analysed the women's role in household decision on consumption, production and investment to become a entrepreneur in Madurai district of Tamil Nadu. The study revealed that farm women were involved to the extent of about 73 per cent with regard to decisions concerning household consumption. The mean score for involvement of farm women in the decisions related to crop production was 55.74 per cent indicating that half of the women did not involve themselves in the decision making process purely due to male domination in the decisions on crop production and lack of interest on the part of rural women.

Bhuvaneshari and Kannan (1999) examined the participation of women and their role in decision-making process in farm and off-farm activities and the experiences of specific programmes meant for increasing the participation of women in agriculture and employment generation opportunities for them. A sample of 100 farm women from Lalgudi block of Tiruchirapalli district of Tamil Nadu was studied in the year 1997-98. The study revealed that female alone took decisions on par with their husbands on use of seed (39 per cent), seed storage (28 per cent), sowing (23 per cent), application of manure (24 per cent) and taking care of animals (34 per cent). The farm women's active participation in decisions on these operations was due to the effective skill and knowledge gained through organized programmes by government and non-government organizations.

Jyothi *et al* (1999) examined the economic empowerment of farm women and their role in decision making in farm financial and household activities through Integrated Rural Development Programme (IRDP) and Development of Women and Children in Rural Areas (DWCRA) in Kolar district of Karnataka. It was found that women belonging to the small farms and agricultural labour took decisions on important matters as they earned cash income and had control over resources. The logit analysis performed to identify the socio-economic factors that have bearing on the decision making process revealed that women's participation in farm and financial decisions was positively associated with education of husband and the empowerment of women. However, the participation of women in decision-making was negatively associated with size of family, land holding and husband as a head of household. The magnitude of empowerment index of women showed that among the large farm category, only three per cent had a high level of empowerment, while 83 per cent had a medium level of empowerment. Women belonging to the small farm and agricultural labour categories with a high empowerment score formed 20 and 27 per cent of total respondents, respectively. It was also concluded that mere participation of women in different economic activities of the households did not empower women. They need access to assets, income and skills to seek empowerment.

Naresh and Narayanagowda (1999) conducted a study on the knowledge level of farm women about improved sericulture practices based upon the primary data collected through interviews of 60 trained and 60 untrained farm women of Bangalore district of Karnataka. Results indicated that 61 per cent of trained farm women had a high knowledge of improved sericultural practices as against 7 per cent of untrained farm women. High exposure to mass media and overall knowledge of trained farm women was significantly related to their decision-making ability.

Rajkishor *et al* (1999) examined the role of rural women in the decision making process in agriculture based on data collected in Khairabad and Machharehta development blocks of Sitapur district in Uttar Pradesh. The data revealed that participation of farm women in the decision making in case of preparation of land was as less as 13 per cent. It was further observed that the involvement of farm women in decision making was zero in the activities namely selection of crops and varieties to be sown, proper time and method of sowing of seed, means of irrigation, manure and fertilisers to be used, purchase and sale of farm machinery and engaging hired labours. It was also noted that matters related to storage, marketing of farm produce, purchase and sale of animals and land, majority of women (28 per cent) were consulted by the family head while taking decisions. The respondents belonging to middle age (36-45 years) and above 45 years age had participated more in decision making (about 18-27 per cent) as compared to younger age group (about 7 to 9 per cent). Education was found to be an important variable influencing the involvement of farm women in farm decision making. It was due to their having more knowledge and experience about improved farm practices. Level of participation of farm women in decision making was higher in nuclear families as compared to intermediate and joint family, in higher caste (22.45 per cent) as compared to lower caste (3.70 per cent) and Medium caste (13.40 per cent), comparatively more in medium size of land holding (1-2 ha) followed by large size of holding. It was concluded that, level of participation of women in decision making was influenced by age, level of education, joint or nuclear family, caste, large size of land holding and higher socio-economic status of farm women.

Sheokand *et al* (1999) conducted a study of 300 dairy farmers in the paddy belt of Haryana comprising three district viz. Kaithal, Karnal and Kurukshetra during 1996-97. It was revealed that decisions taken by husbands, wife and jointly, respectively in Kaithal district were 79.7 per cent, 5.9 per cent, and 14.4 per cent, in Karnal district 66.6 per cent, 4.3 per cent and 29.1 per cent and in Kurukhetra district 69.3 per cent, 6.3 per cent and 24.4 per cent. The corresponding figures in these three districts by farm size wise indicated that in case of landless 65.5 per cent, 9 per cent and 25.5 per cent; in marginal farms 70 per cent, 4.5 per cent and 25.5 per cent; small farms 70 per cent, 5 per cent and 25 per cent; medium size farms 72.5 per cent, 7 per cent and 20.5 per cent and large size farms 80 per cent, 3 per cent and 17 per cent. On an average, the contribution of male, female in performing various livestock activities was 45.2 per cent and 54.8 per cent, while their average participation in decision-making was 71.9 per cent and 28.1 per cent respectively. The study concluded that farm women from the three districts were least involved in decisions.

Singh and Singh (1999) conducted a study to analyse the impact of women participation in agricultural work and their role in decision-making process about economic and household matters in Chamoli and Almora district of Uttarakhand. The study revealed that the total working hours spent by adult females accounted for 85 per cent of agricultural work, 81 per cent related to animal husbandry and domestic work. The female labour contributed as much as 80 per cent of value of productive work and nearly 90 per cent of the value of domestic work. Though the women performed more than four-fifth of agricultural work, their decisions were accepted only in less than one-third of the cases. The power to take or influence the decisions by farm women were found to be high in the matters related to seed selection (29 per cent), purchase of agricultural implements (30 per cent) and sale and purchase of livestock (34 per cent).

Tuteja (2000) based on the study in Haryana state concluded that decision making of farm women about sales and purchase of land was positively related to farm size, i.e., higher the size of farm better the involvement. Farm women of the big households involved in the decision on farm credit (61.54 per cent) and on sale and purchase of animals (77 per cent). The participation of female labourers in decision making was poor in those fields where women had low exposure such as variety to be sown, farm credit and marketing of produce. In relation to financial powers on their earned income, 44 per cent women were free to spend, while women from landless and small households had to surrender their earned income to the family pool due to weak economy which did not have any scope for saving.

Logamatha (2001) carried out his study in Namakkal district of Tamil Nadu to estimate the pattern of employment, income generation and decision making behaviour of farm women and its determinants in crop, dairy and poultry based farming system. The multinomial Logit model analysis indicated that the education of male head and gross income of farm had positive influence on farm women's decision making but gross cropped area and age of farm women had negative influence on farm women decision making on selection of farming system.

Boreth *et al* (2002) carried out an investigation in Rajasthan state with a view to study the role of farm women in decision making related to various agricultural aspects. The data collected from 743 farm women highlighted that in 72.80 per cent cases, women were consulted by their counterparts in decisions related to the harvesting of crops, selection of crops and crop rotation.

In more than 50 per cent cases, women were not involved in decision-making activities requiring technical competence viz. seed rate, soil treatment, seed treatment, use of rhizobium culture, method of sowing and fertilizer application. This was due to lack of technical knowledge on the part of women and their limited exposure to training and other information sources. Decisions regarding agricultural marketing were taken predominantly by male members. This might be because of unawareness of women about marketing practices. Male took decisions related to farm credit. Besides, it was generally thought by men that women did not understand much about money matter as they were confined to the home, hence women could not take such decisions.

Vaish *et al* (2002) carried out a study to identify the constraints pertaining to the involvement of rural women in decision-making relating to adoption of rice production technology in Faizabad district of Uttar Pradesh. They observed that cent per cent (100 per cent) respondents were of the opinion that lack of technical know how was a common constraint considered as barrier for involvement of farm women in decision relating to rice production technology. This was followed by lack of education (92.00 per cent), men's thinking that they know better than women (72.00 per cent), dominance of men in agriculture (69.00 per cent), opportunities were not provided by men (59 per cent), women's thinking that men know better than them or it is men's job (54 per cent). It was recommended to consider these constraints while designing developmental programmes especially for rural women.

To sum up, it can be said that farm women had higher participation in decision making in the activities like purchase and sale of animals, type of feed of animals, purchase and sale of land, marketing of farm produce, process and storage of farm produce as observed by Alcober and Perrilla (1989), Nand (1994), Thakor (1996), Bhuvaneshari *et al* (1999) and Rajkishor *et al* (1999).

Farm women were not allowed to participate or not consulted by family head in decisions related to major farm operations because of dominance of men in family, illiteracy of farm women, less exposure to outside world, lack of knowledge of improved farm practices as indicated by Kadlag (1994) and Alagumani (1999). Vaish *et al* (2002), Lack of economic sources in their command, lack of extension support and low education (*Talukdar et al*, 1997) and limited exposure to information sources (*Boreth et al*, 2002) were the major factors contributed to low decision making of farm women.

Various socio-economic factors were responsible for higher participation of farm women in decision making on farm and family affairs such as higher education of farm women, farm women of age between 30 to 45 years, small family size, more farm experience, higher technical knowledge, more contacts with mass media, skills gained through training, farm women of higher caste, large landholding as observed by Shirodkar (1993), Kadlag (1994), Chakravarty and Chakravarty (1996), Khatik and Pandey (1997), Bhuvaneshari *et al* (1999), Rajkishor *et al* (1999), Naresh and Narayanagowda (1999) and Logamatha (2001).

To increase the decision-making ability of farm women and encourage them to participate in decision making process, Rimawi (1998) argued for more training programmes, intensification of extension programmes and involvement of farm women in development programmes.

Regarding the socio-economic empowerment of farm women, it was observed that women had to accept the male subordination within the households with nil or low entitlement of earned income and low decision making ability of farm women. This phenomenon was closely associated with the empowerment level of farm women (Jyothi *et al*, 1999). Mere participation of farm women in different economic activities of households did not empower the farm women unless they have access to credit, assets, income and different skills (Tuteja, 2000).

2.2 Impact of the Development Programmes on Farm Business Economy

The adoption of technological innovations in agriculture has received considerable attention among development economists because new technologies seem to offer opportunities to increase production and income substantially. Variation in productivity of crops has been traditionally explained by using factors like size of holding, quality of land, yield increasing inputs, area under irrigation, human and bullock labour and weather condition. Human resource factors such as farmers' education, skill and knowledge were not considered as important factors for explaining the productivity of crops. Schultz (1964) and Mellor (1976) argued that investment on education and extension in rural areas was important to improve the agricultural productivity. It was presumed that due to awareness of beneficiary farm women about the latest farm technology, there could be significant difference in resource use, crop yield and resources use efficiency on beneficiary farms than that on non-beneficiary farms. Keeping this in view, the past research was reviewed critically in the context of the present study and it is presented below:

2.2.1 Resource Use in Crop Production

Talathi and Veerkar (1992) conducted a study on the response of yield of rice to the use of different inputs in the Konkan region of Maharashtra. The data collected from 110 cultivators under the Cost of Cultivation Scheme revealed that the overall size of the holding was 0.54 ha. The per hectare quantities of inputs used were 237 human labour days, 74 kg of seed, 28 kg. of NPK and 24 pair days of bullock labour. The cultivators allocated higher proportion of available resources to the HYV's and achieved about 29 quintals of yield per hectare, which was 64.58 per cent higher than the local variety (17.62 q). It was further observed that plot size and fertiliser used influenced the productivity of HYV rice positively and significantly, whereas in the production of local varieties of rice, plot size, hired labour and seed influenced the productivity positively.

Atibudhi and Singh (1994) conducted a study to assess the impact of technological changes in rice cultivation on different farm sizes in Balasore district of Orissa. The study revealed that the use of different inputs and output at mean level differed significantly between different levels of technology. The productivity of the farm using the high yielding variety (HYV) technology was two times higher than those using local technology. The technology farms employed more labour per hectare than traditional ones by 32.4 per cent, 36 per cent and 49.7 per cent on marginal, small and large farms respectively. The results of production function analysis indicated a significant structural break in shifting from local technology to new technology. In other words, with the given level of inputs, more output can be produced by HYV technology or the said output can be produced with less use of input applying new technology.

Mohamed (1996) attempted to examine the impact of Southern Roseires Agricultural Development Project in Sudan on farm women. The findings reflected the differences in some socio-economic characteristics of the farmers based on gender, level of education, annual income and farm size. Chi-square analysis showed that there was a highly significant difference between male and female farmers in the services provided by the project such as land, credit, mechanization services and improved seeds. This reflects a high level of discrimination based on gender. In addition to this, analysis of results reflected that the women development programmes failed to reach objective envisaged by the project. The study concluded that women development could not be achieved since women remained isolated from the mainstream of development and planning and they would continue to be in a disadvantaged position. Accordingly, it was recommended that women could be fully integrated in the development process through giving more attention to their real roles and needs.

Narayanamoorthy (1999) examined the data from Pudukottai district of Tamil Nadu to assess the impact of farmers' education on the productivity of the crops. The bi-variate analysis indicated that the input use pattern by farmers was significantly higher in High Educated Group of Farmers (HEGF) when compared to Less Educated Group of Farmers (LEGF). As regards fertilizer use, it was 83 kg /ha and 73 kg /ha in HEGF and LEGF respectively. The significant difference was also observed in the use of other resources since HEGF were relatively rich and, therefore, they adopted higher amount of yield increasing inputs. The coefficient of education implied that one per cent increase in education level of farmers had an effect of only 0.038 per cent in productivity of paddy. This suggested that farmers' education only had limited role in increasing the productivity. Among the different factors included in the function, fertilizer and irrigation had a positive and significant influence on paddy output. The results of the study were not in conformity with Schultz's hypothesis that the education of the farmers will have a strong effect on the productivity of the crops in a dynamic agricultural set-up than in traditional agriculture.

2.2.2 Labour Utilisation Pattern in Crop Production

Rathore and Gaur (1996) studied the nature and extent of contribution of farm women in agriculture by comparing the time utilization pattern of males and females in farm operations in tribal and non-tribal areas of Udaipur and Chittorghar districts of Rajasthan. Data were obtained from 180 tribal and non-tribal respondents. It was noted that farm women worked for longer hours than men i.e., 15-18 hours a day. Most of the farm women were performing intercultural and post- harvesting activities in both tribal and non-tribal villages. There was a significant difference in performance of home and farm activities between tribal and non-tribal women.

Kaur and Punia (1998) examined the participation of women in home, dairy and farm activities in three districts of Haryana. It was revealed that on an average, farm women spent 8 to 10 hours in household activities. The level of rural development, caste, per capita income, socio-economic status and level of household technology were found to be positively and significantly related with the time spent in house holds activities. About 60 per cent respondents were involved in activities related to agriculture. The paddy transplanting, weeding harvesting and winnowing emerged as female dominated activities, while women were equal partners in harvesting and threshing.

Beohar *et al* (1999) attempted to study the contribution of farm women in paddy cultivation based on the data collected from sample of 50 farm women from Sendari village in Chattisgarh. The study revealed that both the family and hired female labour were used in sowing and transplanting, intercultural operation, harvesting, transporting and winnowing operations. With the increase in the farm size, the involvement of family women labour in paddy cultivation decreased but it was reverse for hired women labour. Use of female labour was observed to be more than male labour in transplanting, intercultural operation and harvesting of paddy crop.

Mishra *et al* (1999) examined the extent and proportion of women labour participation in paddy cultivation and the gaps in wages between men and women labour in Kymore Plateau and Satpura hill region of Madhya Pradesh. It was observed that the participation of farm women was higher in the transplanting of paddy, intercultural operation and harvesting while operations like preparatory tillage, sowing, manuring and fertiliser application, irrigation and threshing operations were performed jointly with men. The use of women labour (both family and hired labour) in paddy cultivation constituted 53 per cent of the total human labour employment. The participation of family women decreased as the size of farm increased but the total employment hours of women increased as the size of farm increased. The hiring of female labour was highly associated with the increased in the size of farm. The results of the study also showed that lower wages were paid to women for all the operations as compared to men and the wage gap was more than 71 per cent. It was suggested that diversified farming such as dairy, poultry etc. could help to increase the employment opportunities of farm women.

Panghal *et al* (1999) conducted a study to compare the efficiency of 200 male and female labour in performing different crop operations in major crops of Haryana. The comparative working efficiency of male and women labour in performing different farm operations was calculated based on time taken per hectare to perform only those operations where the participation of women labour existed. The study concluded that women labour participation is quite high in some of the crop operations like transplanting, weeding and picking. The total women labour participation increases with the size of the farm. Women labour was also found relatively more efficient than men labour in these operations. There was no participation of women labour in irrigation and ploughing operations in all the zones of Haryana and in almost all the crops.

Singh *et al* (1999) examined the pattern of employment of men and women farmers in rice-wheat production system based on the data collected from Kausambi district of Uttar Pradesh. The study revealed that farm women were intensively involved in crop and livestock production and in processing of farm produce such as cleaning, drying, grinding and selling of rice and wheat. The introduction of technology in rice-wheat farming system has led to the reduction in the male labour demand and increased the use of hired female labour. The differential pattern of wage structure between women and men was largely determined by nature and duration of agricultural task. The study suggested that there was a need to evaluate technologies for reducing women drudgery and to increase labour saving–gender–adjustable technology in agricultural development in future.

Seema *et al* (2000) conducted a study of twelve villages on participation pattern of rural women in post-harvest activities in Haryana State. The study revealed that, the activities like cleaning, drying and storage were done independently by 37.7 per cent farm women and jointly with husband by 53.9 per cent farm women. Threshing was carried out jointly by 56.1 per cent of farm women and some of the activities were monopolized by farm women like dehusking (69.71 per cent), shelling (96.7 percent), grading (92.9 per cent) and marketing (92 per cent). It was inferred that farm women were responsible for most of the post-harvest activities.

Sobha (2001) on the basis of her study in Chittor district of Andhra Pradesh, reported that women belonging to lower socio-economic groups being landless had to perform labour intensive activities. Women performed sowing (55 per cent), winnowing (90 per cent), transplanting (85 per cent) and poultry care (75 per cent). Caring of milch animal was not a major activity for farm women of lower socio-economic strata. However, poultry care was undertaken by 46 per cent of women.

2.2.3 Gaps in Technology Adoption

Rai *et al* (1999) examined the impact of central sector scheme 'Women in Agriculture' in Hissar district of Haryana on different aspects of farm women. The study brought out that the scheme was found to be very effective with respect to increase in knowledge regarding various agricultural technologies, their adoption and resources used by the farm women. On an average, about 60 per cent of farm women had adopted improved varieties of seeds. All the farm women adopted seed treatment, weed control, use of fumigants, rat control measures and kitchen gardening. The use of correct seed rate and Rhizobium culture was reported by 97 per cent. The adoption of plant protection measures, balance use of fertilizers and soil and water testing was reported by 78 per cent, 65 per cent and 55 per cent of the selected women farmers. The overall use of farm inputs was increased due to the implementation of the scheme.

Shriram and Chouhan (2000) conducted a study on adoption gaps in improved practices of wheat cultivation among tribal and non-tribal farms in the most backward districts of Rajasthan. He observed that the maximum adoption gap was reported in the use of high-yielding varieties (69.47 per cent) followed by plant protection measures (67.19 per cent), seed treatment (65.01), water management (49.85 percent), sowing (49.39 per cent), application of manures and fertilizers (49.39 per cent) and harvesting (45.57 per cent). The adoption gap was higher in tribal population than that in non-tribal respondents in all major areas.

2.2.4 Cost and Returns Analysis in Farm Business

The resource use structure influences the cost and return structure of the crop production activity. The quantum and proportions of out of pocket expenses and imputed costs in total cost structure either increase or decrease, depending upon changes in the use of different resources and substitution of one form of resource for another. The proportion of cash expenditure in the total cost of production of different crop enterprises also increases depending upon the process of transformation. The studies indicating the cost and return structures of crop enterprises have been reviewed and briefed below.

Santha (1993) studied the economics of rice cultivation in Puzhakkal block, Trichur district of Kerala. He compared the production cost, input use and profitability of rice production in three seasons: Viruppu (first crop), Mundakan (second crop) and Punja (third crop). Rice is mainly grown as a transplanted crop during the Mundakan season and as a direct sown crop in the other seasons. The study revealed that cultivation during the Mundakan season was the most profitable in terms of total returns and net income. The Viruppu crop performed best in terms of benefit-cost ratio and cost of production.

Chandravati *et al* (1999) conducted a study to assess the impact of ANTWA (Andhra Pradesh Training of Women in Agriculture) on agriculture development. The study revealed that the per hectare productivity of rice increased by 7.5 quintals, sugarcane by 60.46 quintals, groundnut by 1.17 quintals and that of sesame by 0.47 quintals. The increase in net income per hectare ranged between Rs. 1,027 and Rs. 6,537 in the above crops. The total income from all crops increased from Rs. 18,235 to 30,359 per hectare. Thus, the programme had a positive influence on the crop production.

Gitanjali and Kathy (2001) compiled the impact of the DANIDA supported project 'Women in Agriculture' in four states in India viz. Karnataka, Madhya Pradesh, Orissa and Tamil Nadu. The impact studies in these four states indicated that due to implementation of the project 'Women in Agriculture', the paddy yield was increased up to 25 bags per acre in the farm adopting new techniques against 12 bags per acre on non-adopter's field. It was further observed that there was a greater involvement of trained farm women in decision making both at home and on the farm. A sense of pride was inculcated on being consulted by their husbands and other farmers on agricultural technology. A relatively higher level of awareness among the farm women was noticed about the new farm technologies who were exposed to various trainings.

Korde *et al* (2003) studied the Kal Irrigation Project in Raigad district of the Konkan region in Maharashtra. One hundred respondents (50 beneficiaries and 50 non-beneficiaries) were selected for the study. It was concluded that average productivity of rice on the beneficiary farms was 26.13 q /ha. and 15.18 q/ ha. in case of non-beneficiary farms. The average annual income of beneficiaries was Rs. 42,970 and that of non-beneficiaries was Rs. 22,280. The personal and socio-economic characteristics of the beneficiaries and non-beneficiaries showed that the beneficiaries were better off than non-beneficiaries in respect of land holding, annual income, risk bearing, extension contact and change proneness. Further, it was observed that beneficiaries were better than non-beneficiaries with respect to cropping pattern, input use, use of improved technology, productivity of major crops, investment in agriculture, saving and barrowing.

2.2.5 Resource Use Efficiency in Crop Production

The knowledge about the differences in resource productivities in different regions and at different levels of technology in the same region is of greater importance for deciding policies for rational use of various resources. The significant differences in marginal value productivities of different resources on farms operated with different levels of technology would indicate the possibility of increasing agricultural production by shifting surplus resources and reallocating the same in an optimal manner. Studies conducted in the past were reviewed critically and these are presented below;

Sharma (1987) examined the resource use efficiency of major inputs used for crop production in five tribal villages of Himachal Pradesh. The study revealed that the inputs such as bullock labour, human labour, land and manure were not optimally utilized. He felt that if these inputs coupled with modern inputs were used intensively and optimally, there prevailed a scope for increasing crop output in the area.

Mahitha and Hemachandrudu (1992) probed into the resource use efficiency of the factor of production on paddy farms in Andhra Pradesh by using the data collected by the Cost of Cultivation Scheme, Department of Agricultural Economics, APAU, Hyderabad. Using the Cobb-Douglas type of production function, marginal value productivities were estimated and ratios of marginal value product (MVP) to opportunity cost (OC) was computed to estimate the efficiency of the resource use. The study concluded that the ratio MVP / OC was less than one for all-important resources used for the paddy crop production in Andhra Pradesh indicated the excessive use resulting in low efficiency and high cost. This warranted the need for reorganization of farm resources since the MVP /OC ratios for most of the resources deviate from unity.

Sunandini *et al* (1992) conducted a study to evaluate the efficiency-use of inputs in the production of rice in Andhra Pradesh and to determine as to whether resources could be redistributed in order to improve productivity, profitability or both. The sample consisted of 218 farmers from West Godavari, 213 from Warangal and 180 from Nellore district. Using ordinary least squares technique, a Cobb-Douglas type of production function was estimated and the marginal value product was used to ascertain resource-use efficiency. The results indicated that there was an under-utilization of tractor-power, manure and fertilizers, and a generally high level of resource inefficiency in all the three districts.

Tiwari and Dheer (1994) estimated the resource use efficiency and the marginal value productivity (MVP) of various factors of production of *ratoon* sugarcane in Bihar state. Data were collected from a sample of 40 farmers from Gobind Pitaunjhia village in Runi Saidpur community development block. The estimated parameters of the Cobb-Douglas production function showed that the per hectare elasticities of production were less than one for all inputs, thus indicating diminishing marginal returns for all factors of production. The highest MVP per rupee invested was recorded for labour (Rs. 6.58) followed by manures and fertilizers (Rs. 3.71).

Reddy (1995) analysed the nature and significance of technology in the different size of holdings for paddy crop by studying the resource use efficiency of various input factors for Cuddapah district of Andhra Pradesh. The results revealed that in the case of small farms particularly the application of HYV seeds, irrigation, chemical fertilizers and pesticides should be decreased, whereas, the application of bullock-labour and human labour should be increased in order to produce higher yield. In the case of medium farms, the paddy yield could be increased by higher application of HYV seeds, irrigation and chemical fertilizers and pesticides, and a decrease in bullock and human labour. In the case of large farms, the application of HYV seeds, irrigation, chemical fertilizers and pesticides should be increased in order to produce higher yield.

Wawire *et al* (1996) compared costs and profitability of rain-fed rice production according to planting method in Western Kenya. Data were obtained from 132 rain-fed rice farmers selected randomly from seven districts. The analysis of the resource use efficiency was limited because of differences in pricing units of some statistically significant inputs, but results indicated that farmers could increase profitability of rain-fed rice production by increasing the labour allocation for weeding. Returns to scale appeared constant under the present technical conditions and different sizes of rice plot.

Upendra *et al* (1998) determined the resource use efficiencies of inputs in rain-fed lowland, rain-fed upland, irrigated and deep-water rice systems in three villages in Pusa block of Bihar during 1990-91. Production elasticities and marginal value productivities of inputs were estimated. The results indicated that the farmers did not make the best use of their limited resources. Ample scope existed to readjust resource use to increase income. An additional investment was required on land, manures and fertilizers under rain-fed lowland rice and on land, human labour, manures, fertilizers and plant protection under irrigated rice and on land, manures and fertilizers under deep-water rice.

Birari *et al* (1999) studied the size group- wise and crop-wise changes in resource use levels of major inputs on the sample farms of irrigated and rainfed region in Western Maharashtra. The exercise was based on the data collected form 250 farm-families from 4 different categories based on land holdings. The study concluded that the per hectare resource use levels of crucial inputs viz., human labour, bullock labour, manure and fertilizers were relatively higher in the irrigated region. The use of seed was relatively more in the rain-fed region. The production function analysis indicated great variation in the production elasticities of resource inputs. In general, human labour, manure and fertilizers and other working capital were the major resource inputs influencing the output. The degree of resource use inefficiency was relatively more for land in both the regions and annualised capital investment and cropping intensity in the rain-fed region. There was no specific relationship observed between the use level of resources and size group of farms.

Yerriswamy and Hugar (2001) revealed from the analysis of input use efficiency in selected rice farming systems during 1997-98 in Tungabhadra Project area, Karnataka, that the use of chemical fertilizers and plant protection chemicals in kharif rice production were over-utilized in both Highly Intensive Agricultural System (HIAS) and Semi Intensive Agricultural System (SIAS). However, they were under utilized in Traditional Intensive Agricultural System (TIAS). In the case of rabi rice, land and labour had significant influence in TIAS against chemical fertilizers in HIAS. They suggested that the over-use of chemical fertilizers and plant protection chemicals in HIAS and SIAS needs to be addressed by educating the farmers about the higher use of organic manures, appropriate crop rotation, and judicious use of both chemical fertilizers and plant protection chemicals.

To sum up, Atibudhi (1994) observed higher productivity of HYV technology which was two times more than that of the local technology. Modern technology led to higher level of output as observed by Rai *et al* (1999), Chandravati *et al* (1999), Gitanjali and Kathy (2001), Korade *et al* (2003). While, Narayanmoorthy (1999) indicated a limited role of farmer's education on farm productivity. However, the overall use of inputs increased due to the application of modern farm technology. Further, it was observed by Talathi and Veerkar (1999) that cultivators had educated higher proportion of resources to HYVs and achieved 64 per cent higher yield than the local variety of rice. Shriram (2000) observed that higher inputs were used on non-tribal farms as compared to tribal's farm

Some studies were carried out to find out the extent of involvement of farm women in the different farm operations. Rathore and Gaur (1996) observed that farm women worked for longer hours than men (15–18 hours a days). Participation of farm women was more in the farm operations of paddy crop like transplanting, weeding, harvesting, winnowing and female were equal partners of male in harvesting and threshing as observed by Kaur and Punia (1998). Whereas, Beohar *et al* (1999) and Mishra *et al* (1999) observed that farm women were involved in sowing, transplanting, intercultural operations, harvesting, and winnowing of paddy crop. Besides, women were responsible for post- harvest activities (Seema, 2000). Modern technology in rice-wheat system reduced the demand of male labour and increased the demand for hired female labour (Sobha, 2001). Thus, from various studies it could be concluded that the contribution of farm women was significant in various agricultural operations.

In the crop production, the various resources are required namely human labour, bullock labour, chemical fertilizers, manure, irrigation, plant protection chemicals and working capital. Studies were reviewed to find out the level of utilization of these crucial inputs in paddy crop production. It was observed by Reddy (1995) that HYV seed, fertilisers, pesticides were over-utilised on small farms, while under-utilized in medium and large farms. All inputs were under-utilised in the rice crop production in Bihar state as reported by Upendra *et al* (1998). While, Yerriswamy and Hugar (2001) indicated that chemical fertilisers and plant protection chemical were over-utilised in the rice crop production. Human labour, manure, fertilisers and working capital were the major inputs influencing the crop output of the major crops in Western Maharashtra (Birari *et al* (1999). Tiwari and Dheer (1994) observed diminishing marginal returns in *ratoon* sugarcane, where as Wawire *et al* (1996) reported constant returns to scale in rice production.

2.3 Differentials in Employment and Income because of Scheme/Programmes

Farm women's involvement in income generating projects has been recognized since long as a part of rural development.

These projects provide employment as well as improvement in the socio-economic status of their family. Various projects were launched to boost the income and employment of farm women. Several studies were also conducted to assess the impact of schemes or projects on income and employment of farm women. Some of these studies were reviewed in the context of the present study, which are enumerated below:

Patnaik and Sailabala (1986) conducted a study on the contribution of farm women to the farm sector in Satyabad block of Puri district in Orissa which revealed that landholding size and working hours of females were inversely related. Females did not to go for employment outside their own farm when farm size was larger. In the case of small sized farm, females tended to seek wage employment outside their own farm since it did not offer adequate employment and earning throughout the year. The contribution of females towards family income from non-family activities was significant. Besides, the contribution of female labour towards agricultural production was always more than the male labour, which tends to decrease with increase in land holding size. In the regression model, land emerged as the most significant variable. It was observed that one per cent increase in female labour would lead to 0.68 per cent increase in total output when other variables, i.e., land, irrigation and male labour were constant. When the households were landless, one per cent increase in female earning led to the increase of 0.58 per cent of the total family income, while one per cent increase in male earning would increase the family income by 0.42 per cent.

Kalaimati (1988) based on his study on labour force participation of women in agriculture concluded that women participation in all the agricultural operation remained the same over a long period. In the past, they were either labourer or they assisted their husbands in some agricultural operations. Today, in contrast, in addition to performing various agricultural operations, women are managing large farms of many acres by themselves and now they are consulted on many aspects of agricultural marketing. Ignorance, traditional attitude, illiteracy, lack of skill, seasonal nature of employment, heavy physical work and long hours of work with limited payment, discrimination in wage structure, lack of job security, lack of comprehensive legislation, competition in employment and resultant deprivation of real wages, lack of minimum facilities at work place, bondage or alienation were the main problems faced by the farm women and women workers in agriculture.

Kaur (1988) studied the impact of technological advancement in the areas of agriculture, communication and health on the status of rural women in Haryana. The data based on a comparative analysis of the most developed and least developed regions of Haryana, revealed that partial mechanization in agriculture had favourable influence on income and employment pattern of farm women from all socio- economic groups, while full mechanization had exerted an adverse influence on poorer women. The conclusion that emerged from the analysis was that the level of regional development, caste system, class position and gender emerged as significant factors in determining access to technology and thereby consequent gains with respect to income and employment.

Wimalasena *et al* (1989) examined the impact of the People's Participation Project in Sri Lanka. It was revealed that women's participation in development activities was strengthened in cluster villages and there was visible socio-economic development. Economic activities were diversified with the inflow of the technology particularly in agriculture.

Thimmaiah and Hadimani (1990) studied socio-economic impact of mechanized tillage by way of a case study of two villages in Dharwad district of Karnataka. It was concluded that the increased nominal income had improved the standard of living of the mechanized households and enabled the agricultural labour families to earn more wages. The literacy rate among the younger generation was improved dramatically among the mechanized households. Mechanization had increased diversification of economic activities and the increased saving led to the land acquisition.

Singh *et al* (1992) conducted a study in 10 villages of Kanpur district where IRDP was in operation since 1980-81. The study revealed that female workers employment was 68.30 per cent, which was higher than the male employment (31.33 per cent). The level of women employment was on upkeep of draft and milch animals by small and marginal farmers and to adopt intensive agriculture by following modern farm technology. Thus, it was concluded that IRDP had increased the participation of rural women largely by raising their level of employment.

Ghosh (1993) studied impact of Integrated Rural Development Programme (IRDP) on rural women in Birbhum district of West Bengal. It was reported that about 33 per cent of the respondents were benefited due to training programme and their status had been increased while 67 per cent respondents were of the opinion that there was no change in their status.

Mehta and Joshi (1993) on the basis of their study on impact of the scheme 'Tribal Sub-Plan Area' conducted in three districts of Rajasthan State showed that there is substantial increase (27.96 per cent) in income of the beneficiaries under IRDP against 6.71 per cent income increase of non-IRDP beneficiaries. The shift matrix showed that the government programme had helped in reducing the poverty gap by approximately 25 per cent. However, poorest of the poor had not gained significantly from the programme. Decomposition analysis revealed that the major gain had been achieved due to business and livestock and gain in agricultural income was due to increased productivity.

Tawade and Nalband (1993) conducted a study of 135 beneficiaries under IRDP in Dahanu tahsil (tribal block) and Palghar tahsil (non- tribal) of Thane district in Konkan region of Maharashtra. It was observed that 68.18 per cent of the tribal block beneficiaries and 49.28 per cent of the non-tribal block beneficiaries had started dairy enterprise after having benefits of IRDP. It clearly indicated that after taking the benefits of IRDP, most of the beneficiaries had crossed the poverty line and moved from low-income group to higher income group.

Raut *et al* (1995) conducted a study on employment, income and expenditure of tribal in Igatpuri tahsil of Nashik district of Maharashtra state. They observed that the annual income per family was Rs. 7,801. In the total income, the share of agriculture was 58.67 per cent followed by wages (24.80 per cent), service and business (13.91 per cent) and miscellaneous sources (2.62 per cent). The per family average annual income worked out to Rs. 3,208, Rs. 7,494, and Rs. 8,689 for landless, small, medium and large size groups, respectively. The wages was the main source of income to the landless workers as it contributed 74.28 per cent in the total income, whereas agriculture was the major source of other three size classes of groups.

Chauhan and Sirohi (1999) examined the impact of Intensive Cattle Development Programme (ICDP) on female employment in rural areas. The data were collected from 300 rural households selected from three districts of Haryana. It was revealed that beneficiary female participation in dairy farming was 108.5 man- days, 158.37 man- days, and 151.42 man- days per year for small, medium and large herd size farm categories constituting about 50 per cent, 52 per cent and 42 per cent of total man-days employment, respectively. On the other hand, female participation among the non-beneficiaries households was lower at about 96 man-days a year. It was concluded that employment generation in dairy sector resulting from the implementation of ICDP had benefited a female more than a male.

Puhazhendhi and Jayaraman (1999) examined the employment generation through the farm women groups in Chitradurga district in Karnataka and Periyar district of Tamil Nadu. They observed a positive impact on the employment generation on 42 per cent of group members who had undertaken the income generating activities and generated employment of 172 man-days per members. By undertaking supplementary activities such as animal husbandry, poultry and non-farm activities like petty shops, kirana shop, flowers setting business had provided employment to greater extent. The annual employment available for the group members increased to 85 per cent during post-group formation period. Estimated employment elasticity work out to 0.31 during the initial period of group formation, had increased to 0.72 during post- phase of group formation. Such a positive response to the employment reaching closer to the optimum level indicates the multiplier effect of the project in terms of employment generation.

Anita *et al* (2000) studied the 80 beneficiaries of central sector scheme 'Women in Agriculture' in Haryana which revealed that 22.50 per cent trainees put the mushroom production technology into practice and 6.25 per cent respondents tried the technology after some persuasion. Modern technology adoption in mushroom production was responsible for increase in income and employment of farm women.

Singh and Prasad (2000) studied the sample of 200 beneficiaries of the IRDP in Samasthipur block of Bihar state. The study revealed that the minor irrigation enterprise was the most profitable in 83.32 per cent of beneficiaries who crossed poverty line. Agriculture was the second most profitable sector in which 41.66 per cent beneficiaries crossed poverty line. The least profitable sector was the rural artisan. The beneficiaries perceived the changes in the selected areas such as improved standard of living (72.5 per cent), dietary standard (66.5 per cent), consciousness about education of children (61.5 per cent), status in caste and community improvement (44 per cent), habit of small saving (29 per cent).

Khorate and Hardikar (2003) conducted an impact study of Development of Women and Children in Rural Areas (DWCRA) scheme in terms of income and employment generation in Sindhudurg district of Maharashtra state. The study revealed that 59.09 per cent beneficiaries had an additional employment of 31 to 60 man-days, 20 per cent beneficiaries had 91 man-days and 20.91 per cent beneficiaries had an additional employment for 57.05 man-days. The inferences were drawn that DWCRA scheme had brought positive change in the income and employment generation for the beneficiaries. However, the increase was not satisfactory. Hence, it was recommended that DWCRA groups should be motivated to undertake labour intensive and remunerative enterprises.

Mali *et al* (2003) carried out a study on gender employment pattern and income of the 108 households in irrigated area of

Western Maharashtra for the period of three years i.e., 1999-2002. The study revealed that the average annual employment of female was 196 days in which crop production and livestock activities were to the tune of 71 per cent. On an average, male workers were employed for 269 days in which the share of own farm activities were 57 to 83 per cent. The average annual gross family income of farm families was Rs. 1,80,548 and Rs. 44,860 for non-farm families. Of the total income, 58 to 73 per cent was from crop production in case of farm families while in case of non-farm families, 73 per cent share of income from wage earning. The regression coefficient of employment function of farm and non-farm families in respect of livestock activity and gross cropped area of farm families in irrigated area were observed to be positive and significant. Thus, it was recommended that the livestock activity and labour intensive crops such as fruits, vegetables and flowers could be included in cropping pattern.

Subhas Chand (2003) carried out an investigation of two projects namely the Drought Prone Area Programme (DPAP) and Comprehensive Watershed Development Project (CWDP) in Tamil Nadu. Both the programmes were implemented by Tamil Nadu Agricultural University. It was observed from the study that 1.8 lakhs of casual labour man-days were generated during the implementation of the various works in 15 DPAP watersheds. After the implementation of the project, the income was increased considerably i.e., from Rs. 27,163 to Rs. 41,484 over a period in CWDP areas and about 10 to 25 per cent increment in income was noticed in DPAP watershed. Further, it was observed that women's participation in decision making of different activities were increased by 85 per cent in household activities, 87 per cent in agriculture, 57 per cent in social activities and 41 per cent in educational activities. Because of the project support, farm women were encouraged to participate in the project activities.

To sum up, several studies as cited above have pointed out that the level of income and employment of farm women were mainly dependent upon farm size, level of technology adoption in agriculture, live stock and socio-economic factors like level of

regional development, caste system, class position, education of beneficiary were identified by Patnaik and Sailabala (1986), Kalaimati (1988), Kaur (1988), Thimmaiah and Hadimani (1990) and Mali *et al* (2003) in their studies.

Several rural development projects were launched to encourage and enhance the employment and income in rural areas. Some especial schemes and projects were exclusively designed for farm women and their implementation has yielded positive results on income and employment of farm women. The review of different studies indicated that beneficiaries of Integrated Rural Development Programme (IRDP), DWCRA, Women in Agriculture, DPAP etc had significant effects on female employment (Singh *et al*, 1992), status of farm women increased as shown by Ghose (1993), government programmes helped in reducing the poverty line by approximately 25 per cent (Mehta and Joshi, 1993) and Tawade and Nalband (1993), Chouhan and Sirohi (1999), increased in standard of living of farm women as observed by Singh and Prasad (2000), Khorate and Hardikar (2003), Subhas Chand (2003). Anita and Mehta (2000) revealed that due to the implementation of Women in Agriculture scheme, the adoption of mushroom technology was increased which led to more income and employment.

2.4 Constraints Observed by Beneficiaries while Availing the Benefits of the Projects/Schemes

Arya and Shah (1984) examined the main constraints in the adoption of new technology in dry land agriculture in Himalayan region of Uttar Pradesh. The study revealed that the yield gap between the existing and potential level of food production was due to slow take up of new dry land technology, old cropping system and traditional farm technology. By adopting the technology, yield could be increased by 1.5 to 3.3 times above the present level. The main constraints identified were (1) small and skewed distributed holdings, (2) fragmented and scattered holdings, (3) shortage of labour, (4) lack of availability of inputs and funds and, (5) lack of education, extension and training to farm women.

Kumavat and Sharma (2000) conducted a study in Jaipur district of Rajasthan to identify the constraints faced by both beneficiaries and non-beneficiaries in getting the benefits under the poverty eradication programmes. It was revealed that 67 percent respondents viewed as no active participation of people in programme implementation, lack of awareness among people (66 per cent). The other constraints observed by the respondents were selling of their produce (63 per cent), lack of supervision and proper evaluation by the officials (32 per cent), selection criteria was not strictly followed (16.66 per cent).

Gaikwad and Dhane (2001) reported from his study on the impact of IRDP in Ambegaon block of Pune district that majority of the beneficiary farmers faced problems like lack of knowledge (88 per cent), excess time for approval of scheme and subsequent benefits (81.83 per cent), lack of technical knowledge regarding plant protection implements obtained through the schemes (96 per cent). Further it was observed that the interruption in work due to lack of capital (62 per cent), excess of documentary requirement (55.33 per cent), un-availability of sanctioned loan at a time (50 per cent), lack of scientific knowledge regarding the use of inputs (45.35 per cent).

Ramkrishanan and Reddy (2002) attempted a study to ascertain problems perceived by 120 trainees during the training programmes under Tamil Nadu Women in Agriculture programme in Madurai district of Tamil Nadu state. It was revealed that majority of the trainees (80.83 per cent) perceived inadequate duration of training programme, less frequency in organizing the training programme, inconvenient place of training and inadequate use of audio-visual aids. Nearly half of the respondents (49.66 per cent) stated that boarding facilities were inadequate and lack of uniformity in coverage of programme content.

Dhuware and Pande (2003) conducted a study to identify the major constraints in the adoption of the recommended practices as perceived by selected beneficiaries (120) of Sunderpur watershed of Jabalpur district in Madhya Pradesh. The study indicated that major constraints observed by the beneficiary farmers were the lack of irrigation facilities (57.50 per cent), untimely availability of watershed based production technology (35.08 per cent), high cost of inputs like seed, fertilizers and pesticides (33.33 per cent), lack of finance (15.83 per cent), uncertainty about the availability of irrigation water (30 per cent), lack of transportation facilities (25.83 per cent), and lack of a training institute (20.00 per cent). Based on the constraints, it was recommended that watershed technology be made available by means of different extension approaches and support from the government to solve the problems of finance for inputs.

Sujatha *et al* (2003) attempted to study the shortcomings in the execution of scheme "Development of Women and Children in Rural Areas (DWCRA)" in Guntur district of Andhra Pradesh. The data collected from 676 DWCRA beneficiaries for the period 1994-95 to 2002-03. The major constraints faced by the beneficiary women groups were lack of training facilities, inadequacy of finance, poor identification of beneficiaries, non-availability of raw material, and poor marketing facilities. Thus, it was recommended for proper identification of beneficiaries, increasing the amount of revolving funds, provision of raw materials and appropriate training facilities.

Thomas *et al* (2003) examined the socio-economic constraints of watershed development programme in the Polakad district of Kerala through a personal interview of 120 project beneficiaries. It was revealed that the most prominent strengths of the programme were the co-operation of the farmers as perceived by 89.17 per cent of the sample respondents, followed by the right selection of inputs as perceived by 56.67 per cent respondents. The analysis of negative perceptions about the programme by the beneficiaries showed that untimely distribution of the inputs was perceived as the most important weakness of the programme by 84.17 per cent respondents and 77.50 of the sample respondents were unaware of the rationale underlying the project components. The lack of the technical support was reported as another weakness of the programme as perceived by 76.67 per cent of respondents.

To sum up, major constraints in the adoption of technology as noticed by Arya and Shah (1984) were small and scattered holding, shortage of labour, lack of availability of inputs and funds, lack of education, extension and training to farm women. Lacks of awareness, difficulties in selling of their produce, lack of supervision were the constraints in participation of farm women in project implementation as observed by Kumawat (2000). The majority of farmers faced problems as observed by Gaikwad (2000) and Thomas *et al* (2003) were lack of knowledge, capital and excess documentary requirement, lack of transportation facilities, high cost of inputs (Dhuware and Pande, 2003), lack of marketing and inadequacy of input (Sujatha *et al*, 2003). Ramkrishanan and Reddy (2002) identified constraints like inadequate duration of training, less frequency of training, inconvenient place of training and lack of boarding facilities during training programmes.

3

Methodology

This chapter is devoted to the discussion in brief of the methodology adopted for the present study. It provides an insight into description of sampling procedure, source of data, method of data collection, definition of variables and analytical approach adopted to accomplish the objectives under study. An attempt is made to explain the above said issues to make the plan of investigation crystal clear in the discussion that follows.

3.1 Location of the Study

The present study is undertaken in Thane district of Maharashtra State. The three tahsils namely Dahanu, Palghar and Wada were selected purposively for the study as a central sector scheme 'Women in Agriculture' was being implemented in these three tahsils since 1994-95. The location of the tahsils and the villages selected for study is depicted in the map of Thane district (Fig. 1).

3.2 Selection of Sample

3.2.1 Selection of Villages

The central sector scheme 'Women in Agriculture' was being implemented in six villages of Wada tahsil, four villages of Palghar and eight villages of Dahanu tahsil of Thane district in Maharashtra State since 1994-95. In the beginning of the scheme, 200 farm women were selected in each tahsil comprising ten groups. Each group consisted 20 farm women representing small, medium and large farm family of tribal and non-tribal households. Thus, in these three tahsils of Thane district, 600 farm women have been benefited through 30 groups. During 1999-2000, additional 5 farm women were added as a beneficiary in each group making a total of 750 farm women in the district.

One village from Palghar, two villages from Wada and three villages from Dahanu were randomly selected in proportion to the total number of villages covered under the scheme in three tahsils of Thane district for the present study.

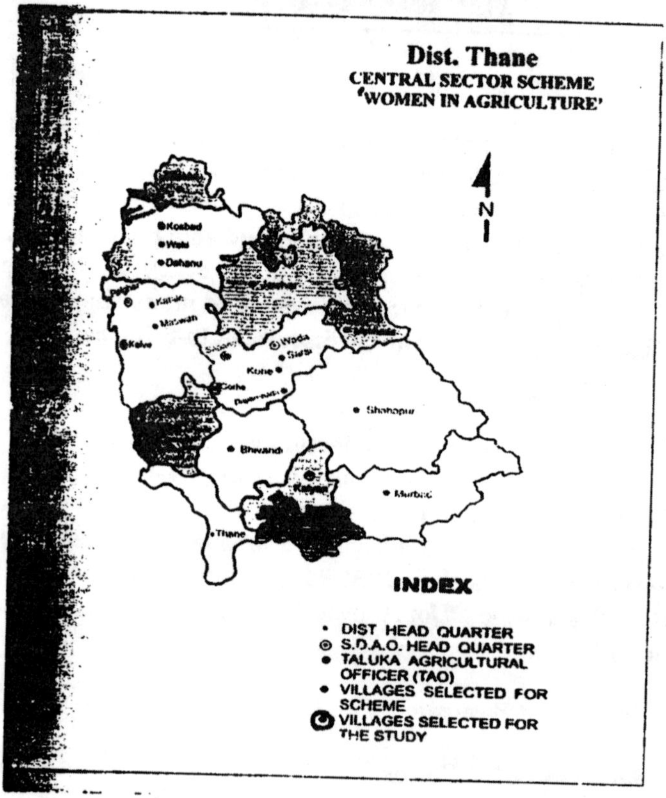

Fig. 1. Map of Thane District Showing the Village in Which Scheme-Women in Agricultre is in Operation and the Villages Selected for the Study.

3.2.2 Selection of Sample Households

The central sector scheme 'Women in Agriculture' was operated in 18 villages comprising 750 farm women. However, 120 farm women out of 600 farm women who were benefited since the beginning of the scheme i.e., 1994-95 were taken for the study. It is, thus, clear that a total sample of 120 beneficiary farm women of the scheme comprising 40 sample households (two groups) from Wada, 20 (one group) from Palghar and 60 (three groups) from Dahanu tahsil were selected for the present study. In order to assess the impact of the scheme, it was required to have equal number of non-beneficiary farm women households belonging to the same village and having the same socio-economic status. Thus, 120 farm women were selected as a non-beneficiary, therefore, the total sample of 120 non-beneficiary farm women households comprising 40 households from Wada tahsil, 20 households from Palghar and 60 from Dahanu tahsil were selected by simple randomisation for the study.

Thus, the total sample for the study became 240 households comprising 120 beneficiary and 120 non-beneficiary farm women of the scheme spread over six villages of Thane district in Maharashtra State as shown in Table 3.1.

Table 3.1
Distribution of Sample Households According to the Selected Villages in Thane District

Tahsils	*Selected villages*	*No.of groups*	*No. of sample households*		
			Beneficiaries	*Non-Beneficiaries*	*Total sample size*
Dahanu	Korpatpada / Bordi	1	20	20	40
	Lilakpada / Ghatalpada	1	20	20	40
	Tokepada / Gholwad	1	20	20	40
Palghar	Kelve	1	20	20	40
Wada	Gorhe	1	20	20	40
	Sapne	1	20	20	40
Total	**6**	**6**	**120**	**120**	**240**

3.3 Source of Data

The data for the present investigation were collected from 240 farm women households (120 each of beneficiaries and non-beneficiaries) located at six villages of three tahsils, i.e., Dahanu, Palghar and Wada. The secondary data regarding features of the Thane district and tahsils under the study were collected from the office of District Superintending Agriculture Officer (DSAO) and Taluka Agriculture Officer (TAO) of Dahanu, Palghar and Wada. Various statistical reports of the Thane district were also referred for getting the requisite information.

3.4 Method of Data Collection

A pre-tested interview schedule was used to collect the information from the respondents. The data were collected regarding decision-making process in the farm business management, economic empowerment, farm business economy, employment and income pattern of both beneficiary and non-beneficiary households and constraints in implementation of scheme at various levels. The data were collected for the year 2001-2002 through personal interviews keeping in view the objectives of the study. The discussion with the officials of the agricultural department at different level in Thane district also provided insight into the performance of the scheme under study.

3.5 Method of Analysis

The sample households have been categorized into three size classes based on operational holdings viz. small (upto 0.50 ha.), medium (0.51–1.0 ha) and large (1.01 ha. and above) for the purpose of analysis of data.

To attempt the first objective of the study, the Decision Making Index is employed to find out the involvement of farm women in decision-making and factors influencing the decision making process. The Karl Pearson's correlation coefficient (r-value) was calculated to establish the level of relation between decision-making index and twelve socio-economic parameters. The significance was tested by 't' test. The socio-economic empowerment brought out in farm women because of scheme implementation was analyzed by simple tabulation and percentages.

The second objective of the study was fulfilled by estimating per hectare resource use for paddy and farm as a whole, per hectare labour use, operation-wise labour use, computation of different costs by applying the standard cost concepts. Input—output relationship was sutdied by Cobb- Douglas type of production fuctionand resources use effciency was estimated by computing the Marginal Value Product (MVP). The Chow's test was employed to test whether the two production functions were different in their slope and intercepts.

The third objective of the study regarding the impact of the scheme on employment and income of the sample households was done by simple tabulation and percentages.

The fourth objective regarding different factors responsible for the employment and income was fulfilled by applying the multiple regression analysis method and was tested for its significeance by 't' test. The regression equation of beneficiaries and non-beneficiaries households was compared by the use of dummy variable technique.

The fifth objective regarding the constraints while availing benefits of the scheme at the beneficiary's level was studied by simple tabulation.

3.6 Farm Women in Decision-Making

The decision- making in farming is not as easy a job as it appears. It is a thinking process. Nevertheless, farm women knowingly or unknowingly participate in decision-making process in the farming enterprise, which is based on her long-standing field experience, taking decisions involved the following steps (Dube *et al.* 1988):

- Desire for change,
- Getting initial information,
- Recognition of problems,
- Getting additional information,
- Consideration of alternative means,
- Consideration of resources,
- Consideration of alternative uses of means, and
- Taking final decision.

3.6.1 Decision Making Index (DMI)

The beneficiary farm women under the scheme 'Women in Agriculture' were exposed to various agricultural technologies through exposure visits, mass media, village level training and through the continuous contacts with the extension agency. Acquisition of more technical knowledge regarding various agricultural production technologies develops the confidence which leads in more participation in decision-making process. Considering the cropping patterns, farm business and family activities, 21 important activities were selected on which the respondent farm women were likely to take decisions. Of these 14 activities were related to crop production, four activities were related to dairy and animal husbandry, three activities were on family affairs. Besides, two activities exclusively related to the decisions regarding the participation in the scheme activities were taken for beneficiary farm women. Thus, 23 activities in case of beneficiaries and 21 activities in case of non-beneficiaries were identified for the study.

The level of decision-making by farm women was decided by using Decision Making Index (DMI). Farm women with no participation in the decision making was given zero score, if the farm women are consulted one score was given and two score was given if the farm women take decisions independently (Shirodkar, 1993) which is as under:

Decision Making Index (DMI)

$$= \frac{\text{Decision making score obtained by farm women}}{\text{Maximum possible score of farm women}} \times 100$$

The farm women were classified into the following categories according to the score of Decision Making Index (DMI):

- Low decision-making .... Score up to 15
- Medium decision-making .... Score 16 to 30
- High decision-making .... Score 31and above

3.6.2 Estimation of Correlation Coefficient and Test of its Significance

The decision making process is influenced by various socio-economic factors. Twelve important socio-economic variables viz.

age, education, status in family, extension contacts, social participation, technical knowledge, annual family income, caste, family size, farm size, occupation of family head and education of family head were considered for ascertaining the correlation between decision making and these socio-economic factors.

The Karl Pearson's Coefficient of Correlation formula (Gupta, 1997) was employed to find out the correlation between the socio-economic factors and decision-making which is as under:

$$r_{XY} = \frac{\left(\sum XY\right) - \frac{\left(\sum X\right)\left(\sum Y\right)}{N}}{\sqrt{\left\{\left(\sum X^2 - \frac{\left(\sum X\right)^2}{N}\right)\right\} \times \left\{\left(\sum Y^2 - \frac{\left(\sum Y\right)^2}{N}\right)\right\}}}$$

The **t test** is used to test the significance of an observed correlation coefficient (Gupta, 1997).

$$t_{cal} = \frac{r\sqrt{n-k}}{\sqrt{1-r^2}}$$

Where, n = no. of observations and k = parameter, but here k=2

3.6.3 Construction and Standardization of Socio-Economic Scales

Several attempts have been made to prepare socio-economic status scales both outside and within the country. The level of income has been used by Taussing (1928) and occupation by Cattle ((1942). Among the multifarious measuring devices the scale prepared by Chapin (1928), Swell (1940), Shea (1936), Lewiss and Dhillon (1955), Freeman (1961), Trivedi (1963) and Chorge (1985) were used for rural and social studies.

In all, twelve important socio-economic variables were identified to test the relative influence on the decision making process of farm women.

3.6.3.1 Age

With the advancement of the age, the decision making power of the individuals certainly increases. Several complex decisions are required to be taken in agriculture especially on farms where crop production and livestock activities are carried out. In certain decisions, age may have significant relationship. It was thought that the farm women in the higher age group might participate more in taking decisions about farm production and family affairs. The respondent farm women were categorised into three groups as suggested by Laxmidevi (1988) and Sethi (1991) as below:

(a) Up to 30 years

(b) 31 to 50 years

(c) 51 years and above

3.6.3.2 Education of Farm Women

Education is hypothesized to affect the agricultural productivity in two ways, firstly, via a choice of better inputs and output (allocative effect) and secondly, through a better utilisation of existing inputs (technical efficiency aspect). It was thought that educational level would influence the decision making of the farm women in different farm operations. Hence, the education level of both husband and wife have been taken separately to assess the influence on the decision making process of farm women. Accordingly, farm women were categorized and given score as follow:

(a) Illiterate .... = 0

(b) Primary (1 to 7 Std.)......................... = 1

(c) Secondary (8 to 10 Std.)...... .... = 2

(d) Higher secondary (11 to 12 Std) .... = 3

(e) Graduate and above .... = 4

3.6.3.3 Education of Family Head

The family heads were also classified with the same scale as discussed in 3. 6. 3. 2 above to study their relationship between the educational level of family head and decision making of farm women.

3.6.3.4 Status of Farm Women in the Family

It refers to the position that farm women occupy in the family while taking rational decisions. The farm woman who is the head of family has to take almost all the decisions in the family. In the nucleus family, farm-women act as a family co-head, who is generally involved in the decision making process. If the farm woman occupies the status of daughter or daughter-in-law is dominated by the elder members of the family because of her subordinate position in the family. Thus, it can be said that the position occupied in the family by a farm woman gives her power to take a decision in farm and family matters.

Thus, farm women were classified into three catagory and accordingly the score was given to them as under:

(a) Daughter/Daughter-in-law .... = 1

(b) Family co-head .... = 2

(c) Family head .... = 3

3.6.3.5 Extension Contacts

By contacting the extension agencies, individual may gain knowledge and motivation for adoption of new ideas. An increased number of contacts with extension agencies enable an individual to bring clarity in his thinking and to take accurate decisions. In the present study, for measuring the extension contact of the farm women, fifteen extension activities / information sources were considered like number of exposure visits, technical training's attended, number of demonstrations organized, listening of radio and television etc. for the scoring. The respondent farm women were categorised into three groups based on their contacts with extension agencies as suggested by Kaur (1988). Accordingly, the sample households were classified into three groups:

(a) Number of information sources less than 7

(b) Number of information sources between 8 to 15

(c) Number of information sources 16 and above.

3.6.3.6 Social Participation of Farm Women

Social participation or cosmopoliteness is the tendency of an individual to be in contact with the outside world based on the belief that individual's needs cannot be satisfied in his group, family and community. It may have an effect on his knowledge, experience, and broadening the horizon of his views. For measuring the cosmopoliteness, respondent's association with six social and political groups like Gram panchayat, Panchayat Samiti, Zilla Parishad, Co-operative societies, women's Self Help Groups (SHG) and any social group in village were considered. It was assumed that cosmopoliteness influences the decision-making behaviour of the farm women in the family. Accordingly, sample households were divided into three groups;

(a) No membership of any organization .... = 0

(b) Member of atleast one organizations .... = 1

(c) Member of more than one organisations ...... = 2

3.6.3.7 Technical Knowledge of Farm Women

The technical knowledge of farm women especially about paddy crop cultivation and dairy practices were measured by computing the knowledge score. The data were collected on 28 statements (questions), i.e., 23 statements in respect of paddy cultivation and 5 for animal husbandry and dairy practices. If the farm women has given correct answer to any sub-questions under the head, the 'two' score was given and 'one' score was given for partial correct answer and 'zero' score was given for those who had given incorrect and no answer. Accordingly, the total knowledge score of an individual farm women for all 28 statements was worked out. The maximum possible score of individual farm women was 56.

In order to determine the level of knowledge of farm women about improved technology of paddy cultivation and different practices in the areas of animal husbandry and dairy, a Knowledge Index was calculated by using the following formula (Rahane, 1996; Deepti, 2002);

Knowledge Index

$$= \frac{\text{Knowledge score for all correct answers}}{\text{Maximum possible knowledge score of respondent farm women}} \times 100$$

The farm women were categorised into the following three groups;

(a) Low knowledge : Knowledge Index up to 20

(b) Medium knowledge : Knowledge Index between 21 to 40

(c) High knowledge : Knowledge Index 41 and above.

3.6.3.8 Annual Gross Income of Family

Though the annual gross income is the resultant effect of economic status of sample farms. Adoption of innovations always involves additional expenditure. Farmers with better economic condition can afford to purchase TV sets, newspapers, farm magazines for seeking latest agricultural information. It is, also possible for these farmers to go on educational tours to increase their technical competence. It is therefore, expected that better economic condition influences farmers in seeking the information and their communication behaviour. Based on gross family income, farm households were classified into the following three categories and this variable was taken as such without any score:

(a) Annual income up to Rs. 40,000

(b) Annual income up to Rs. 40,001 to 80,000

(c) Annual income more than Rs. 80,001 and above

5.6.3.9 Caste

Castes are the hereditary groups, which had a direct bearing on the individual's socio-economic status in the society. The higher caste farmers are more social than middle caste and low caste farmers. It is assumed that decision-making process is also influenced by the caste. Hence, respondents were classified into the following three groups and scored as follows:

(a) Lower caste (SC / ST) = 1 score

(b) Middle caste (OBC) = 2 score

(c) Higher caste (Gen) = 3 score

3.6.3.10 Family Size

Family is the basic unit of the society. The size of family also affects the individual personality. It was assumed that a small family having husband, wife and one or two kids treated as a nuclear family in which farm women play a significant role in decision making than the large and joint family. In the present investigation respondent's households were classified into three classes as suggested by Laxmidevi (1988), Gupta (1988), Sethi (1991), Malviya (1991) and they were scored as under:

(a) Members in family up to 4

(b) 6 members in family

(c) Members above 7

3.6.3.11 Farm Size

In India, land holding is the most important indicator of socio-economic status of an individual. Size of land holding is closely associated with the level of income and standard of living of the households and is a source of social prestige in rural society. The access and control of land has been influenced by a historical and political factors and its association with caste in the Indian situation has made an important variable of rural social stratification (Cohn, 1979). Hence, it was assumed that land holding has influence on the decision making process of farm women of sample households. Land variable was taken as such without any score.

3.6.3.12 Occupation of Family Head

Male member in the family is usually a main bread earner and decisions are influenced by his type of profession and level of earning. Hence, the profession of family head was considered as one of the factors which influence the decision making by farm women. Accordingly, three prominent professions like wages, agriculture and service were considered and scored as under.

(a) Working on others farm (Wage earning) ...... = 1

(b) Agriculture .... = 2

(c) Agriculture + allied .... = 3

(d) Service .... = 4

3.7 Socio-Economic Empowerment of Farm Women

The socio-economic empowerment brought out in farm women because of scheme implementation was analysed by simple tabulation and percentages. Different variables which contribute towards socio-economic empowerment of farm women were taken for the study. These were viz; access to money/ credit, ownership and control over resources, right to do the expenditure, access to communication media, contacts with extension agencies and skill acquired by farm women through training (Jyothi *et al*, 1999)

3.8 Farm Business Analysis

The costs, returns, and net returns from the paddy crop and farm business as a whole which includes paddy, vegetable and horticultural crops were estimated by adopting usual farm management concepts of cost and measures of income. The total input costs in crop production have been worked out at three stages of costs, i.e., cost A, cost B and cost C. These concepts of costs are useful for measurement of returns to different factors of production. The costs and returns for the farm business have been estimated on per hectare basis for the individual size classes of farms under study.

3.8.1 Production Function Analysis

The adoption of improved technology in agricultural sector has brought a significant change in the pattern of agricultural production in the country. The nature and intensity of use of inputs with the pattern of disposal of production have undergone tremendous changes. Therefore, the production in agriculture has become more and more market oriented today. The production of agriculture sector has become increasingly dependent on the use of purchased inputs. Therefore, the relationship between inputs and production has assumed considerable importance.

Production function analysis was carried out by using primary data collected for this purpose. A series of production function studies have been conducted in India with the major objective of determining the productivity of resources and allocation efficiency of farm inputs for crops or for the farm business as a whole. One of the most widely used production function for empirical estimation is the Cobb-Douglas type of production function. This function was originally used by C. W. Cobb and P. H. Douglas ("A Theory of Production", *American Economic Review*, Vol. 18, March Supplement 1928, pp. 139-165).

By now, the choice of Cobb-Douglas form has become a convention in production function analysis mainly because of its theoretical fitness to agriculture and its computational manageability. The specification of function in its stochastic form is as follows;

$$Y = a X_1^{b1} X_2^{b2} X_3^{b3} X_4^{b4} X_5^{b5} X_6^{b6} X_7^{b7} e^{u}$$

in logarithmic form, it becomes a log linear equation as under,

$$\text{Log } Y = \log a + b_1 \log X_1 + b_2 \log X_2 + b_3 \log X_3 + b_4 \log X_4 + b_5 \log X_5 + b_6 \log X_6 + b_7 \log X_7 + \log e$$

Where,

Y = Value of gross output in Rs. for a farm business as a whole and in quintals for paddy crop

X_1 = Nitrogen (kg)

X_2 = Phosphorus (kg)

X_3 = Potash (kg)

X_4 = Farm Yard Manure (tonnes)

X_5 = Human labour (man-days)

X_6 = Bullock labour (pair days)

X_7 = Other working capital (Rs)

a = intercept term

e = error term

b_1 to b_7 =elasticity coefficients of respective inputs.

The individual coefficients were tested with the help of 't' test, while the overall significance of fitted equation was tested with the help of 'F' test. The relevant F* ratio is

$$F^* = \frac{R^2 / (K-1)}{(1 - R^2) / (N - K)}$$

which is compared with $F_{0.05}$ with $v_1 = (K-1)$ and $V_2 = (N-K)$ degree of freedom (Koutsoyiannis, 1977).

3.8.2 Specifications of the Variables

A great deal of caution needs to be exercised in selection, classification and aggregation of input variables used in production function analysis for studying the resource productivity. A brief description of inputs used as explanatory variables in the present study is given below;

(a) **Dependent Variable:** The output (Y) was taken in quintals for paddy crop and in rupees for farm business as a whole.

(b) **Independent or explanatory variables**

1. *Nitrogen* (X_1): In the present investigation nitrogen has been taken as an explanatory variable in kilograms for paddy crop and in monetary terms for the farm as a whole.
2. *Phosphorus* (X_2): This variable has been taken as an explanatory variable in kilograms for paddy crop and in monetary terms for the farm as a whole.
3. *Potash* (X_3): This variable has been taken as an explanatory variable in kilograms for paddy crop and in monetary terms for the farm as a whole.
4. *FYM* (X_4): The farmyard manure in tonnes has been taken for paddy crop and in monetary terms for farm as a whole. The prevailing rates in that locality during reference year was taken for value calculation.
5. *Human labour in man days* (X_5): In the present study, human labour used from the land preparation to harvesting operations has been used in terms of man-days in paddy crop and the actual wages prevailed in the locality in the

monetary terms for a farm as a whole. One man-day consists of eight hours of work per adult male. Thus, for the present study, female labour hours were converted into man equivalent days considering the wages prevailing in the villages. The wage rates for male and female were different and based on the wage rate ratio of male and female, the female labour hours were converted into man equivalent days. Female labour day was considered as equivalent to 0.87 man-days.

6. *Bullock labour* (X_6): Bullock labour both owned plus hired used for different farm operations was considered as a separate input and it was measured in pair days. Hence one pair day means eight hours of work by a pair of bullocks. This variable was taken in bullock pair days for paddy crop and in monetary terms for farm as a whole.

7. *Other Working capital* (X_7): The cost in rupees of pesticides, seed, machine, irrigation, incidental charges and repair of machinery were included and taken for calculation purpose for paddy crop and farm as a whole.

3.8.3 Statistical Test for Comparing Production Function Relationship

In order to know whether the sample beneficiaries and non-beneficiaries belong to different production function relationships, the **Chow's test** of equality has been applied (Chow, 1960). The Chow's test proceeds as follows:

Step I: Combining all the n_1 and n_2 observations, and obtain its residual sum of squares (RSS), say S_1 with df = ($n_1 + n_2$—k), where k is the number of parameters estimated.

Step II: Run the two individual regressions (1) and (2) and obtain their RSS, say S_2 and S_3 with df = (n_1—k) and (n_2—k) respectively. Add these two RSS, say $S_4 = S_2 + S_3$ with df = ($n_1 + n_2$—2k)

Step III: Obtain $S_5 = S_1$—S_4

Step IV: Given the assumption of Chow's test, it can be shown that

$$F = \frac{S_5 / k}{S_4 / (n_1 + n_2 - 2k)}$$

If the computed 'F' with df = $(k, n_1 + n_2 - 2k)$ exceeds the critical 'F', the hypothesis that the two regressions are the same can be rejected. In other words, such regression differs in intercepts, slopes or both.

3.8.4 Estimation of Returns to Scale

In the Cobb-Douglas type of production function, the returns to scale are measured by adding the elasticity of all the inputs. Thus, for the production function

$$Y = a X_1^{b1} X_2^{b2} X_3^{b3} X_4^{b4} X_5^{b5} X_6^{b6} X_7^{b7} e^{u}$$

$b_1, b_2 \ldots\ldots b_n$ are the regression coefficients or elasticity of production and returns to scale is;

$$\sum b = b_1 + b_2 + \ldots \ldots\ldots + b_n$$

Depending upon the sum of the regression coefficient as less than, equal to or greater than unity, the prevailing returns to scale may be considered as decreasing, constant or increasing respectively. Since the elasticities of coefficients are constant in the Cobb-Douglas production function, the scale returns so indicated simply representing the average condition for the sample farms. The sums of regression coefficients were further tested for their deviation from unity (Koutsoyiannis, 1977). The test is applied as follows:

$$Z^{*} = \frac{| bi - 1 |}{SE.\sum (bi)}$$

Where,

bi = Sum of the production elasticities.

SE of (bi) =The standard error of the sum of the production elasticities.

3.8.5 The Estimation of Marginal Value Product (MVP)

The regression coefficient or elasticity of production of inputs obtained from crop production function has been used to calculate the Marginal Value Products (MVP) of individual resources at their geometric means for the average farms. The formula used for the purpose is as given below (Dhawan and Bansal, 1977).

$$\text{MVP P}xi = \text{MPP } xi \times Py$$

$$\text{MVP of } xi = bi.\frac{\text{Geometric Mean of } Y}{\text{Geometric Mean of } xi} \times Py$$

Where bi = Elasticity of production of ith input.

Py = per unit price of output.

The resource use efficiency of the average farmer has been judged on the neo-classical criterion that each factor of production is paid equal to its marginal productivity. It is pointed out that this test is relevant for knowing whether agricultural production of the region could be increased profitably to a significant extent by making adjustments in the existing use of inputs. A resource is considered to be used most efficiently, if its MVP is sufficient to offset its cost. This criterion was used as a test of resource use efficiency. If the MVP of particular resource is positive, it means that there exits scope for further increase in the use of inputs to the point where MVPxi = Pxi. The ratio of Marginal Value Product (MVP) to the factor cost (Pxi) is higher than unity indicating that the resources are efficiently used.

3.9 Estimation of Gross Family Employment and Income Functions

The differentials in income and employment of sample households have been estimated by simple tabular analysis, while the factors influencing these economic parameters have been identified by using the dummy variable approach (Gujrathi, 1995 p.512).

3.9.1. The Annual Gross Family Employment Function

The annual gross family employment function in respect of beneficiary and non-beneficiary households has been deduced not only to identify the factors influencing the employment in both the categories, but also to compare these two regression relations at the same time with the help of an estimation of analysis of covariance employment model based on pooled observations which is specified as under:

$$Y = a + b_1 X_1 + b_2 X_2 + b_3 X_3 + b_4 D_1 + b_5 (D_1 X_1) + b_6 (D_1 X_2) + b_7 (D_1 X_3) + u$$

Where;

Y= Annual gross family employment in man-days.

X_1 = Gross cropped area in hectare.

X_2 = Working capital investment in Rs (Agriculture and agro-based activities)

X_3 = Working adult units (number)

D_1 = 0, if non-beneficiary

D_1 = 1, if beneficiary

a = Intercept and U = error term.

b_1, b_2 and b_3 are the regression coefficients of the respective variables of the base category i.e. non-beneficiaries. The b_4 is the differential intercept coefficient and b_5, b_6 and b_7 are the differential slope coefficients of X_1, X_2 and X_3 variables, respectively. The differential intercept and slope coefficient indicate that how the intercept and slope coefficient of respective variables of beneficiaries employment function differs from the intercept and slope coefficient by the non-beneficiaries employment function. Here, the dummy variable D_1 is introduced to measure the shift not only in intercept but also in the slope coefficient of the beneficiaries function because of implementation of scheme under study. If the differential intercept coefficient (b_4) is statistically non-significant then, we may accept the hypothesis that the two regressions have a common intercept. Similarly, if the differential slope coefficient, say b_5 is statistically significant, and then we may reject the hypothesis that the slope coefficients in respect of X_1 variable in both regressions are the same. It is expected that this model may enable us to find out whether implementation of the central sector scheme *Women in Agriculture* has made any difference in the gross family employment of the sample households under study, assuming of course, all other variables were held constant.

3.9.1.1 Estimation of Mean Employment Functions of Beneficiaries and Non-Beneficiaries

From the above said single regression model, the individual employment function of the two different categories can easily be deduced as under.

Assuming that E(Ui) =0, then mean employment function of **non-beneficiaries** would be:

$$E\,(Yi / D_1 = 0, X_1, X_2, X_3) = a + b_1X_1 + b_2X_2 + b_2X_3$$

Similarly, the mean employment function of **beneficiaries** would be:

$$E\,(Yi / D_1 = 1, X_1, X_2, X_3) = (a + b_4) + (b_1 + b_5)\,X_1 + (b_2 + b_6)\,X_2$$
$$(b_3 + b_7)\,X_3$$

This is how the estimation of a single employment model enables us to estimate two individual employment functions with the help of a dummy variable technique.

Specification of Variables

A. Dependent Variable:

Annual Family Gross Employment in Day (Y)

Gross family employment from all sources (farm and non-farm) during the year 2001-2002 was estimated and expressed in terms of man-days of eight hours. 300 man-days in a year has been considered as a full employment norm according to time criteria. The day-to-day work done by children (10-15 years), Adult male and female (16 to 60 years and above) has been recorded in terms of hours as suggested by Ghosh, B. N. (1977), Bindu and Thakur (1996).

B. Independent Variables

1. Gross cropped area in hectares (X_1)

This variable has been considered as an explanatory variable with an intention of knowing the contribution of gross cropped area in the annual family employment.

2. Working capital investment in agriculture and agro-based activities in rupees (X_2)

This variable included the expenditure on inputs such as labour both human and bullock, seed, manure, fertilizer, irrigation, crop protection and repairs of machinery and hiring charges of implements and machinery utilized for crop production plus the working expenses made on agro-based activities i.e. Papad making, bee keeping, basket making, etc off-farm and non-farm enterprises which generate the employment and therefore this variable has been taken as an explanatory variable.

3. Family size in adult units (X_3)

As mentioned earlier, the family size of the sample households was measured in adult units. It was expected that increase in size of family of farm households would result in increasing the gross family employment with the view to earn more for meeting increased family expenditure. In other words, the size of family may indicate positive relationship with its gross family employment. To check this presumption, this independent variable has been considered for analysis.

4. Dummy variable (D_1)

The dummy variable has been introduced to compare the difference of two regressions in not only in the intercept but also in the slope coefficient of the variables. The non-beneficiaries group has been considered as a base category by assigning zero value, while the beneficiaries group has been given one value.

3.9.2 Estimation of gross family income function

The gross family income function in respect of two categories of households, i.e., beneficiaries and non-beneficiaries has been estimated and compared on the line of employment function explained earlier.

Specification of Income Model

The multiple linear regression equation of the following type is used.

$$Y = a + b_1X_1 + b_2X_2 + b_3X_3 + b_4D_1 + b_5(D_1X_1) + b_6(D_1X_2) + b_7(D_1X_3) + u$$

Where,

Y = Annual gross family income in Rupees

X_1 = Gross cropped area in hectares

X_2 = Working capital investment in crop and agro-based enterprise in rupees

X_3 = Annual gross family employment (off-farm and non-farm except service) in man-days

D_1 = Dummy variable which has been assigned values as under:

D_1 = 1, if beneficiary

D_1 = 0, if non-beneficiaries.

a = intercept, U = error term.

b_1, b_2, b_3 are the regression coefficients of the respective variables of base category, i.e., non-beneficiaries income function. The b_4 is the differential intercept coefficient and b_5, b_6, b_7 are the differential slope coefficients of the variables X_1, X_2 and X_3 respectively.

3.9.2.1 Estimation of Mean Income Functions of the Beneficiaries and Non-Beneficiaries.

From the above said income model, the individual income function can be derived as under.

Assuming that E (ui) = 0

(i) Mean income function of ***non-beneficiaries*** would be;

$$E(Yi/D_1 = 0, X_1, X_2, X_3) = a + b_1X_1 + b_2X_2 + b_3X_3$$

(ii) Similarly, the mean function of ***beneficiaries*** would be;

$$F(Yi/D_1 = 1, X_1, X_2, X_3) = (a + b_4) + (b_1 + b_5)X_1 + (b_2 + b_6)X_2 + (b_3 + b_7)X_3$$

Specification of Variables

A. Dependent Variable

Annual Gross Family Income (Y)

Annual gross family income from different sources namely, agriculture, wages, off-farm, non-farm and service of the sample households during the year 2001-2002 have been considered.

B. Independent Variables

1. Gross cropped area in hectare (X_1)

This independent variable has been considered to know the contribution of gross-cropped area in the annual gross family income of both the categories of the farms.

2. Working capital investment in crop and agro-based enterprises in ruppes (X_2)

This explanatory variable is identical to that of one used under employment function. It was thought that the increase in working capital investment in farm activities especially crop and agro-based activities may generate income in respect of both the categories of farms.

3. Annual family employment from off-farm and non-farm activities in man days (X_3)

This variable included the gross family employment from off-farm and non-farm activities except service (private and government) and is expressed in man-days of eight hours. It was expected that the gross family employment through these activities might indicate positive association with the gross family income.

4. Dummy variable (D_1)

This variable is introduced to measure the shift in intercept as well as slope coefficient of the above said variables in beneficiaries income function because of the scheme implementation.

3.9.2.2 Test the Significance of Difference between the Mean of Annual Income of Two Sample Households

To test the significance of difference between the means of annual household income of beneficiary and non-beneficiary sample households was carried out by applying the simple 't' test with the following formula. (Gupta, 1997 p. A-336)

$$t = \frac{\overline{X_1} - \overline{X_2}}{S} \times \sqrt{\frac{n_1 \times n_2}{n_1 + n_2}}$$

X_1 = mean annual income of beneficiaries households

X_2 = mean annual income of non-beneficiaries households

S = combined standard deviation

n_1 = number of observations (beneficiaries)

n_2 = number of observations (non-beneficiaries)

The value of S was calculated by the following formula.

$$S=\sqrt{\frac{\sum(X_1-\overline{X}_1)^2+\sum(X_2-\overline{X}_2)^2}{n_1+n_2-2}}$$

The degree of freedom= (n_1 +n_2–2)

If calculated t > table t, it could be concluded that, two means of annual income of beneficiaries and non-beneficiaries differed significantly from each other.

3.10 Constraint Analysis

While designing the project /scheme, every care is taken to be a flawless in implementation. However, it has been experienced that at the implementation stage some lacunae are observed. The constraint analysis gives an insight to both the beneficiaries and implementers for the mid- term corrections.

To attain this objective of the study, the views of beneficiary farm women were gathered regarding the problems being faced while participating in the scheme under study, their perceptions about the way of implementation and suggestions for improvement in the scheme implementation. Information was also gathered regarding general problems faced by the beneficiary and non-beneficiary farm women in availing the benefits of the development schemes. Non-beneficiary farm women were requested to give their opinions for improving the participation of rural women in different projects. While collection of data and reviewing the scheme, some discrepancies were noted at the field level which were taken as a general types of constraints. The data were compiled by simple the tabulation and percentage method.

4

Socio-Economic Features of the Sample Households

Agro-physical and socio-economic conditions have profound influence on the production of crops and livestock. Therefore, in scientific investigation concerning to these enterprises in a particular tract, the study of economic background is necessary to understand the implications of physical conditions under which production is carried out. The various factors like topography, location, climate, rainfall, soil, irrigation, marketing and communication facilities etc. decide the suitability of a particular enterprise to that area. Therefore, a brief account of the agro-physical and socio-economic conditions prevailing in the district is given in this chapter so as to have better knowledge about the region and to help interpretation of results and drawing inferences.

4.1 Socio-economic Features of study Area:

The Central sector scheme 'Women in Agriculture' was implemented in Dahanu, Wada and Palghar talukas of Thane district in Maharashtra State, which have been taken for the study. (Fig 2 and 3)

Thane district is one of the four districts of Konkan region, which receives annual rainfall upto 2500 mm. This district is highly urbanized as 72.58 per cent of population lives in urban area. The district consists of 14.74 per cent tribal population and six tahsils have more than 50 per cent of tribal population in their total population. Paddy is grown as a main food crop

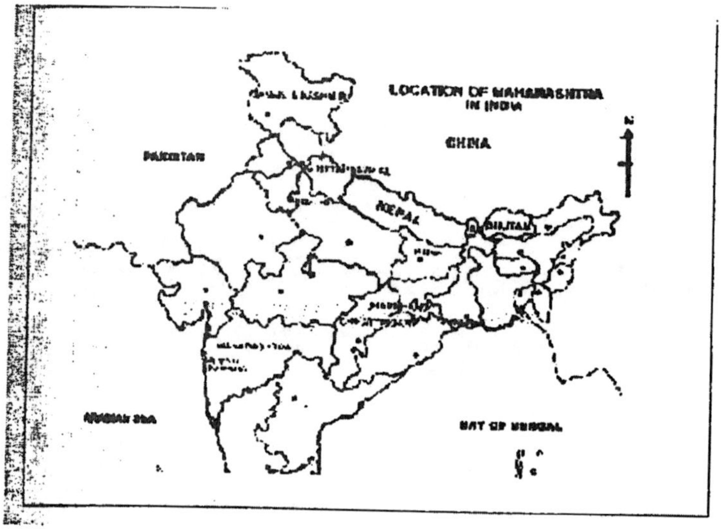

Fig. 2 Location of Maharashtra State in India.

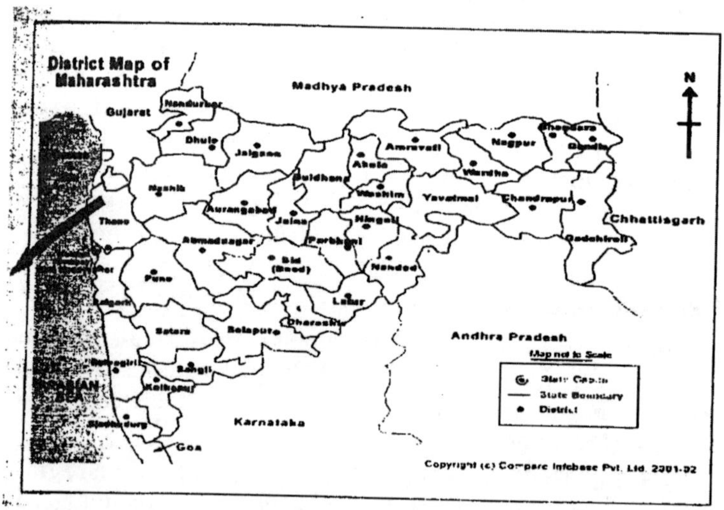

Fig. 3 Map of Maharashtra State Showing a location of Thane District.

followed by vegetables and fruit crops. Cropping intensity is restricted due to limited irrigation potential created in the district. Despite several efforts for mechanization, the spread of important farm machinery and implements was not encouraging.

4.2 Socio-Economic Features of Sample Households

As a prelude to the main analysis concerning to deployment and use of farm resources and their productivities, income and employment of the sample households, some important aspects of the structure of farms and their organisation must be studied. It is always essential to know the details of the composition of the selected sample farm families along with their capital assets, land use pattern, cropping pattern and socio-economic characteristics of sample households before going to further analysis.

This section has been devoted to examine some important aspects of the farms and their organization in respect of both beneficiary and non- beneficiary sample households. The aspects examined are related to average size and composition of sample farm families, caste of sample households, per farm value of capital assets, land use pattern of sample farms and cropping pattern of the sample households based on analysis of data for the year 2001-2002. It is expected that this information will enable to understand distinct socio-economic characteristics of the beneficiary in relation to non- beneficiary sample households.

4.2.1 Size and Composition of Sample Farm Families

The size of a family denotes the total number of members living together under one common headship and sharing food under one roof of a family. In the present study, it refers to the family members of the respondent farm women. The information on family size and its composition is presented in Table 4.1 with the view to ascertain the pressure of population on land and availability of owned labour at farm level.

It is revealed from the Table 4.1 that at the overall level, the average family size of the sample households did not differ significantly, which shows the nucleus type of family pattern. The male members were 25.32 per cent in beneficiary and 23 per cent in non-beneficiary households. The proportion of females and children were 28.33 per cent and 46.35 per cent in beneficiary and 27.98 per cent and 49.02 per cent in non-beneficiary households.

Table 4.1
Average Size and Composition of the Sample Farm Families

(Numbers)

Sex	*Beneficiaries*				*Non-Beneficiaries*			
	Small (N=48)	*Medium (N=43)*	*Large (N=29)*	*Overall (N=120)*	*Small (N=48)*	*Medium (N=43)*	*Large (N=29)*	*Overall (N=120)*
Adult Male	1.10 (22.87)	1.18 (25.87)	1.31 (28.60)	1.18 (25.32)	1.02 (23.23)	1.02 (22.67)	1.20 (23.26)	1.06 (23)
Adult Female	1.36 (28.27)	1.32 (28.95)	1.27 (27.73)	1.32 (28.33)	1.27 (28.93)	1.23 (27.33)	1.41 (27.33)	1.29 (27.98)
Children	2.35 (48.86)	2.06 (45.18)	2.0 (43.67)	2.16 (46.35)	2.10 (47.84)	2.25 (50)	2.55 (49.41)	2.26 (49.02)
Average per family	4.81 (100)	4.56 (100)	4.58 (100)	4.66 (100)	4.39 (100)	4.50 (100)	5.16 (100)	4.61 (100)

(Figures in the parentheses indicate the percentages to the respective average size of family)

The average size of the family at the overall level was 4.66 in beneficiaries and 4.61 in non-beneficiaries. Importantly, the average size of family was a bit more in small size class of beneficiaries and large size class of non-beneficiaries. The adult females were a bit more than adult male in both the categories.

4.2.2 Caste

Caste is an endogamous group where the status of an individual in a group is determined by his or her birth. The castes are 'discrete categories' because they are no more related to each other organically, nor are they segmentary entities. In order to uplift the socio-economic status of a large number of castes traditionally belonging to the lowest ladder in the Indian society, they have been scheduled in the constitution for granting state benefits to them. The scheduled castes and scheduled tribes are categories constructed by the Indian state. Recently, the Other Backward Classes (OBCs) have also created to extend the state benefits to the castes in the middle and lower hierarchy of traditional Indian society (Bhagat, 2003). Thus, castes are classified for this study in the following categories depending upon their privileges granted through constitutional means.

1. General Castes- Marathas, Brahmins and Muslims
2. Other Backward Castes (OBC)- Bari, Kunbi, Wadwal, Teli, Bhandari, Agari, Kumbhar etc.
3. SC, ST : Mahar, Chambhar, Katkari, Malhar Koli and Warli

The information was collected to assess the social stratification of the sample households as the education, social status, land holding and family income are closely associated with the caste of the individual. The sample households were broadly classified according to their caste group and it is presented in Table 4.2 below.

Table- 4.2
Caste-wise Composition of Samples Households

(Numbers)

Caste group	*Beneficiaries (N=120)*				*Non-beneficiaries (N = 120)*			
	Small	*Medium*	*Large*	*Overall*	*Small*	*Medium*	*Large*	*Overall*
STs	20.00 (41.67)	9.00 (20.93)	5.00 (17.24)	34.00 (28.33)	21.00 (43.75)	14.00 (32.56)	1.00 (3.45)	36.00 (30.00)
SCs	2.00 (4.17)	1.00 (2.33)	---	3.00 (2.5)	2.00 (4.17)	4.00 (9.30)	4.00 (13.79)	10.00 (8.33)
OBCs	25.00 (52.08)	33.00 (76.74)	22.00 (75.86)	80.00 (66.67)	25.00 (52.08)	24.00 (55.81)	24.00 (82.76)	73.00 (60.83)
GEN	1.00 (2.08)	---	2.00 (6.90)	3.00 (2.5)	---	1.00 (2.33)	---	1.00 (0.84)
Total	48.00 (100)	43.00 (100)	29 (100)	120 (100)	48.00 (100)	43.00 (100)	29 (100)	120.00 (100)

(Figures in the parentheses indicate percentages to the respective total)

It was examined from the Table 4.2 that at the overall level, the tribal and Other Backward Caste (OBCs) was predominant in the sample households as both of these castes jointly represented about 95 per cent in beneficiaries and 90.83 per cent in case of non-beneficiaries. Among the tribals, *Warli, Katkari* and *Malhar Koli* were prominent tribes while *Kunbi* and *Wadwal* were in majority under OBC categories. It was interesting to note that majority of the tribal was small holders in both the sample households and a few of them were large landholders which indicate the fragile resources base. The farmers belonging to the OBCs category represented 66.67 per cent in beneficiaries and 60.83 per cent in non-beneficiaries which indicates their strong economic base in the rural area as OBCs are considered the traditionally agrarian community. Farmers from SCs and General category were poorly represented in both the sample households. The castewise composition of the sample households in graphically shown in the Fig. 4.

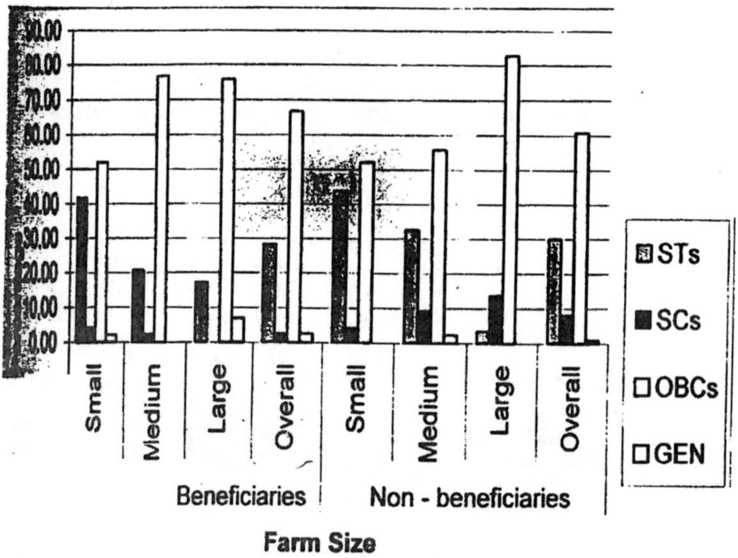

Fig. 4: Caste-wise composition of sample households.

4.2.3 Per Farm Value of Capital Assets

Capital assets with the farmers influence the adoption of modern technology leading to increase in crop productivity. The details of the capital assets possessed by the sample households during the year 2001-2002 are given in the Table 4.3.

It was observed from Table 4.3 that at the overall level, beneficiary household possessed more capital assets (Rs.1,39,934.04) than non-beneficiary farm women households (Rs. 1,05,987.73) and the total value of assets increased with an increase in the farm size. The residential house emerged as the most valuable asset in both the households. Next to residential house, implements and machinery was the important asset which alone shared 13.91 per cent in beneficiary and 15.53 per cent in case of non-beneficiary farms. The livestock asset shared only 2.22 per cent and 2.01 per cent in beneficiary and non-beneficiary household respectively. It was also seen that at the overall level, the value of important assets was higher in case of beneficiaries than non-beneficiaries.

4.2.4 Land use Pattern of the Sample Farms

The details of the average land use pattern for the year 2001-02 of the sample farms are given in Table 4.4.

It could be revealed from Table 4.4 that at the overall level, the average size of holding was 0.89 and 0.81 in beneficiary and non-beneficiary respectively. The proportion of gross irrigated area to gross cropped area was 0.04 per cent in beneficiary and 0.02 per cent in non-beneficiary. The cropping intensity was 102.27 per cent and 101.68 per in beneficiary and non-beneficiary households respectively, which indicated the poor irrigation status in the study area.

4.2.5 Cropping Pattern of the Sample Households

The cropping pattern within a homogeneous agro-climatic area is influenced by soil type, size of holding, source of irrigation, level of investment and availability of resources. However, in the changing scenario of agriculture, the new agricultural

Table 4.3
Per Farm Value of Capital Assets of the Sample Farms during the Year 2001-02

(Rupees)

Assets	*Beneficiaries*				*Non-Beneficiaries*			
	Small	*Medium*	*Large*	*Overall*	*Small*	*Medium*	*Large*	*Overall*
Residential house	54895.83 (71.80)	100186.0 (75.02)	133034 (67.26)	96038.64 (68.63)	35006 (72. 51)	87650 (75.28)	110223 (73.72)	77623 (73.24)
Farm house	1354 (1.77)	465.11 (0.35)	20213.79 (10.22)	11344.3 (8.11)	--	3200 (2.75)	4300 (2.88)	3750 (3.54)
Irrigation structure	2516 (3.29)	3283.72 (2.46)	7941.37 (4.01)	4580.36 (3.27)	1200 (2. 49)	2356.12 (2.02)	6530.20 (4.37)	3362.10 (3.17)
Oil Engine /Electric motor	3802 (4.97)	3999.99 (3.0)	7413.78 (3.75)	5071.92 (3.62)	1320 (2. 73)	2635.21 (2.26)	3480.23 (2.33)	2478.48 (2.34)
Pipe line	202 (0.26)	305.10 (0.23)	480 (0.24)	329 (0.24)	120 (0. 25)	156 (0.13)	261 (0.17)	179 (0.17)
Implement and machinery	11595 (15.17)	22015.55 (16.49)	24781.26 (12.53)	19463.93 (13.91)	8650 (17. 92)	18130.32 (15.57)	22620.30 (15.13)	16466.87 (15.53)
Livestock	2091.66 (2.74)	3295 (2.47)	3931.03 (1.99)	3105.89 (2.22)	1980. 30 (4. 10)	2301.10 (1.98)	2103.45 (1.40)	2128.28 (2.01)
Total assets	76456.49 (100)	133550.4 (100)	197795.23 (100)	139934.04 (100)	48276. 3 (100)	116428.75 (100)	149518.18 (100)	105987.7 (100)

(Figures in parentheses indicate the percentages to the respective totals of capital assets)

Table 4.4

Per Farm Land use Pattern of the Sample Households in Different Farm Size Groups

(ha)

Particulars	*Beneficiaries*				*Non-Beneficiaries*			
	Small (N=48)	*Medium (N=43)*	*Large (N=29)*	*Overall (N=120)*	*Small (N=48)*	*Medium (N= 43)*	*Large (N=29)*	*Overall (N=120)*
Total holding	0.37	0.81	1.85	0.89	0.32	0.75	1.69	0.81
Permanent Fallow Land	--	---	0.01	0.01	---	0.01	0.05	0.02
Cultivable Land	0.37	0.81	1.84	0.88	0.32	0.74	1.64	0.79
Net Cropped area (NCA)	0.37	0.81	1.84	0.88	0.32	0.74	1.64	0.79
Area cropped more than once	0.01	0.03	0.04	0.02	--	0.03	0.01	0.01
Gross Cropped Area (GCA)	0.38	0.84	1.88	0.90	0.32	0.77	1.65	0.80
Area under irrigation	0.004	0.030	0.13	0.045	---	0.029	0.0724	0.027
Proportion of gross irrigated area to the gross cropped area (%)	0.023	0.083	0.24	0.041	---	0.086	0.15	0.028
Cropping intensity (GCA/NCA) *100	102.70	103.70	102.17	102.27	100	104.05	100.61	101.68

(Figures in parentheses indicate the percentage)

technology plays a vital role in determining the cropping pattern and the intensity with which the land is utilized. The new agricultural technology generally influences cropping pattern in two ways: firstly, by shifting the area away from less remunerative crops to more remunerative crops and secondly, by shifting from single/mono cropping to double or multiple cropping.

The cropping pattern and intensity of cropping brought about by new technology and vice–versa were examined in detail for sample households as a whole and is given in Table-4.5

It is indicated from Table 4.5 that paddy was the main staple food crop grown on a large scale as it was grown on 87.10 cent on beneficiary farms and 92.77 per cent on non-beneficiary farms of the total cropped area, which supports the livelihood of the sample households. The mono-cropping system was adopted in the Thane district because of high rainfall in which paddy is traditionally the best-suited crop. Other crops grown were like vegetables mainly chilli and brinjal on small scale. Sapota was grown mainly in the Dahanu tahsil and other fruit crops like mango, jackfruit, jamun were planted especially on bunds. Among other crops were pulses, betelvine, minor millets, which were taken on very small area.

To sum up, it is seen from the above description of sample households that the average size of family at the overall level was 4.66 members and 4.61 members in beneficiary and non-beneficiary households. Tribal and Other Backward Caste farmers had the majority in the sample households followed by farmers from SCs and general category. Regarding the capital assets possessed by the sample households, beneficiaries had possessed more capital assets, i.e., higher by Rs. 33946.31 as compared to non-beneficiaries. The average size of holding was 0.89 ha. and 0.81 ha in beneficiaries and non-beneficiaries respondents. Due to poor irrigation facilities, cropping intensity was 102.27 per cent and 101.68 per cent on beneficiary and non-beneficiary farms. Paddy was the main crop as it had occupied more than 85 per cent of total cropped area. This crop was followed by the crops such as vegetables, fruits and pulses grown on a small scale.

Table 4.5
Cropping Pattern of Sample Households during the Year 2001-02

(ha)

Crops	*Beneficiaries*				*Non-Beneficiaries*			
	Small	*Medium*	*Large*	*Overall*	*Small*	*Medium*	*Large*	*Overall*
Paddy	17.57 (97.29)	31.9 (86.87)	48.63 (84.06)	98.1 (87.10)	15 (97.40)	30.35 (96.66)	45.35 (88.97)	90.7 (92.77)
Other cereals	---	0.05 (0.14)	---	0.05 (0.04)	---	0.02 (0.06)	0.07 (0.14)	0.09 (0.09)
Pulses (Beans)	---	0.10 (0.27)	0.30 (0.52)	0.40 (0.36)	--	0.10 (0.32)	0.20 (0.39)	0.30 (0.30)
Oilseeds	--	0.05 (0.14)	0.12 (0.21)	0.17 (0.15)	--	0.03 (0.10)	0.05 (0.10)	0.08 (0.08)
a. Chilli	0.47 (2.60)	2.92 (7.95)	5.5 (9.51)	8.89 (7.89)	0.35 (2.27)	0.40 (0.32)	3.50 (6.87)	4.25 (4.35)
b. Brinjal	0.02 (0.11)	0.1 (0.27)	0.40 (0.69)	0.52 (0.46)	0.05 (0.32)	0.10 (0.32)	0.20 (0.39)	0.35 (0.36)
Total Vegetables	0.49 (2.71)	3.02 (8.22)	5.9 (10.20)	9.41 (8.35)	0.40 (2.60)	0.50 (1.59)	3.70 (7.26)	4.6 4.70)
a. Chikku	--	1.4 (3.81)	2.50 (4.32)	3.9 (3.46)	--	0.40 (1.27)	1.50 (2.94)	1.90 (1.94)
b. Mango	--	0.20 (0.54)	0.40 (0.69)	0.6 (0.53)	--	---	0.10 (0.20)	0.10 (0. 0)
Total horticulture		1.6 (4.36)	2.90 (5.01)	4.5 (4.0)	---	0.40 (1.27)	1.60 (3.14)	2.0 (2.05)
Total	18.06 (100)	36.72 (100)	57.85 (100)	112.63 (100)	15.40 (100)	31.40 (100)	50.97 (100)	97.77 (100)

(Figures in parentheses indicate the percentage)

4.3 Socio-Economic Characteristic of the Farm Women

This section of the chapter is devoted to study the socio-economic attributes like age, education and occupational status of the respondent farm women.

4.3.1 Age

Age denotes the chronologically completed calendar year by the respondents. Age influences the behaviour of the individual by exposing to varied situations number of time and therefore, the age of the farm women was considered as an essential aspect in this study. The distribution of sample farm women according to age groups is given in Table 4.6.

Table 4.6
The Distribution of Farm Women According to their Age Group

Sr. No.	*Age group*	*Beneficiaries (N=120)*		*Non Beneficiaries (N=120)*	
		Number of Farm Women	*Per cent*	*Number of Farm Women*	*Per cent*
1.	Young aged (Up to 30 yrs)	37	30.83	38	31.67
2.	Middle aged (31to 50 yrs)	75	62.50	67	55.83
3.	Old aged (51 yrs and above)	8	6.67	15	12.5
	Total	**120**	**100**	**120**	**100**

It is noted that sample farm women from the categories of beneficiaries and non-beneficiaries had by and large the same proportion in the first age group, i.e., upto 30 years. In the second group, i.e., 31-50 years, there were 75 farm women, i.e., 62.50 per cent farm women from the categories of beneficiaries. The proportion of non-beneficiary farm women was 55.83 per cent in this age group. The farm women belonging to old age group, i.e., 51 years and above was 6.67 per cent in beneficiaries and 12.5 in non-beneficiaries.

It is clear that the majority of farm women were belonging to middle age group, i.e., 31 to 50 years.

4.3.2 Educational Status of Respondent Farm Women

Education is a prerequisite for adoption of technology. The objectives of the education are to bring about desired changes in the farmers knowledge, skill and attitude. The process ultimately helps in accelerating crop production and making the community better off. Considering these aspects, the formal education of farm women was studied. The data in these respects are presented in Table 4.7.

It is noted that the proportion of sample farm women having primary education was 40 per cent in beneficiaries and 38.33 per cent in non-beneficiaries. Besides, the farm women having secondary education, i.e., 8th to 10th std. had the proportion of 37.5 and 31.67 per cent in the above categories respectively. This clearly indicates that bulk of farm women belonging to both the categories had the primary and secondary education. Interestingly, the proportion of illiterate farm women were 9.17 per cent in beneficiaries and 21.67 per cent in non-beneficiaries which indicates relatively more illiteracy in non-beneficiary farm women.

4.3.3 Occupational Status of the Farm Women

Occupation refers to trade or professional activities in which the entire family is traditionally engaged. In ancient times, occupation in rural areas was closely associated with the caste system. However, in modern times occupation continues to be an important source of status and prestige along-with its determining role influencing the level of income of an individual in society. However, with the increase in modernization and diversification, it has become problematic to classify different occupations into meaningful categories. Although, the occupations depending upon natural endowment and level of economic development, major categories could nevertheless be identified as given in Table 4.8

Table 4.7
Educational Status of Beneficiary and Non-beneficiary Farm Women of Sample Households

Educational Status	*Beneficiaries (N=120)*				*Non-Beneficiaries (N=120)*			
	Small (N=48)	*Medium (N=43)*	*Large (N=29)*	*Overall (N=120)*	*Small (N=48)*	*Medium (N=43)*	*Large (N=29)*	*Overall (N=120)*
Illiterate	10.00 (20.83)	1.00 (2.33)	---	11.00 (9.17)	14.00 (29.17)	11.00 (25.58)	1.00 (3.45)	26.00 (21.67)
Primary (Std 1-7)	19.00 (39.58)	21.00 (48.84)	8.00 (27.59)	48.00 (40.00)	25.00 (52.08)	11.00 (25.58)	10.00 (34.48)	46.00 (38.33)
Secondary (Std 8-10)	17.00 (35.42)	16.00 (37.20)	12.00 (41.38)	45.00 (37.5)	9.00 (18.75)	16.00 (37.21)	13.00 (44.83)	38.00 (31.67)
Higher Secondary (Std 11-12)	2.00 (4.17)	2.00 (4.65)	5.00 (17.24)	9.00 (7.5)	---	3.00 (6.98)	3.00 (10.34)	6.00 (5.00)
College)	---	3.00 (6.98)	4.00 (13.79)	7.00 (5.83)	--	2.00 (4.65)	2.00 (6.90)	4.00 (3.33)
Total	48.00 (100)	43.00 (100)	29.00 (100)	120.00 (120)	48.00 (100)	43.00 (100)	29.00 (100)	120.00 (100)

(Figures in parentheses indicate the percentage)

Table 4.8
Distribution of Sample Farm Women According to Their Occupation

Occupation	*Beneficiaries (N=120)*				*Non-beneficiaries (N=120)*			
	Small	*Medium*	*Large*	*Overall*	*Small*	*Medium*	*Large*	*Overall*
Agriculture	30.0 (62.5)	26.00 (60.47)	15.00 (51.72	71.00 (59.17	25.00 (52.09	29.00 (67.44)	19.00 (65.52)	73.00 (60.83)
Agril +Wages	12.00 (25.00	5.00 (11.63)	---	17.00 (14.16	19.00 (39.58	10.00 (23.26)	10.00 (34.48)	39.00 (32.50)
Agril. +Allied	6.0 (12.5)	12.00 (27.90)	14.00 (48.27	32.00 (26.67	4.00 (8.33)	4.00 (9.30)	–	8.00 (6.67)
Service (Pvt/ Govt.)	–	--	---	--	---	---	--	--
Total	48.00 (100)	43.00 (100)	29.00 (100)	120 (100)	48.00 (100)	43.00 (100)	29.00 (100)	120 (100)

(Figures in parentheses indicate the percentages)

It is observed that in case of beneficiary farm women at the overall level, the proportion of farm women having agriculture as a occupation was 59.17 per cent followed by agriculture + allied activities to the extent of 26.67 per cent and agriculture + wages was 14.16 per cent.

As regards non-beneficiaries, the occupation of agriculture showed the dominance since 60.83 per cent of farm women had agriculture as a main occupation followed by agriculture +wages as occupation for 32.50 per cent of farm women. Importantly, the proportion of farm women having agriculture + allied activities was meagre, i.e., 6.67 per cent. It is also noted that, not a single farm woman belonging to these two categories was engaged in service either in private or in government organization.

To sum up, it can be said that agriculture and agriculture+allied activities in beneficiaries and agriculture, agriculture + wages were main occupation to the non- beneficiary sample farm women.

In brief, from the socio-economic status of the sample farm women respondents, it is seen that, 93.33 per cent of beneficiary and 87.50 per cent of non-beneficiary farm women were below the age of 50 years. The beneficiary farm women were at little bit higher literacy level as compared to non-beneficiary farm women. Agriculture was a major source of employment for both the sample households.

5

Impact of the Scheme on Decision-Making of Farm Women and their Socio-Economic Empowerment

In the modern age, the decision-making of the farm enterprises and family affairs should be done by all economically active family members in a democratic spirit. Several studies conducted in India and abroad suggested that in order to increase the role of farm women in decision making for agricultural production, dairy and other allied activities of technical nature, it is necessary to equip them with latest information so that they can play a vital role in decision making in the family (Uta Hoffmann and Vogler 2001; Kazakopoulos, 2001). It was also observed that house wives/ farm women were consulted more on the agricultural activities which are mostly carried out and supervised by them (Rimawi, 1998). Farm women are little consulted in the matter of technical nature due to lack of knowledge or training among the farm women. (Talukdar *et al*, 1997; Boreth et al, 2002).

Decision–making as a mental process requires conscious reasoning. Rational decision involves the use of deliberation, planning and best available sources of information and advice in arriving at a decision as a means of achieving maximum economic and other allied ends.

The successful launching of Central Sector Scheme viz. Women in Agriculture has provided much impetus for agricultural development in the Thane district of Maharashtra State. However, if the condition of farm women has to improve considerably, the efficiency of their decision making skill must be enhanced in respect of how to produce, how much to produce and when to produce and how to allocate the income resulting from their farm business among family living needs, debt payment and capital investment.

The decision-making ability of an individual might be influenced by the possession of farm related technical knowledge, skills and socio-economic characteristics. Therefore, in order to assess the extent of participation of farm women in making decisions about the different aspects of agricultural operations, certain statements were included in the schedule. The participation of farm women in decision-making was measured by computing the Decision Making Index (DMI) explained in the methodology chapter. Keeping these issues in mind, the impact assessment of the scheme under study on the decision making of farm women and ascertaining the factors responsible for decision-making was taken as one of the objectives of present study.

It was also assumed that due to implementation of scheme ***Women in Agriculture*** in Thane district, the beneficiary farm women might have been socio-economically empowered. The gap in these types of empowerment was studied by comparing beneficiary farm women with non-beneficiary farm women of the sample households. Details of analysis on these aspects are presented in sub-head 5.4 of this chapter.

5.1 Participation of Farm Women in Decision Making on Different Farm and Non-Farm Activities

Information regarding decision-making was collected from beneficiary farm women on 23 selected activities related to farm operations, dairy enterprise, family activities and participation in the scheme activities and 21 activities were studied for non-beneficiary farm women. The results are presented in Table 5.1.

Table 5.1

Participation of Farm Women in Decision–Making on Different Farm and Non-farm Activities

(Per cent)

	Decision making activities	*Beneficiaries (N=120)*			*Non–Beneficiaries (N=120)*		
		Not Involved	*Joint Decision*	*Independent Decision*	*Not Involved*	*Joint Decision*	*Independent decision*
(A) Crop production activities							
1.	Sale / purchase of land	47. 50	45. 00	7. 50	70. 00	21. 70	8. 30
2.	Selection of crop	11. 70	65. 00	23. 30	72. 00	8. 00	20. 00
3.	Selection of variety	3. 30	33. 30	63. 40	67. 50	13. 30	19. 20
4.	Purchase of agricultural inputs	20. 00	41. 70	38. 30	59. 20	25. 80	15. 00
5.	Use of chemical Fertilizers	5. 00	28. 30	66. 70	51. 20	29. 60	19. 20
6.	Use of FYM	3. 30	67. 50	29. 20	25. 80	53. 30	20. 90
7.	Irrigation management	16. 70	50. 00	33. 30	50. 00	28. 00	22. 00
8.	Plant protection	2. 50	42. 50	55. 00	65. 00	13. 30	21. 70
9.	Intercultural operation	1. 70	42. 50	55. 80	28. 30	49. 20	22. 50
10.	Crop harvesting and transport	20. 80	58. 30	20. 90	75. 80	0. 90	23. 30
11.	Food processing	5. 80	65. 00	29. 20	69. 20	15. 00	15. 80
12.	Sale of produce	10. 00	66. 70	23. 30	33. 30	50. 00	16. 70

Cont/....

	Decision making activities	Beneficiaries (N=120)			Non–Beneficiaries (N=120)		
		Not Involved	Joint Decision	Independent Decision	Not Involved	Joint Decision	Independent decision
13.	Choice of market	15. 80	66. 70	17. 50	32. 50	54. 20	13. 30
14.	Decision on grading of farm produce	15. 00	16. 70	68. 30	39. 20	49. 10	11. 70
(B) Animal husbandry and dairy							
15.	Selection of milch animals	20. 00	75. 00	5. 00	78. 90	10. 60	10. 50
16.	Sale of milk	30. 00	62. 50	7. 50	15. 80	78. 90	5. 30
17.	Preparation of milk products	10. 00	17. 50	72. 50	----	100. 00	----
18.	Preparation of cattle feed	20. 00	52. 50	27. 50	15. 80	73. 70	10. 50
(C) Family affairs and other activities							
19.	Purchase of garments for self	5. 80	79. 20	15. 00	20. 80	69. 20	10. 00
20.	Purchase of Jewellery	25. 00	70. 80	4. 20	25. 00	66. 70	8. 30
21.	Spending of own earnings	----	20. 00	80. 00	33. 30	35. 00	31. 70
22.	Study tour	1. 70	18. 30	80. 00	----	----	----
23.	Working for women's Self Help Group	2. 50	5. 80	91. 70	----	----	----

It is revealed from the Table 5.1 that beneficiary farm women took independent decisions in the activities of technical nature like grading of produce (68.30 per cent), use of chemical fertilisers (66.70 per cent) and selection of variety (63.40 per cent). In addition, they were involved more than 60 per cent in joint decision making process prominently in the activities like use of FYM, sale of produce, choice of market, food processing and selection of crop. Higher level of decisons making by the beneficiary farm women was due to enrichment of their technical knowledge. These findings are in conformity with the findings of Bhuvaneshari and Kannan (1999) who concluded that the active participation of farm women in the decision making on the operations of technical nature was due to the effective skill and knowledge gained through organized programmes by government and non-government organizations.

Their counterpart i.e. non-beneficiary farm women were comparatively less involved in decision-making. Less than 25 per cent farm women took independent decisions. Nearly 65 to 75 per cent of farm women were least involved in the decision making process or sometimes they were not allowed to take an independent decisions. It was further observed that most of the decisions related to farm operations were taken by their husbands or family heads and the farm women had a very little role to play in the same. This dominance of husbands in decision-making process was due to the fact that for taking farm related decisions, one should have technical knowledge and skill about the same. Moreover, husbands are more exposed than their wives to different sources of informations. Further, decisions on many of these items involving expenses and risks for which husbands were in a better position to decide than their wives. Thus, the least involvement of the non-beneficiary farm women in the decision making process was due to lack of technical knowledge and their limited exposure to training and other information sources

The farm women of both the sample households were least involved in the decisions regarding sale and purchase of land and purchase of agricultural inputs. The reasons for the least participation of the farm women in these activities were attributed to involvement of money.

In the area of animal husbandry, beneficiary farm women were taking decisions either independently or were involved in decisions making in the activities of technical nature like preparation of milk products and preparation of feed for cattle. It is also observed that sizeable number of farm women of both the sample were involved in decision making process in the areas of animal husbandry and dairy. These findings are in contrast with the findings of Sheokand *et al* (1999) who concluded that despite high level of participation of farm women in animal husbandry and dairy activities, they were least involved in the decision making.

The involvement of farm women from both the categories of sample households in decision-making was quite satisfactory with respect to purchase of garments and jewellery. However, the beneficiary farm women were comparatively more involved in taking decisions on these aspects.

Sizeable percent of beneficiary farm women were taking an independent decisions regarding their study tours and working with farm women's group.

The beneficiary farm women were enjoying more previlages in spending their earning as compared to the non-beneficiary farm women. These findings are in contrast with the findings of Ghose (1993) who noted that 65.42 per cent of the beneficiary farm women of IRDP were not consulted by the male members while spending their income.

The sizeable number i.e.more than 50 per cent of farm women of both the sample households were involved in joint decision making regarding the sale of produce and chice of market. These findings are inconsistent with the findings of Boreth *et al* (2002) who observed that decisions regarding the agricultural marketing were taken predominantly by male members, which was due to unawareness of women about marketing practices.

Therefore, it can be concluded that the beneficiary farm women had an upper hand in decision making either jointly with other family members or independently due to acquisition of technical knowledge about farm activities through training, demonstrations and study tours.

5.2 Decision Making Index (DMI)

The Decision Making Index (DMI) was computed by applying the formula as described earlier under methodology chapter to examine the gaps in the decision making between beneficiary and non–beneficiary farm women. The DMI score was grouped as a low (15-30), medium (31- 45) and high (46 and above) based on range of DMI score. In computing the DMI, 23 major activities for beneficiary farm women and 21 activities for non-beneficiary farm women were selected on which farm women were likely to take decisions. The details of the results are presented in Table 5.2.

Table 5.2
Distribution of Beneficiary and Non-Beneficiary Respondents by their Decision Making Index

DMI Score	*Beneficiaries (N=120)*		*Non-beneficiaries (N=120)*	
	Number	*Per cent*	*Number*	*Per cent*
Low (15–30)	01	0. 85	05	4. 16
Medium (31-45)	10	8. 33	54	45. 00
High (46 and above)	109	90. 82	61	50. 83
Total	120	100	120	100

It is observed from the Table 5.2 that more than 90 per cent beneficiary farm women were highly involved in decision making process (DMI Score 46 and above) while only 50.83 per cent of non-beneficiary farm women were categorized under high DMI score. It is thus amply affirmed that beneficiary farm women were either taking decisions independently or were actively involved in joint decisions with their husbands / family heads. This led to the conclusion that, beneficiary farm women were generally taking decisions regarding the activities requiring technical competency since they have access to technical knowledge, skills, various resources and economic independence which are the parameters for enhancing decision-making ability.

5.3 Relationship between the Personal and Socio-Economic Characteristics and Decision -Making of Farm Women

Karl Pearson's correlation coefficient *'r'* was worked out for ascertaining the relationship between socio-economic characteristics of farm women and their decision making. Twelve important socio-economic variables viz. age of farm women, education of farm women, status of farm women in family, extension contacts, social participation, technical knowledge, annual family income, caste, family size, farm size, occupation of family head and education of family head (Puri, 1972) were considered to find out the extent of influence of these variables on the decision-making process of farm women of beneficiary and non-beneficiary sample households. The ***'r'*** value was tested for its significance at 1, 5 and 10 per cent level of significance by applying the *'t' test.*

5.3.1 Age of Farm Women and the Decision Making

Age is an important basic characteristic of an individual linked with participation in social and economical activities. It is also linked with one's maturity and experience of physical participation in a particular activity. The correlation between age and the Decision Making Index (DMI) is given in Table 5.3 below:

Table 5.3
Relationship Between Age of Farm Women and Decision Making

Age of farm women	*Beneficiaries*	*Non-beneficiaries*
	Average value of DMI	*Average value of DMI*
Up to 30 yrs	45. 92	27. 41
31 to 50 yrs	47. 10	31. 75
51 yrs and above	44. 45	29. 11
Overall	45. 82	29. 42
'r' value	0. 053 ^{NS}	0. 052 ^{NS}

***, **, * Significant at 1, 5 and 10 per cent level of probability,
NS = Non- Significant

It is observed from the Table 5.3 that beneficiary farm women in the age group of 30 to 50 years were more involved in the decision making process as average DMI was highest in this age group. On comparison of average DMI of both the samples, it is observed that an average DMI of beneficiaries farm women was high indicating the higher level of decision making by them in the family. The 'r' value of beneficiaries (0.053) and for non-beneficiaries (0.052) turned out to be positive but statistically non-significant. This means that participation of farm women in decision making was not influenced by their age as younger farm women were tended to take more decisions than old age farm women. These findings endorsed the findings of Punia *et at* (1991), Shirodkar (1993) and Kadlag (1994) who concluded from their study that majority of farm women had actively participated in decision making belonging to younger age group (30 to 45) than older farm women. These findings led us to conclude that while selecting the farm women as beneficiaries of any programmes, preference could be given to relatively younger farm women.

5.3.2 Educational level of Farm Women and Decision Making

Education develops personality of an individual and brings about mental development. The individual with higher education acquires more knowledge and is eager to accept new ideas more quickly. He also offers solutions to certain problems more quickly because of rational thinking while taking decisions. The ability to read and write gives individual access to vivid body of the knowledge, expose to social life outside the family and provide entry into other opportunities.

Hence, it was presumed that the decision-making process is largely influenced by the level of education of farm women. Accordingly, the data were collected from the respondents and analysed. The findings are presented in Table 5.4

It is quite apparent from the Table 5.4 that the formal education played a major role in decision-making process. The average DMI increased with an increase in the level of education of farm women of both the sample households. However, the average DMI in all groups and at the overall level was quite higher in case of beneficiaries farm women as compared to non-beneficiaries farm women.

Table 5.4
Relationship Between Education of Farm Women and Decision Making

Level of education	*Beneficiaries* *Average value of DM*	*Non-beneficiaries* *Average value of DM*
Illiterate	36. 98	22. 67
Primary (0-7 Std)	43. 69	28. 09
Secondary (8-10 Std)	48. 09	29. 22
Higher secondary (11-12 Std)	49. 13	30. 12
Graduate and above	51. 22	37. 01
Overall	45. 82	29. 42
'r' value	0. 39 ***	0. 32 ***

***, **, * Significant at 1, 5 and 10 per cent level of probability.
NS = Non-Significant.

The 'r' values turned out to be statistically significant in both the sample households indicating the significant relationship between education of farm women and decision making. It showed that education played a major role in decision-making process due to more articulation in agriculture and the home management front. These findings are having the conformity with the findings of Khatik and Pandey (1997) and Rajkishor *et al* (1999) who reported that education of farm women had shown a significant and positive relationship with their decisions.

5.3.3 Status of Farm Women in Family and Decision-Making

The status of the farm women means the position of women in society or in family. It refers to the position of an individual in the social structure defined by his designated rights and obligations. In the sociological point of view, this concept implies a hierarchical arrangement in family involving a set of rights and obligations, which the occupant is expected to fulfil. It was hypothesized that the farm women who occupy the status as a head or co-head of the family, daughter-in–law and daughter who were the beneficiary of the scheme under study also influence the process of decision making in the family. The relation between the status of farm women in family and decision making is given in Table 5.5.

Table 5.5
Relationship Between the Status of Farm Women in Family and their Decision-Making

Status in family	*Beneficiaries*	*Non-beneficiaries*
	Average value of DMI	*Average value of DMI*
Family head	50. 44	38. 13
Family co-head	45. 25	31. 15
Daughter-in-law/ Daughter	41. 77	19. 00
Overall	45. 82	29. 42
'r' value	0. 11 NS	0. 42 ***

***, **, * Significant at 1, 5 and 10 per cent level of probability.
NS = Non-significant.

It is indicated from the Table 5.5 that the farm women of beneficiary households having a status as a head, co-head of the family, daughter and daughter-in-law were also actively involved in decisions related to farm and family affairs. It implied that daughter–in–law and daughter in the family played a significant role in decisions by sharing technical knowledge with other family members.

In case of non-beneficiary households, it was observed that farm women as a head of family or co-head played a dominant role in decision making as ***r** value* turned out positively significant which implied that the daughter-in law and daughter had little or no say in decision making process. The farm women who was the co-head of the family also played a little role in decision making as compared to the farm women as a head of the family. These findings are in conformity with the findings of Punia (1991) who observed that younger and unmarried farm women who were considered as an inexperienced and did not involve in decision-making process in the family.

It can be concluded that the beneficiary farm women irrespective of their family status were highly involved in decision making due to technical knowledge gained through the scheme than non-beneficiary farm women.

5 3.4 Extension Contacts of Farm Women and Decision-Making

Increased numbers of contacts with extension personnel and agencies enable an individual to bring clarity in his thinking to take concrete decisions. Thus, it was hypothesized that the farm women with more extension contacts vis-à-vis; more sources of information might be participated actively in taking decisions about agriculture and household activities. The results are presented in the Table 5.6.

Table 5.6

Relationship Between Extension Contacts and Decision-Making

Level of extension contacts (Number of extension agencies)	*Beneficiaries*	*Non-Beneficiaries*
	Average DMI	*Average DMI*
Low–Number of information sources between 0 to 7	34. 24	28. 07
Medium–Number of information sources between 8 to 15	49. 10	29. 21
High-Number of information sources 16 and above	54. 12	31. 00
Overall	45. 82	29. 42
'r' value	0. 58 ***	0. 11 NS

***, **, * Significant at 1, 5 and 10 per cent level of probability.

NS—Non-Significant.

Table 5.6 revealed that more extension contacts of the beneficiary farm women led to higher level of decision making as average DMI increased with an increase in level of contacts with the extension agencies or sources of information. In case of non-beneficiary farm women the average DMI also increased with an increase in level of extension contacts, however average DMI was lower in all three groups and also at the overall level as compared to DMI of beneficiaries. The 'r' value of beneficiary farm women shows the significant positive relationship between the use of sources of information by the farm women and their participation in decision making. In case of non-beneficiary farm women, the ' r ' value turned out to be non-significant indicating the poor extension contacts which led to the poor involvement of farm women in the decision making process.

These findings indicated that the beneficiary farm women were highly exposed to the various extension agencies and institutions for getting technical knowledge. High levels of awareness about the technical knowledge had developed the confidence, which provided sound base for decision-making. These findings are consistent with the findings of Bhuvaneshari and Kannan (1999) who observed the positive and significant association between the extension contacts and decision-making pattern of farm women.

5.3.5 Social Participation of Farm Women and Decision Making

Social participation refers to the degree, with which the respondents were involved in formal organisations as a member or office bearer and regularity in their attendance to meeting (Laximi Devi,1988). This indicates the extent and nature of contacts of an individual with the external world. The cosmopolite persons are generally early adopters and venturesome. It was viewed that farm women as members of social and political institutions would have positive bearing upon the decision-making. Thus, farm women having a membership of Self Help Groups, Co-operative society, Social groups in village, Gram Panchayat, Panchayat Samiti and Zilha Parishad were taken into consideration to measure the degree of social participation of farm women. The degree of influence of social participation on decision-making process of farm women was worked out and the results are presented in Table 5.7.

Table 5.7
Relationship between Social Participation and Decision-Making

Level of social participation	*Beneficiaries*	*Non-Beneficiaries*
	Average DMI	*Average DMI*
No membership of any organisation	----	26. 01
Members of one organisation	44.72	30. 21
Member of two or more organisations	46. 92	32. 04
Overall	45. 82	29. 42
'r' value	0. 63 ***	0. 10 NS

***, **, * Significant at 1, 5 and 10 per cent level of probability.
NS = Non – Significant.

It is evident from the Table 5.7 that all the beneficiary farm women were the members of women self help group and a few were the members of other social groups in village and few of them were the members of Panchayat Raj Institutions like Grampanchayat, Panchayat Samiti and Zilla Parishad and the village level cooperative society.

The results strongly supported the assumption that membership of social and political institutions have positive bearing on decision-making as 'r' value (0.63) shows statistical significant relationship between social participation of farm women and their decision making. This implies that the more social exposure through the scheme under study could make a positive impact on beneficiary farm women in the process of decision-making. The 'r' *value* in case of non-beneficiaries was non-significant, which indicated the low level of social participation than the beneficiaries.

Thus, it is concluded that the beneficiary farm women were found to have increased exposures to the outside world which led them to take decisions either independently or jointly with the family head.

5.3.6 Level of Technical Knowledge of Farm Women and Decision-Making

A knowledgeable person is capable of clear and balanced thinking. He is able to take right decisions at the appropriate time. The scheme under study is knowledge intensive and aimed at to upgrade the technical knowledge of farm women by way of different extension strategies. It was therefore hypothesized that the beneficiary farm women with higher level of knowledge about agriculture and dairy enterprise are likely to participate more in decision making process in family. The DMI values were grouped according to the level of Knowledge Index (KI) and correlation coefficients were worked out to test the significance of relationship between level of technical knowledge and decision-making. Results are presented in Table 5.8 below:

Table 5.8
Relationship Between Knowledge and Decision-Making by Farm Women

Level of Knowledge Index (KI)	*Beneficiaries*	*Non-beneficiaries*
	Average value of DMI	*Average value of DMI*
KI up to 20	40. 28	26. 91
KI (21 to 40)	44. 95	29. 30
KI (41 and above)	52. 23	32. 07
Overall	45. 82	29. 42
Ƴ' value	0. 48 ***	0. 09 NS

***, **, * Significant at 1, 5 and 10 per cent level of probability.

NS = Non– Significant.

It is seen from the Table 5.8 that the average value of DMI increased with an increase in the knowledge index in case of both the sample households. However, the average DMI values of beneficiary farm women are observed to be higher than average DMI values of non-beneficiaries.

This shows that the beneficiary farm women had more technical knowledge about agriculture and dairy enterprise. It is further noted that the level of decision making of farm women increases as the knowledge level of farm women increases which shows the direct positive relationship. This relationship was further tested by estimating the 'r' value which has indicated significant positive correlation at one percent level in case of beneficiary farm women and positive but not significant in case of non- beneficiary farm women. Thus, it can be said that, higher the technical knowledge of farm women, greater they participate in taking decisions about farm and family affairs. This finding is similar to the findings of Bhuvaneshari and Kannan (1999), Naresh and Narayanagowda (1999) who revealed that high level of knowledge about agricultural practices by farm women had positively associated with their decision making.

5.3.7 Annual Gross Income of Family and the Decision-Making

Annual gross income of family decides the life style of farmer and farm and family requirements depend upon the income, which he earns. A better financial position enables the farmer to avail more number of information sources and use of more number of communication channels, which have a positive bearing on the decision-making process. In the present investigation, family income was referred to as the annual monetary income received by the respondents family from both agriculture and other sources. It was hypothesized that the level of gross annual income of the family would influence the decisions of farm women. The data pertaining to this aspect were collected and analysed to arrive at the results, which are presented in the Table 5.9

It is observed from Table 5.9 that in case of the beneficiary farm women, the annual gross income did not influence the decision making as 'r' value turned out to be non-significant.

In the case of non–beneficiary farm women, the decision making of the farm women was highly influenced by the gross income of family as 'r' value turned out to be positive and highly significant indicating a positive relationship between gross family income and decision making. This inferred that higher the farm size, higher the farm income and higher level of involvement of farm women in the decision making process.

These findings are in conformity with the findings of Logamatha (2001).

Table 5.9
Relationship Between Annual Gross Income of Family and Decision-Making by Farm Women

Level of annual gross income (Rs)	*Beneficiaries*	*Non-beneficiaries*
	Average value of DMI	*Average value of DMI*
Up to Rs 40,000	44.40	21.50
Rs. 40,001 to 80,000	46.45	32.70
Rs. 80,001 and above	46.61	34.08
Overall	45.82	29.42
'r' value	0.039 NS	0.26 ***

***, **, * Significant at 1, 5 and 10 per cent level of probability.

NS = Non- significant

The beneficiary farm women had participated actively in decision making process irrespective of their gross family income. However, in the case of non-beneficiary farm women, a positive significant correlation has been noted between gross income and decision making. It looks that the beneficiary farm women had an equal opportunities for acquiring the technical knowledge irrespective of their income levels of families which led them for higher levels of decision-making.

5.3.8 Caste and Decision-Making

It was presumed that farm women of higher caste having more social and political exposure take leading roles in family decisions than lower castes and tribal farm women. In view of this, the influence of the caste on decision making of farm women was assessed and the results are presented in Table 5.10

It is seen from the Table 5.10 that in case of beneficiary households, the involvement of farm women in decision making process was not governed by the caste. This is because the beneficiary farm women were working in a group of 20 farm women in the scheme under study, which was basically a heterogeneous group and the technologies were disseminated by the extension agencies irrespective of their caste. Thus, it could be concluded that, imparted technology was caste neutral.

Table 5.10
Relationship Between Caste and Decision Making by Farm Women

Caste	*Beneficiaries*	*Non-beneficiaries*
	Average value of DMI	*Average value of DMI*
Scheduled Caste and Scheduled Tribe (SC&ST)	39. 48	18. 75
Other Backward Caste (OBC)	48. 95	34. 64
General Category	49. 03	34. 89
Overall	45. 82	29. 42
'r' value	0. 09 NS	0. 38 ***

***, **, * Significant at 1, 5 and 10 per cent level of probability.
NS = Non- Significant.

In case of non-beneficiary farm women, the DMI value increased with an increase in the caste status. The DMI value for the farm women belonged to SC/ST appeared to be small as compared to the DMI of OBC and general caste. This led to the conclusion that a higher caste farm women dominate in the decision-making process than the tribal and scheduled caste farm women, which could be attributed to more social exposure led to higher socio-economic status of higher caste farm women leading to higher level of decision making.

5.3.9 Family Size and the Decision-Making

The size of family referred here as the total number of individuals having relations and living under a common roof. An individual from a small sized family gets more chances to take more decisions. However, in case of large size families, responsibility is divided among a large number of persons in the family, thus they get limited opportunities to play their role in a particular aspect. It was therefore, presumed that the farm women belonging to smaller size families might have higher participation in decision making when compared with the farm women in the large sized families. The findings are presented in Table 5.11

Table 5.11
Relationship Between Family Size and Decision-Making

Family size	*Beneficiaries*	*Non-beneficiaries*
	Average value of DMI	*Average value of DMI*
Small (up to-4 members)	45. 98	37. 00
Medium (5 to 6 members)	45. 87	34. 00
Large (7 & above)	45. 61	17. 28
Overall	45. 82	29. 42
'r' value	0. 023 NS	0. 051 NS

***, **, * Significant at 1, 5 and 10 per cent level of probability.

NS — Non-Significant.

It is examined from the Table 5.11 that the average DMI value of both the sample households appeared to be higher in case of small family as compared to medium and large size family which has strongly supported the assumption that smaller the size of farm women families, more they would participate in decision making.

The average value of DMI is higher in small, medium and large size family and also at the overall level in case of beneficiary as compared to non-beneficiary households indicating a higher level of involvement of beneficiary farm women in decision making process in the family.

The 'r' value for both the categories of households turned out to be non-significant which has indicated that there is no relation between the family size and decision making by farm women. However, the level of decision-making by non-beneficiary farm women decreased with an increase in family size. These findings are similar to those of Jyoti *et al* (1999) who reported that, the decision-making was negatively associated with the size of family.

5.3.10 Farm Size and Decision-Making

Land is a basic resource of income to farmers. The size of land holding and area under the crops decide to some extent the level of their income and social status and a symbol of economic standing of a person in the social system. An individual having a large holding is naturally required to give attention to a variety of fieldwork. Thus, it was therefore thought that the farm women from the families with a large size holdings might participate more in decision making due to diversity of farm activities. The relationship between the farm size and the decision making of farm women is analysed and presented in Table 5.12.

Table 5.12
Relationship Between Farm Size and Decision-Making by Farm Women

Farm Size	*Beneficiaries*	*Non-beneficiaries*
	Average value of DMI	*Average value of DMI*
Small (0 to o. 50 ha)	45. 44	27. 05
Medium (0. 51 to 1. 00 ha)	45. 67	28. 19
Large (1. 01ha. and above)	46. 35	33. 04
Overall	45. 82	29. 42
'r' value	0. 16 **	0. 12 *

***, **, * significant at 1 , 5 and 10 per cent level of probability.
NS = Non-Significant

It is seen from Table 5.12 that the average DMI increased with an increase in the farm size of both the sample households, which implied positive correlation between the farm size and decision making of farm women. However, the average DMI value is observed to be much higher in beneficiary farm women as compared to non-beneficiary farm women. It is further observed that the farm women of large size farms having higher DMI value showed the higher level of participation in decisions though these decisions involved more monetary inputs having higher risk.

The 'r' value of both the households turned out to be positive showing significant relationship between the farm size and making of decisions by farm women. These findings are in contrast with those of Chakravarty and Chakravarty (1996); *Jyoti et al* (1999) as they concluded that farm size and decision making had inverse relationship as lower the farm size higher the involvement in decision making of farm women and vice- versa.

5.3.11 Occupation of Family Head and the Decision-Making

The occupation of the family head is a determinant of family income. Usually the level of standard of living and expenditure depend on the profession of family head. Thus, it was presumed that family head with good profession coupled with the high returns enjoys maximum decisions in the family as compared to other members of family. The relationships thus worked out between the profession of family head and involvement of farm women in decision-making are presented in Table 5.13.

Table 5.13

Relationship Between the Occupations of Family Head and Decision-Making by Farm Women

Occupation of family head	*Beneficiaries*	*Non-beneficiaries*
	Average value of DMI	*Average value of DMI*
Work on others farm (Wage earning)	20. 97	18. 17
Agriculture	31. 17	18. 31
Agril. + allied	39. 12	23. 70
Scrvicc	46. 20	28. 10
Overall	45. 82	29. 42
'r' value	0. 48 ***	0. 29 ***

***, **, * Significant at 1, 5 and 10 per cent level of probability.

NS = Non-Significant

It is revealed from Table 5.13 that the DMI value has increased with an increase in the level of profession of family head in both the sample households. This indicates that the decisions of farm women are positively correlated with the level of profession of the family head. This has also been confirmed from the positive and significant 'r' value of both the sample households. It is further observed that the DMI value of beneficiary farm women at the overall level appeared to be higher indicating the higher level of decision making by beneficiary farm women.

The participation of farm women of both the sample households in the decisions was observed to be higher in case of family heads with service as a profession which was due to inadequacy of time to devote for family activities and farm operations which provided opportunities for farm women to take decisions.

5.3.12 Educational Level of Family Head and Decision-Making of Farm Women

Family head is a person who decides the day-to-day affairs of his family. Every strategic decision taken by the family head influences the personality make-up of individuals in the family. It was presumed that the education level of the family head affects the level of involvement of family members in decision-making process. If the head of family possesses the higher education, generally he or she takes decisions alone. The results in this regard are presented in Table 5.14.

It is noted that by and large, the average value of DMI showed some decline with an increase in the level of education of family heads in both the sample households. This means that farm women having illiterate family heads were likely to take more decisions in the family. The DMI values of beneficiary households appeared to be relatively higher than the DMI values of non-beneficiary households. This indicates the higher level of participation of beneficiary farm women in decision making process. The 'r' value for beneficiaries turned out to be non-significant which means that farm women were involved in decision making irrespective of the educational levels of their family heads.

Table 5.14
Relationship Between Educational Level of Family Head and Decision-Making of Farm Women

Level of education of family head	*Beneficiaries*	*Non-beneficiaries*
	Average value of DMI	*Average value of DMI*
Illiterate	47.92	32.49
Primary (0-7 Std)	44.73	28.41
Secondary (8-10 Std)	45.85	31.51
Higher secondary (11-12 Std)	45.83	27.75
Graduate and above	44.80	26.98
Overall	45.82	29.42
'r' value	0.03 NS	-0.14 *

***, **, * Significant at 1, 5 and 10 per cent level of probability.

NS—Non-Significant.

In case of non-beneficiaries, the 'r' value is negative but statistically significant which shows that the decision making of farm women was negatively correlated with the educational levels of their family heads. This led to the conclusion that the farm women, whose family head is highly qualified, did not involve them in decision making. This finding are in contrast to those of Jyoti *et al* (1999) and Logamatha (2001) who showed that education of male family head had a positive and significant relationship with the decision making of farm women. However, these findings are similar to thoec findings of Rimawi (1998) who argued that farm women of illiterate husbands had participated more in decision making.

To sum up, it is observed that in case of beneficiaries farm women at overall level, six attributes namely education of farm women, extension contacts, social participation, technical knowledge of farm women, farm size and occupation of the family head had a positive and significant impact on decision-making of farm women. This led to the conclusion that beneficiary farm women having age between 30 to 50 years, well educated and highly cosmopolite in nature, having good contacts with the extension agencies and belonged to large farm size with well remunerative profession of family head were taking an independent decisions and were also involved in decision-making process. These findings are in commensurate with the findings of Rajkishor *et al* (1999) who observed that the level of decision making of farm women was positively influenced by level of education of farm women, joint or nuclear family, higher caste, large size of land holding and higher socio-economic status of farm women.

In case of non-beneficiary farm women, six attributes namely education of farm women, status of farm women in family, annual gross income of family, caste, farm size, occupation of family head showed a positive and significant impact on decision making of farm women. Thus, decision-making of non-beneficiary farm women was highly influenced by the level of education of farm women coupled with high annual gross family income and belonged to the OBC or higher caste with a large farm size and high level of profession of family head.

Six parameters such as age of farm women, status of farm women in family, annual gross family income, caste, family size and educational level of the family head had positive but non-significant relationship with decision making of the beneficiary farm women. As regards non-beneficiary farm women, four socio-economic parameters namely age, extension contacts, social participation and technical knowledge had positive but non-significant relationship with decision-making of farm women while family size turned out to be negative and non-significant. The education of family head showed negative but significant relationship with the decision making of farm women indicating inverse relationship between decision making by farm women and the level of education of the family head. The major reasons for low participation of non-beneficiary farm women in decision taking were less extension contacts, low level of technical knowledge, low social participation, large family size and older age of farm women. These findings are similar to the findings reported by Boreth *et al* (2002) who observed that the lack of technical knowledge, limited exposure to training and other information services were the factors responsible for low decision making by farm women. Talukdar *et al* (1997) identified problems responsible for low decision making of farm women were like lack of support of extension agencies, low educational status of farm women. Logamatha (2001) concluded that age of farm women had negative influence on decision making.

From the above said findings, it can be recommended that to enhance the role of farm women in decision making, increase in women's access to technical knowledge for which training, support of extension services and development programmes targeted at farm women farmers needs are needed. It is also recommended to consider these constraints while designing developmental programmes especially for rural women.

High level of decision making by beneficiary farm women as compared to non-beneficiary farm women proved the hypothesis that the continuous training, result demonstrations, exposure visits, mahila gosthis and contacts with extension agencies have helped to enhance the knowledge of beneficiary farm women and also led to greater involvement in decision making and family management.

5.4 Impact of the Scheme on Socio-Economic Empowerment of Farm Women

"Women make up 60 per cent of the world's poor. Experience has shown that when women are empowered, the benefits are felt in entire families and communities. It is essential to promote access to and use of information and communication technologies among women" (Kofi Anaan, 2002)

The word 'empowerment' has the most conspicuous feature containing the word 'Power', which means control over material assets, intellectual resources and ideology. The process of challenging existing power relations and of gaining greater control over the sources of power may be termed as empowerment. Empowerment is an effective strategy to cope with gender–centric discrimination and attain gender equality. The incidence of gender based discrimination or subordination of women is very much rooted in the economic dependence of women. Thus, the economic empowerment is one of the primary conditions for improving the social status of women. Unless the women become economically independent or make substantial contributions to the family for its sustenance, they cannot be treated equal to men in all aspects of life.

The major approaches to women's empowerment are envisaged as integrated development, economic empowerment and consciousness raising and organizing of farm women. It also focuses on improving women's control over material resources and strengthening women's positions as workers and income earners by mobilizing, organizing and providing access to support services.

'Empowering farm women' is the commitment made by the Government of India in the Ninth and the Tenth Five-Year Plan. The 'Women in Agriculture' project is exclusively targeted at increasing the skill of poor and marginal farm women. In the present investigation, it was hypothesized that the socio-economic empowerments have been brought in the farm women due to implementation of the scheme under study in Thane district. The parameters which indicates the socio-economic empowerment viz; access to credit, ownership and control over the resources, right to do the expenditure, access to communication media, contact with extension agencies, training attended and skills acquired have been taken for present study to see the extent of socio-economic empowerment acquired by farm women due to scheme implementation. The details of each parameter are described as below.

5.4.1 Access to Money/Credit

One factor hindering farm women's empowerment is their limited access to credit and saving schemes. This problem restricts their access to technology, income generating project, land possession and allotment of resources required for development. Collectivisation has been recognized as a tenet of women's empowerment. It has been defined as a process of bringing a group of women togather at a base to become an integral part of an economic activity.

In the present study, the saving habit among the beneficiary farm women was promoted by introducing Self Help Group (SHG) concept as an inbuilt component of the scheme under study. Accordingly, the beneficiary farm women were organized into thrift group of 20 farm women and monthly saving of certain amount was being circulated among the group members in case of exigency. In case of non-beneficiaries, it was presumed that saving habit was being promoted through the other rural development projects. The details of the savings on the account of farm women in the different agencies are given in Table–5.15.

Table 5.15
Average Saving According to Different Sources by Sample Farm Women

(Rs.)

Sr No	*Particulars*	*Beneficiaries*	*Non-beneficiaries*
1.	Bank Saving	1199. 49	220
2.	Post office saving	121. 12	----
3.	Saving with women's Self help group (SHG) account.	2024. 17	----
4.	Overall saving	1486. 56	220

It is seen from Table 5.15 that due to the implementation of scheme 'Women in Agriculture', the beneficiary farm women could be organized into Self-Help-Group (SHG) which pursued in average saving of Rs. 1199.49, Rs. 121.12 and Rs. 2024.17 in banks, post office and with farm women's self help group (SHG) account respectively. At the overall level, the average saving of beneficiary farm women was Rs. 1486.56. On the other hand, the average saving of non-beneficiary farm women was very meagre i.e. Rs. 220.

It could thus be concluded that beneficiary farm women had better access to money and control over financial resources than non-beneficiary farm women.

5.4.2 Ownership and Control Over Resources

Farm women need to have control over productive resources i.e. land, house, critical inputs / machinery and equipment and milch animals etc which create a sense of security, belongingness and owning. Other impacts of control over resources are to enhance their decision-making ability to meet some psychological needs like self-esteem and confidence. The details of the possession of productive assets like land, house, critical inputs, farm machinery and equipment and milch animal are presented in Table 5.16.

Table 5.16
Distribution of Farm Women According to Possession of Productive Assets

Sr No.	*Particulars*	*Beneficiaries (N = 120)*		*Non-Beneficiaries (N = 120)*	
		No.	*Per cent*	*No.*	*Per cent*
1.	Land	11	9. 16	3	2. 5
2.	Residential or farm House	14	11. 66	6	5
3.	Critical agri. inputs / Equipments	97	80. 83	10	8. 33
4.	Milch animals	85	70. 83	26	21. 66

It is seen from Table 5.16 that the beneficiary farm women had possessed more productive assets than non-beneficiary farm women. The higher number of beneficiary farm women having machinery /inputs and milch animals was due to stimulus that had been inculcated through training and exposure visits of beneficiary farm women and the facilities availed through various subsidies under the scheme.

On the other hand, the non-beneficiary farm women were holding comparatively less assets than beneficiary farm women. However, the control over land and residential house was not so encouraging since 9.16 per cent and 11.66 per cent of beneficiary farm women and 2.5 per cent and 5 per cent of non-beneficiary farm women had possessed these important assets. The lack of ownership of such important resources with farm women has barred them from the access of the formal credit system thus limiting their scope to acquire other productive resources such as cattle, poultry or working capital for trade in farm products.

5.4.3 Right to do the Expenditure

The farm women participate in economic activities to earn some income for personal use or for family commitment. It is seen that farm women do not have any rights to do expenditure by their own will. In most of the cases, the income earned by them has to be surrendered to the family pool (Ghose, 1993).

It was presumed that due to implementation of scheme under study, beneficiary farm women had acquired enough strength to assert themselves for spending their own earned income as well as some of the farm women enjoyed liberty to spend family income on garments, jewellery, purchase of animals and household items etc. The data in this regard are presented in Table 5.17.

Table 5.17
Distribution of Farm Women by their Right to Spent

Sr. No	*Particulars*	*Beneficiaries (N = 120)*		*Non-Beneficiaries (N = 120)*	
		Number of farm women	*Per cent*	*Number of farm women*	*Per cent*
1.	Garments	86	71.66	22	18.33
2.	Jewellery	65	54.16	15	12.50
3.	Purchase of milch animals	70	58.33	10	8.33
4.	Household items	85	70.83	36	30.00

It is observed from the Table 5.17 that beneficiary farm women had asserted their right to spend own earned income or family income on garments (71.66 per cent), jewellery (54.16 per cent), purchase of milch animals (58.33 per cent) and expenditure on household items (70.83 per cent). On the contrary, non-beneficiary farm women had liberty to spend either their own income or family income to the extent of 18.33 per cent on garments, 12.5 per cent in purchase of jewellery, 8.33 per cent in purchase of milch animals and 30 per cent on household items.

The beneficiary farm women were enjoying more liberty in incurring the expenditure on various assets which was due to the more exposure to the outside world through exposure visits, study tours and knowledge up-gradation through various trainings and seminars organised from time to time by the scheme implementing agency.

5.4.4 Access to Communication Media

Access to communication media helps women for improving their communication and upgrading skill to strengthen their capacity to contact and mediate with external world. The results in this regard are presented in Table 5.18

It is noted from Table 5.18 that the beneficiary farm women had better access to the extension agencies and communication media as compared to the non-beneficiary farm women. The utilization of media like television and radio was quite satisfactory as more than 40 per cent beneficiary farm women were regularly listening radio and 53.33 per cent were watching television programmes especially related to agriculture. On the other hand, 13.33 per cent of non- beneficiary farm women were listening radio and 25 per cent were regularly watching television. Less number of non-beneficiary farm women using these electronic media was because of unawareness of specific programmes and non-possession of radio and television sets.

Further, it was observed that the beneficiary farm women had regularly visited exhibitions (33.33 per cent), attended various trainings (91.66 per cent) and availed study tours (16.66 per cent).

Table 5.18

Distribution of Farm Women According to Exposure to Various Communication Media

Sr. No	Source of Information	Beneficiaries (N=120)			Non-Beneficiaries (N=120)		
		Regularly	Sometimes	Never	Regularly	Some times	Never
1.	Radio listening	50 (41.67)	18 (15.00)	52 (43.33)	16 (13.33)	10 8.33)	94 (78.34)
2.	Television Watching (agril. Programme)	64 (53.33)	8 (6.67)	48 (40.00)	30 (25.00)	6 (5.00)	84 (70.00)
3.	Educational Films	----	46 (38.33)	74 (61.67)	---	---	120 (100)
4.	Farm Publications	120 (100)	--	--	--	10 (8.33)	110 (91.67)
5.	Exhibitions	40 (33.33)	43 (35.83)	37 (30.84)	--	8 (6.67)	112 (93.33)
6.	Trainings	110 (91.67)	10 (8.33)	--	2 (1.67)	10 (8.33)	108 (90.00)
7.	Study tour	20 (16.66)	56 (46.67)	44 (36.67)	--	--	--

(Figures in parentheses indicate the percentages to the respective totals of sample households)

On the contrary, majority of the non-beneficiary farm women had never got such opportunities to avail these facilities. Regarding the use of farm magazines, cent percent of beneficiary respondents had subscribed 'Setkari' farm magazine published in Marathi language by the state department of Agriculture. These observations are similar to the findings of Vinkare and Antwal (2002) who observed that very negligible percentage (less than 5 per cent) of rural women regularly view agricultural programmes.

Watching of television by beneficiary farm women was due to awareness created and motivation brought due to exposure to extension agencies. The viewing behaviour of farm women could be greatly influenced by mass media exposure and contact with extension agencies (Sadamate and Sinha, 1977; Meenakshisundaram *et al*, 2001). It could be concluded that, due to the scheme under study, beneficiary farm women had effectively utilised communication media like radio, television and farm publications. Though radio and television were the established mass media, however, farm women of both the households failed to explore them fully.

5.4.5 Contacts with Extension Agencies

In general, approaches promoted by the conventional agricultural extension programmes have not yet reached up to the women farmers. In India, extension services are directed to pass on the information and skills to women. In reality, this does not happen. Some of the constraints observed in access to extension by farm women are the difficulties in dealing with the male extension workers, hesitation and cultural barriers among the employed extension agents to contact female farmers and unavailability of the female extension agents (Shivamurthy, 1999). It was presumed that because of the implementation of the scheme 'Women in Agriculture,' the beneficiary farm women might have acquired better access to the various extension agencies than non-beneficiary farm women. Hence, data were collected regarding the sources of information for the latest agricultural technologies and results are presented in Table 5.19

Table 5.19
Distribution of Farm Women by their Extent of Exposure to Various Extension Agencies

	Source of information	Beneficiaries (N=120)			Non-Beneficiaries (N=120)		
		Regularly	Some-times	Never	Regul-arly	Some-times	Never
1.	VEW & Facilitators	112 (93.33)	8 (6.67)	--	10 (8.34)	20 (16.66)	90 (75.00)
2.	Gram Sewak	--	25 (20.83)	95 (79.17)	--	38 (31.67)	82 (68.33)
3.	Taluka Aagricultur al Officer (TAO)	20 (16.66)	40 (33.33)	60 (50.00)	--	5 (4.16)	105 (87.5)
4.	BDO	--	10 (8 .33)	110 (91.66)	--	--	120 (100)
5.	Sub Divisional Agricultural Officer (SDAO)	5 (4.16)	15 (12.50)	100 (83.34)	---	--	120 (100)
6.	SAU Scientist	39 (32.50)	40 (33.34)	41 (34.16)	--	--	120 (100)
7.	KVK personnel	42 (35.00)	40 (33.33)	38 (31.67)	3 (2.50)	5 (4.16)	112 (93.34)
8.	Family Members	25 (20.83)	38 (31.66)	57 (47.51)	60 (50.00)	50 (41.66)	10 (8.34)
9.	Relatives	45 (37.5)	38 (31.66)	37 (30.84)	60 (50.00)	40 (33.33)	20 (16.66)
10.	Friends and Neighbours	10 (8.33)	15 (12.50)	95 (79.17)	90 (75.00)	10 (8.33)	20 (16.67)
11.	Village opinion Leaders	--	--	--	30 (25.00)	45 (37.50)	45 (37.50)
12.	Farm Women Self Help Groups	97 (80.83)	18 (15.00)	5 (4.17)	30 (25.00)	70 (58.34)	20 (16.66)

(Figures in the parentheses indicate per centages to the respective totals of sample households).

It is observed from the Table 5.19 that 93.33 per cent beneficiary farm women were getting farm information regularly through village extension workers and facilitators, Taluka Agricultural Officer (16.66 per cent), experts from B.S. Konkan Krishi Vidyapeeth (35 per cent), family members (20.83 per cent), relatives (37.5 per cent), friends and neighbours (8.33 per cent) and from the members of farm women groups (80.83 per cent)

In case of non-beneficiary farm women, they were getting farm information through various sources predominately from friends and neighbours (75 per cent) followed by the family members and relatives (50 per cent each) and village opinion leaders (25 per cent) and members of the farm women groups (25 per cent). The institutional sources played a little role in disseminating the regular farm information to the non-beneficiary farm women as only 8.34 per cent of the non-beneficiary farm women were in contact with Village Extension Workers (VEW), 2.5 per cent with the experts from the Krishi Vigyan Kendra, Kosbad. The beneficiary farm women regularly attend the training and workshops and share their experiences as illustrated in Fig. 5(a) and 5(b).

The beneficiary farm women had a greater access over the communication sources as compared to the non-beneficiary farm women. The department of agriculture was the major source of information in case of beneficiary farm women. The beneficiaries enjoyed more access to the formal communication media like mass media and institutional extension system than the non-formal media i.e. friends, relatives, and village leaders.

In case of non-beneficiary farm women, the major sources of information were friends and relatives. The preference of non-institutional source of information over institutional sources and media was due to the fact that non-beneficiary farm women usually get the information on agricultural aspects through their men which tends to be always distorted. The other reasons could be inability of non-beneficiary farm women to approach the institutional sources either due to the lack of awareness, non-willingness of family men or conservative nature of farm women.

Fig. 5(a) Experience Sharing.

Fig. 5(b) Beneficiary farm women participation in the district level saminar (Mahila Gosthis organised once in a year).

5.4.6 Skill Acquired by Farm Women through Training

The training prepares farm women for undertaking activities outside the sphere of the manual labour sector. Generally, the earning capacity of the trained farm women is higher than those of not trained. A similar argument would hold for skill as well, that more skilled farm women have the capacity to earn more and command the higher social status in the society. Hence, both trained and skilled farm women command a higher socio-economic status (Acharya, 2002). The details of the trainings attended by the sample farm women and thereby skill acquired by them are presented in Table 5.20.

Table 5.20
Distribution of Farm Women According to the Training Attended and Skill Acquired by them (1995 –2002)

Sr.	*Particulars*	*Beneficiaries (N=120)*		*Non-Beneficiaries (N=120)*	
		Number	*Per cent*	*Number*	*Per cent*
A	*Trainings Attended*				
1.	Crops	120	100.00	26	21.66
2.	Vegetables	120	100.00	16	13.33
3.	Horticulture	120	100.00	12	10
4.	Honey bees	112	93.33	-	-
5.	Mushroom	117	97.50	-	-
6.	Goat rearing	119	99.16	5	4.16
7.	Vermiculture	108	90.00	-	-
8.	Fisheries	116	96.66	-	-
9.	Animal husbandry	118	98.33	7	5.83
10.	Food Processing	116	96.66	-	-
11.	Poultry	120	100.00	18	15
12.	Study Tours	76	63.33	-	-
13.	Farm Women Gosthi	120	100.00	-	-
14.	Demonstrations	120	100.00	5	4.16
B	*Skill Acquired*				
15.	Agriculture	91	75.83	10	8.33
16.	Horticulture	89	74.16	11	9.16
17.	Animal husbandry	91	75.83	5	4.16
18.	Poultry	90	75.00	-	-
19.	Food Processing	118	98.33	15	12.5

It is observed from the Table 5.20 that the beneficiary farm women had availed maximum facilities of trainings organized by the department of agriculture and line departments, State Agriculture Universities (SAU), Krishi Vigyan Kendras (KVKs). On the other hand, similar opportunities were not made available to the non-beneficiary farm women as their participation in the various training programmes seems to be very low. It is further observed that the beneficiary farm women had high level of skills in various technical aspects as compared to the non-beneficiary farm women. The beneficiary farm women had acquired skills of insecticides sprayings on Sapota fruit harvesting as shown in Fig. 6(a) and 6(b).

Empoerment of Farm Women Through Skill Base Training Programme

6 (a) Beneficiary farm women have acquired skill of insecticides spraying

6(b) Beneficiary farm women have acquired skill of harvesting of Sapota fruits

To sum up, beneficiary farm women had socio-economically empowered due to implementation of the scheme 'Women in Agriculture' in Thane district of Maharashtra state. It was further observed that beneficiary farm women had better access to the credit facilities and majority of farm women had a ownership of economically important resources like land, house, machinery and milch cow. As beneficiary farm women were more cosmopolite in nature and good social exposure encouraged them to enjoy more liberty in incurring the expenditure. It was further observed that beneficiary farm women had a better access to communication and print media, institutional information sources and continuous up-gradation of technical knowledge through the various training programmes. The technical knowledge and economic independence are the parameters of women empowerment which could develop self confidence among them and lead them to their greater involvement in various farm, economic and social activities.

In case of non-beneficiary farm women, they had little exposure to extension agencies, lack of access to financial resources, communication media and lack of right to do expenditure etc. They didn't have suitable access to and control over farm technology.

Thus, empowerment is a complicated process, which comprises of short- term and long-term strategy. To empower the non-beneficiary farm women there is a need to increase their access to new information as well as to credit and labour market. Furthering their social and institutional participation at all levels by strengthening educational and training programmmes for them, there should be long drawn strategy for increasing their access to and control over appropriate technology.

6

Impact of the Scheme on Farm Business Economy

In the previous chapter, the resource base of the sample households has been discussed. The sample farms used these resources for production of crops which influenced the farm productivity and finally the levels of income. Net returns from the farm business depend on the pattern of response of output to the application of inputs, cost per unit of input and price per unit of output. It would be useful to examine the farm business economy and resource productivity in crop production including resource use pattern, cost and return structure of farm enterprises, profitability and finally the resource use efficiency on the sample households. Besides, it would be helpful to have a further probe into the employment and income structure of the sample farms. With this intention, present chapter is designed to the description of the utilization of farm resources such as labour, manure and fertiliser, cash expenditure in crop production, farm productivity, cost and return structure of crop, farm profitability, resource productivity and resource use efficiency in crop production on the sample households.

Paddy is the staple food crop grown on large scale that supports the livelihood of the rural households. The mono-cropping system has been adopted in Thane district because of high rainfall in which paddy is traditionally considered as the best-suited crop.

During the year 2001-2002, other crops like vegetables, fruit crops were grown where irrigation facilities were available. In vegetables, chilly was taken as a major crop and Sapota was found to be predominant among the fruit crops. Other crops like pulses, betel vine, minor millets were taken on a very small area especially on bunds.

Due to inadequate irrigation facilities, per farm area sown more than once was only 0.02 ha. in case of beneficiaries and 0.01 ha. in non-beneficiaries. Intensity of cropping was 102.27 per cent and 101.68 per cent on beneficiaries and non-beneficiaries farms that indicate a little scope for enhancing the farm income by taking more crops and therefore to increase the productivity of crops was the best option before the farmers.

It is hypothesised that due to implementation of the scheme under study, the resource use on the sample farms has increased resulted into the increase in the crop productivity and thereby farm income and net returns. The impact of the scheme on farm business economy and resource use productivity of major inputs in crop production on sample farms has been proposed to study for paddy and farm as a whole.

6.1 Farm Business Analysis of Paddy Crop

The use of inputs influences the crop productivity. The physical use of some inputs such as labour, manure and fertilizers and cash expenditure used in paddy crop production on the sample farms has been studied and explained as under.

6.1.1 Per Farm and Per Hectare Labour Use for Paddy Crop

Labour is an important resource in crop production. The total labour comprising family and hired male, female and bullock labour used in production of paddy crop grown by the sample farms was consolidated in order to work out average labour utilization per farm and per hectare. The averages so worked out are given in Table 6.1.

Table 6.1
Average Per Farm and Per Hectare Resource Use on Sample Farms for Paddy Crop

Sr. No.	*Resources*	*Beneficiaries*		*Non-Beneficiaries*	
		Per farm	*Per hectare*	*Per farm*	*Per hectare*
1.	Seed (kg)	38.1	44.94	33.4	44.22
2.	Manure (Tonnes)	9.54	6.17	5.67	5.53
3.	Chemical Fertilisers (kg)				
	N	58.22	68.85	43.16	57.10
	P	30.62	36.21	13.13	17.24
	K	18.41	21.76	10.83	14.32
4.	Machinery (Hrs)	3.54	4.19	0.93	1.23
5.	Pesticides (Rs)	306.51	366.76	252.85	334.52
6.	Bullock labour (Pair days)	13.67	16.17	11.18	14.79
7.	Human Labour (man days)				
(a)	Family : Male	16.54 (24.18)	23.11 (25.77)	15.31 (21.79)	20.25 (21.79)
(b)	Female	22.10 (32.31)	30.32 (33.82)	20.80 (29.61)	27.51 (29.61)
	Total Family Labour	38.64 (56.49)	53.43 (59.59)	36.11 (51.41)	47.76 (51.41)
(c)	Hired : Male	10.66 (15.58)	16.16 (18.02)	10.03 (14.28)	13.26 (14.27)
(d)	Hired : Female	19.09 (27.91)	20.06 (22.37)	24.09 (34.30	31.87 (34.30)
	Total Hired Labour	29.75 (43.50)	36.22 (40.40	34.12 (48.58)	45.13 (48.58)
(e)	Total Male labour	27.20 (39.77)	39.27 (43.80)	25.35 (36.09)	33.51 (36.07)
(f)	Total Female labour	41.19 (60.22)	50.38 (56.19)	44.89 (63.91)	59.38 (63.92)
	Gross human labour	**68.39 (100)**	**89.65 (100)**	**70.23 (100)**	**92.89 (100)**

(Figures in parenthesis indicates the percentage in total)

As regards the human labour use for paddy crop on sample farms, it is seen that per farm utilization was 68.39 man-days on beneficiary and 70.23 man-days on non-beneficiary farms. However, the per hectare labour use was 89.65 and 92.89 man-days on beneficiary and non-beneficiary farms respectively. It is also seen that the per farm and per hectare female labour utilisation was quite high as compared to male labour on sample farms.

Family labour plays an important role in paddy crop production. The per farm and per hectare family labour share in total labour utilisation was 56.49 per cent and 59.59 per cent on beneficiary farms and 51.41 per cent and 51.41 per cent on non-beneficiary paddy farms.

Per farm and per hectare bullock labour use was 13.67 and 16.17 pair days on beneficiary and 11.18 and 14.79 days on non-beneficiary paddy farms respectively.

It is noted that on beneficiary farms comparatively less human labour was used than non-beneficiaries because of the increased use of machinery, which was 4.19 hrs and 1.23 hrs per hectare on beneficiary and non-beneficiary farms respectively. However, the use of bullock labour was more on beneficiary farms due to intensification in paddy cultivation.

6.1.2 Use of Manures and Fertilisers

The use of manures, fertilizers, machinery and pesticides per farm and per hectare for paddy crop is shown in Table 6.1.

Manure is the crucial input in paddy production. The use of Farm Yard Mannure (FYM) which is more balanced in its nutrient content is reported to increase the fertilizer productivity. Bhole and Kharche (1992) observed that residual effect of FYM could improve nutrient efficiency of chemical fertilizers by over 20 per cent. Singh *et al* (1992) concluded that FYM is more complementary than substitute to chemical fertilizers because it has residual effect for two to three seasons. It is noted that per farm and per hectare manure application was more on beneficiary farms than the non-beneficiary farms. Also it is seen that the use of chemical fertilizers per farm and per hectare was more on beneficiary farms. Farm machinery especially tractor use was more on beneficiary farms than the non-beneficiary farms indicating that relatively more mechanization of operations in paddy cultivation on beneficiary farms.

The pesticide is one of the most critical inputs for increasing the paddy productivity. Per farm and per hectare use of pesticide on beneficiary farm was more by Rs. 53.66 and Rs. 32.24 than that of non-beneficiary farm. From the above discussion, it is seen that per farm and per hectare resource use was more on beneficiary farms as compared to non-beneficiary farms.

6.1.3 Gaps in Recommended and Actual Use of Inputs on the Sample Farms

Inputs play a significant role in boosting crop production. The production and productivity of paddy depend on the judicious and balance use of inputs. The productivity of the paddy crop is primarily influenced by the factors such as seed, manure, fertilizers, irrigation and labour, etc. Besides, there is a very close complementary relationship among different inputs for increasing production. Therefore, balanced use of all these resources up to the recommended levels is very important. Details regarding the recommendation and gaps in per hectare use of resources such as seed, fertilisers and manures are given in Table 6.2.

The level and pattern in use of the various resources indicate the adoption level of the resources. The gaps in application of resources indicated that (Table 6.2) both beneficiary and non-beneficiary did not use the recommended level of the resources. However, beneficiaries could utilise more resources as compared to non-beneficiaries. This could be because of the adequate finance and technology awareness among the beneficiary farm women.

These results are similar to the findings of Rai *et al* (1999) who observed the positive impact of Central Sector Scheme 'Women in Agriculture' in Hisar district of Haryana. It was noted that due to implementation of the scheme, awareness of farm women had been increased about various agricultural technologies and there was a high level of resource use.

Table 6.2
Per Hectare Use of Resources, Recommended Levels and Gaps in Use for Paddy Crop on Sample Farms

Particulars	*Beneficiaries*				*Non-Beneficiaries*			
	Use level	*Rec*	*Gap*	*% gap*	*Use level*	*Rec*	*Gap*	*% gap*
Seed (kg)	44.94	50	5.06	11.25	44.22	50	5.78	13.07
Manure (Tonnes)	6.17	7.5	1.33	21.55	5.53	7.5	1.97	35.62
N (kg)	68.85	100	31.15	45.24	57.10	100	42.9	75.13
P (kg)	36.21	50	13.79	38.08	17.24	50	32.7	65.52
K (kg)	21.76	50	28.24	56.48	14.32	50	35.6	71.36
Total fertilisers (kg)	126.82	200	73.18	57.70	88.66	200	111.34	125.58

6.1.4 Resource Use for Paddy Crop Production on Different Size of Farm

6.1.4.1 Use of Human Labour and Farm Power

The total labour comprising family and hired male, female and bullock labour used in production of paddy crop grown by the sample farms was consolidated in order to work out average per hectare labour utilization. The averages so worked out are given in Table 6.3.

It is noted that, at the overall level, the gross labour utilisation was 89.65 man-days and 92.89 man-days on beneficiary and non-beneficiary farms for paddy production respectively. Labour requirement across the farm sizes implies that labour utilization showed a decline with an increase in farm size. It is seen that contribution of female labour in total labour utilization for paddy crop production was 56.19 per cent on beneficiary and 63.92 per cent in non-beneficiary farms. Thus, it can be said that cultivation of paddy is largely a feminine activity indicating more female labour intensive operations such as transplanting, weeding and harvesting.

Table 6.3
Per Hectare Resource Use Pattern for Paddy Cultivation according to Size Classes of Sample Farms (2001-2002)

Resources	*Beneficiaries (N=116)*				*Non-Beneficiaries (N=120)*			
	Small	*Medium*	*Large*	*Overall*	*Small*	*Medium*	*Large*	*Overall*
Family labour	34.78	27.24	16.20	23.11	32.2	20.96	15.8	20.25
(a) Male	(34.33)	(29.03)	(19.58)	(25.77)	(32.10)	(21.23)	(18.28)	(21.79)
(b) Female	41.38	33.61	24.16	30.32	39	34	19.3	27.51
	(40.84)	(35.82)	(29.21)	(33.82)	(38.88)	(34.44)	(22.33)	(29.61)
Total family	76.16	60.85	40.36	53.43	71.2	54.96	35.1	47.76
labour (Man days)	(75.18)	(64.85)	(48.80)	(59.59)	(70.98)	(55.67)	(40.62)	(51.41)
Hired labour	10.02	13.98	19.80	16.16	10.9	13.61	13.8	13.26
(c) Male	(9.89)	(14.89)	(23.94)	(18.02)	(10.86)	(13.78)	(15.97)	(14.27)
	15.14	19	22.54	20.06	18.2	30.15	37.5	31.87
(d) Female	(14.94)	(20.24)	(27.25)	(22.37)	(18.14)	(30.54)	(43.40)	(34.30)
Total Hired labour	25.16	32.98	42.34	36.22	29.1	43.76	51.3	45.13
(Man-days)	(24.83)	(35.14)	(51.19)	(40.40)	(29.01)	(44.32)	(59.37)	(48.58)

Contd/....

(Contd table 6.3)

Resources	*Beneficiaries (N=116)*				*Non-Beneficiaries (N=120)*			
	Small	*Medium*	*Large*	*Overall*	*Small*	*Medium*	*Large*	*Overall*
(e) Total Male	44.80 (44.21)	41.22 (43.93)	36.0 (43.53)	39.27 (43.80)	43.1 (42.97)	34.57 (35.01)	29.6 (34.25)	33.51 (36.07)
(f) Total Female	56.52 (55.78)	52.61 (56.06)	46.7 (56.46)	50.38 (56.19)	57.2 (57.02)	64.15 (64.98)	56.8 (65.74)	59.38 (63.92)
Total Human Labour (Man-days)	101.32 (100)	93.83 (100)	82.70 (100)	89.65 (100)	100.30 (100)	98.72 (100)	86.40 (100)	92.89 (100)
Bullock pair	21.40	18.53	12.73	16.17	18	15.55	13.19	14.79
Machinery (hrs)	2.45	2.66	5.82	4.19	1.26	1.02	1.37	1.23
Seed (kg)	41.83	45.86	45.47	44.94	41.2	44.25	45.1	44.22
Mannure (Tonnes)	7.31	6.55	5.51	6.17	7.58	6.47	4.23	5.53
Fertilisers (kg)								
N	73.82	69.53	66.60	68.85	54.9	56.84	57.9	57.10
P	35.40	30.94	39.95	36.21	15.1	21.32	15.2	17.24
K	24.53	22.41	20.34	21.76	16.9	16.87	11.7	14.32
Total Fertilisers	133.7	122.88	126.8	126.82	86.9	95.03	84.8	88.66
Plant protection (Rs)	420	323	376	366.76	372	222	317	334.52

Regarding the family labour utilization, more family labour was engaged (53.43 man-days) by beneficiary farms as compared to non-beneficiary farms (47.76 man-days) for paddy crop cultivation. It is seen that more family labour was utilized on the small size farms as compared to medium and large size of farms. Regarding the share of the family labour in total labour utilization, it is noted that small farms shared 75.18 per cent followed by medium size farms (64.85 per cent) and large farms (48.80 per cent) on beneficiary farms. The corresponding family labour utilization in non-beneficiary farms was more on small farms (70.98 per cent) followed by medium farms (55.67 per cent) and large farms (40.62 per cent).

Thus, it is concluded that the family labour utilization has reduced with an increase in farm size or it is inversely proportional. The small farms engaged more family labour due to inadequate paying capacity for the hired labour indicating their tendency to employ all available family manpower. It is also noted that the family male and female labour use showed a decline on both the sample farms with an increase in farm size. These findings are supported by those of Alcober and Parrilla (1989) as they concluded that the majority of the farmers could not afford to finance farm activities. Thus, most family members worked together in the various agricultural tasks to operate their small farm.

As regards the hired labour, at the overall level, it is observed that the non-beneficiaries could engage more hired labour (45.13 man-days) than the beneficiary farms (36.22 man-days). The use of hired male and female labour showed an increase with an increase in farm size on both the sample households. Use of bullock labour was also more on small farms in both the sample households and subsequently decreased with an increase in farm size. At the overall level, the bullock labour utilisation was 16.17 pair days and 14.79 pair days on beneficiary and non-beneficiary farms, respectively.

6.1.4.2 Use of Manures and Fertilisers

The manures and fertilisers are crucial inputs that directly influence the level of output of the crops. The high yielding varieties of paddy are more responsive to the higher doses of manures and fertilisers. The information regarding the use of manures and fertilisers for paddy production by the sample farms is presented in Table 6.3.

It is noted that the per hectare use of manures at the overall level was 6.17 tonnes and 5.53 tonnes on sample beneficiary and non-beneficiary farms and their use declined with an increase in the farm size on both the sample farms. Comparatively more use of manures by small farms was due to the fact that whatever the quantity produced at the farm was fully applied to the paddy crop. The per hectare use of N, P, K was comparatively more on beneficiary farms (126.82 kg.) than non-beneficiary farms (88.66 kg.). This was mainly because of little more irrigated area, intensification in paddy cultivation due to adoption of improved cultural practices on beneficiary farms.

6.1.4.3 Plant Protection

Thane district is a traditionally paddy growing area. This crop is prone to pests and diseases. However, during data collection it was observed that paddy crop did not face serious pest infestation, which resulted into low use of pesticides. The data were collected on the use of pesticides and its per hectare average expenditure is presented in Table 6.3.

It is observed that per hectare expenditure on plant protection was more (Rs. 366.76) on the farms of beneficiaries than the non-beneficiaries (Rs. 334.52). The pesticides use across the farm size showed that small farms in both the households spent more on plant protection. The sample beneficiaries had spent little more on pesticides due to awareness about the pests and diseases due to increased extension contacts, easy accessibility of pesticides through the schemes than the non-beneficiary farms women.

6.2 Operation-wise Labour Utilization for Paddy Crop

The participation of farm women in the agricultural works can be understood better if we take into account the different agricultural operations. Some agricultural operations are female labour intensive whereas others are male labour intensive because of the gender-based division of labour. Moreover, the different agricultural operations involve different work time and wages. Nine major operations of paddy crops were chosen for the analysis of labour utilization. The operation-wise labour utilisation is given in Table 6.4.

It is noted from the Table 6.4 that for land preparation operation, total human labour used was 6.35 and 10.35 man-days on farms of beneficiary and non-beneficiary farms respectively. The bullock labour utilization for this operation was 3.78 and 4.47 pair days on these farms respectively. Thus, it is noted that relatively less human and bullock labour use was seen on the farms of beneficiaries than that of non-beneficiaries since tractor was used by farmer in ploughing the fields.

After ploughing and preparation of land, raising of seed bed and seeding operation is done. In some cases, rabbing (soil burning) activities are also undertaken, though this practice is being discouraged by the department of agriculture. However, almost all the non-beneficiary and few beneficiary women were still carrying out this operation in the study area. The next important activity is application of manures, which is considered as the most tedious and laborious task by the farmers in the study area, because the manure has to be transported from the house of farmer to the field and spread in two instalments. Tractor or local bullock carts are used for transportation of FYM from house to fields. It is a male activity, however females are also required for loading and unloading the carts.

Both the men and women undertake transplantation of paddy. Transplantation has to be done within a specified period. Therefore, more time is spent on this activity per day. On an average, a person spends ten hours per day in this work. It is also observed that, transplanting required 21.61 and 21.35 man-days of human labour and 5.69 and 4.66 pair days of bullock

Table 6.4
Per Hectare Operation Wise Labour Utilization for Paddy Cultivation

(Man-days)

Sr. No.	Name of Operations	Beneficiaries				Non-Beneficiaries			
		Female	Male	Total Human labour	Bullock pair days	Female	Male	Total Human Labour	Bullock pair days
1.	Land preparation	3.10 (6.15)	3.25 (8.27)	6.35 (7.09)	3.78 (23.37)	5.15 (8.67)	5.2 (15.51)	10.35 (11.14)	4.47 (30.22)
2.	Raising of seedlings	2.90 (5.76)	3.16 (8.04)	6.06 (6.76)	2.41 (14.90)	3.83 (6.44)	2.68 (8.0)	6.51 (7.0)	1.91 (12.91)
3.	F.Y. M. application	1.21 (2.40)	3.06 (7.79)	4.27 (4.76)	2.03 (12.55)	2.02 (3.40)	2.59 (7.33)	4.61 (4.96)	1.78 (14.74)
4.	Transplant-ing	13.79 (27.37)	7.82 (19.91)	21.61 (24.11)	5.69 (35.19)	16.78 (28.25)	4.57 (13.63)	21.35 (22.98)	4.66 (31.50)
5.	Weeding	11.20 (22.23)	1.92 (4.89)	13.12 (14.63)	---	11.41 (19.21)	1.32 (3.94)	12.73 (13.70)	---
6.	Crop Protection	1.20 (2.38)	2.45 (6.24)	3.65 (4.07)	0.06 (0.37)	1.19 (2.00)	2.13 (6.50)	3.27 (3.63)	0.05 (0.34)

Contd /....

Sr. No.	Name of Operations	Beneficiaries				Non-Beneficiaries			
		Female	Male	Total Human labour	Bullock pair days	Female	Male	Total Human Labour	Bullock pair days
7.	Fertilizer application	1.50 (2.97)	3.20 (8.14)	4.70 (5.24)	0.05 (0.30)	1.32 (2.22)	2.36 (7.04)	3.68 (3.96)	—
8.	Crop harvesting	13.02 (25.84)	5.99 (15.25)	19.02 (21.22)	0.64 (3.96)	16.08 (27.08)	3.40 (10.14)	19.48 (20.97)	0.46 (3.11)
9.	Transport and threshing	2.45 (4.86)	8.42 (21.44)	10.87 (12.12)	1.51 (9.34)	1.60 (2.69)	9.21 (27.48)	10.81 (11.63)	1.06 (7.17)
	Total	50.38 (100)	39.27 (100)	89.65 (100)	16.17 (100)	59.38 (100)	33.51 (100)	92.89 (100)	14.79 (100)

(Figures in the parentheses indicate the percentages to respective totals).

labour on the farms of beneficiaries and non-beneficiaries respectively. Transplanting is a labour intensive operation as 24.11, 22.98 per cent of total human labour, 35.19 and 31.50 per cent of total bullock labour were utilised alone for this operation on the farms of beneficiaries and non-beneficiaries respectively. Moreover, transplanting is considered as a female activity as this activity alone shared about 27.37 per cent and 28.25 per cent of total female labour force on the farms of beneficiaries and non-beneficiaries respectively.

Weeding is next in importance in the list of operations undertaken in paddy crop. It requires the pulling out of weeds and wild grasses from the field with the help of 'khurpa'. This activity was done both by male and female labour. However, contribution of female labour to this activity was much higher than that of male labour since 11.20 man-days of female labour were used as against 1.92 days of male labour and 11.41 man-days female against 1.32 man-days of male labour on the farms of beneficiaries and non-beneficiaries respectively.

Plant protection activity is a male activity, even though it is observed that female labour is used in plant protection activities particularly in supply of water. In case of beneficiaries, few farm women were also carrying out dusting and spraying. Pesticide application was carried out at two to three times as per the intensity of pest and diseases on the paddy crop. At the overall level, the labour utilisation for the plant protection of paddy was 3.65 man-days on beneficiary and 3.27 man-days on non-beneficiary sample farms.

The chemical fertilisers are applied mainly at the time of seeding, basal dose at the time of transplanting and two split doses are given after transplanting. Carrying of fertilizers to field and its application is done primarily by males, however, females also carry out this operation in the absence of male labour.

Harvesting is carried out with the help of sickle and is generally undertaken by female labour, though the male is also engage in it. Harvesting is again a labour intensive activity, which is common to both women and men. It is noted that use of female labour for harvesting of paddy was quite more than that of male labour on both the farms.

After the harvest of crop, it is transported and stacked at one place for drying. The grain is threshed and chaff is removed from the grain which is done both by human and machine power. During the data collection, it was observed that the mechanical threshing was adopted on large scale by the beneficiaries as the use of threshers was promoted under the scheme.

It is also noted that, at the overall level, female labour utilization was more than male labour by 11.11 man-days on beneficiary farms and 25.87 man-days on non-beneficiary farms. The three operations namely transplanting, weeding and harvesting alone consumed nearly three fourth of female labours on both the categories of sample farms. These findings are in accordance with the findings of Rathore and Gaur (1996) and Sobha (2001).

This has emphasized the importance of these operations in paddy crop production from female labour point of view. These results may be useful in planning the various operations to ensure labour availability in the peak period.

The contribution of male labour in paddy crop production was 43.80 and 36.07 per cent on the farms of beneficiaries and non-beneficiaries respectively. The five operations out of nine major operations namely land preparation, raising seedbed, transplanting, harvesting and transport consumed nearly 72.91 and 74.76 per cent of total male labours on beneficiary and non-beneficiary farms respectively. Two operations viz., transplanting and harvesting required maximum male, female and bullock labour on both the categories of sample farms.

From the data illustrated in Table 6.4, it is seen that at the overall level, the use of bullock labour for paddy cultivation was 16.17 and 14.79 pair days on the farms of beneficiary and non-beneficiary respectively. Four operations such as land preparation, raising of seedling, manure application and transplanting accounted for 86.01 per cent of total bullock labour use on beneficiary farms and that of non-beneficiary was 89.37 per cent.

It is a proven fact that, knowledge of the practices has greater impact on degree of participation, since knowledge level of any innovations is directly associated with its adoption. These findings give a pointer to the extension organisation to initiate either exclusive programmes of demonstrations, training and allied activities for farm women outside the scheme to educate them about the new agricultural technologies. In other words, well planned continuous extension programme for women need to be necessarily organized by the front line extension system. These findings would enable the extension agency at various levels to formulate the overall extension strategies.

The concerted efforts are also needed to develop better technologies for agricultural operations such as transplanting, weeding, harvesting and cleaning of the produce which are usually performed by farm women to reduce their physical burden and drudgery. Timely completion of these activities helps to enhance the productivity of crops.

6.3 Item-wise Per Hectare Costs and its Share in Paddy Cultivation

It is a worldwide phenomenon that in the process of transformation of traditional agriculture into a modernized one, the technological changes usually take place through increased use of the farm resources.

The costs are incurred in cash when material inputs are purchased and used in production of crops. The main items of cost to be incurred in cash are purchase of material inputs such as seed, manures, fertilizers, fuel and wages of hired labour. The non-cash component of cost consists of depreciation, imputed value of family labour, rental value of land, etc. The crop production cost therefore consists of both the cash and non-cash component of cost.

In order to know the requirement of cash expenditure per cropped hectare according to different items of expenditure, the relevant data for paddy cultivation on the sample farms is presented in Table 6.5.

Table 6.5
Per Hectare Cost of Cultivation and Factor Share in Paddy Cultivation on Sample Farms (2001-2002)

Sr. No.	*Activities*	*Beneficiaries (N =116)*		*Non-Beneficiaries (N=120)*	
		Cost (Rs)	*Per cent*	*Cost (Rs)*	*Per cent*
1.	Hired H. labour				
	Male	646	3.66	530.40	3.59
	Female	702.10	3.98	1111.45	7.55
	Total Hired labour	1348.10	7.64	1493.25	10.01
2.	Bullock labour	1617	9.17	1479	10.03
3.	Machinery	628.50	3.56	184.50	1.25
4.	Seed	396	2.24	408.09	2.77
5.	Manure	3085	17.50	2765	18.71
6.	Chem. Fertilisers				
	a.Nitrogen (N)	682.99	3.87	560.72	3.80
	b Phosphorus (P)	294.02	1.66	134.81	0.91
	c. Potash (K)	177.34	1.0	115.84	0.78
	Total fertilizers	1154.35	6.55	811.37	5.49
7.	Irrigation	105	0.59	41.51	0.28
8.	Plant protection	367	2.08	334.52	2.26
9.	Incidental charges	283.51	1.60	239.48	1.62
10.	Repairs of Implements	149.49	0.84	175.85	1.19
	Working capital	9133.95	51.82	8085.17	54.72

Contd/....

Sr. no.	Activities	Beneficiaries (N =116)		Non-Beneficiaries (N=120)	
		Cost (Rs)	Per cent	Cost (Rs)	Per cent
11.	Int. on W capital	639.37	3.63	565.96	3.83
12.	Depreciation	469	2.66	428.23	2.90
13.	Land Revenue	70	0.40	72.40	0.49
	Cost 'A'	10312.32	58.51	9151.76	61.95
14.	Rental value of land	4944.16	28.05	3641.80	24.64
15.	Int. of fixed capital	383	2.17	208.51	1.41
	Cost 'B'	15639.48	88.73	13001.27	88.00
16.	Family labour				
	Male	924.40	5.24	810	5.48
	Female	1061.20	6.02	962.85	6.51
	Total Family labour	1985.40	11.26	1772.85	13.99
	Cost 'C'	17624.88	100	14774.12	100
17.	Yield (qtl)	39.17	----	30.59	---
18.	Main produce (Rs)	26243.90	-----	19118.75	----
19.	By-product (Rs)	3421	----	2732.084	------
20.	Total Produce	29665	----	21850.83	---

It is noted from the Table 6.5 that the average per hectare cash expenditure for paddy production was Rs. 9133.95 (51.82 per cent of Cost 'C') in case of beneficiaries and Rs. 8085.17 (54.72 per cent of cost 'C') on the farms of non-beneficiaries. This indicates that the per hectare cash expenditure on material inputs on beneficiary farms was relatively more by Rs. 1048.78, i.e, 12.97 per cent than the farms of non-beneficiaries.

In case of beneficiary farms, the item-wise cash expenditure indicates that manures and fertilisers together shared 24.05 per cent of expenditure which was followed by bullock labour (9.17 per cent), hired human labour 7.64 per cent, machinery (3.56 per cent), seed (2.24 per cent) and plant protection (2.08 per cent). The corresponding expenditure on non-beneficiary farms was 24.20 per cent, 10.03 per cent, 11.01 per cent, 1.25 per cent, 2.77 per cent and 2.26 per cent respectively.

The imputed costs such as interest on working capital, depreciation, land revenue, rental value of land and interest on fixed capital were the items of indirect cost. These items constituted 36.91 per cent and 33.27 per cent on beneficiary and non-beneficiary farms respectively.

It can also be said that per hectare cash expenditure on the items viz. machinery, irrigation, plant protection, bullock labour, manures and fertilisers etc was conspicuously more on beneficiary farms indicating that use of material inputs on these farms was higher as compared to that of non-beneficiary farms under study.

6.4 Cost and Returns from Paddy Crop Production

Crop production activity on the sample farms was evaluated by adopting the usual farm management cost concepts and measures of income. The data regarding size group-wise average costs and farm income by using different measures of income from crop production on sample farms are presented in Table 6.6.

It is noted from the Table 6.6 that at the overall level, the per hectare cost of cultivation of paddy crop on the farms of beneficiaries at the level of cost A, cost B and cost C was Rs.10312.32, Rs.15639.48 and Rs. 17624.88 respectively. In case of non-beneficiaries, cost A, cost B and cost C were Rs. 9151.76, Rs. 13001.27 and Rs. 14774.12 respectively indicating that the per hectare average cost of cultivation of paddy crop was quite higher on beneficiary farm. This was mainly due to higher use of inputs on beneficiary farm as explained in the preceding section.

Per hectare average value of gross output and the net income worked out to Rs. 29,665 and Rs.12,040.12 on the farms of beneficiaries and Rs. 21,867.17 and Rs.7,093.05 on non-beneficiary farms. This means that per hectare net income from paddy production was higher by Rs.4,947.07 on beneficiary farms. It is also seen that per hectare net income from paddy cultivation increase with an increase in farm size on both the categories of sample farms.

Further, it is noted that per hectare cost of cultivation of paddy crop at different levels of cost showed decline as the size

Table 6.6
Per Hectare Costs and Returns for Paddy Production on Sample Farms (2001-2002)

(Rs.)

Particulars	*Beneficiaries*				*Non-beneficiaries*			
	Small	*Medium*	*Large*	*Overall*	*Small*	*Medium*	*Large*	*Overall*
Yield (Qtls)	41.20	39.15	38.45	39.17	32.39	31.14	30.31	31.34
Cost A	11259	11061	10414	10312.32	10383	9866	8302	9151.76
Cost B	16987	16366	15611	15639.48	14167	13706	11993	13001.27
Cost C	19820	18625	17015	17624.88	16825	15737	13302	14774.1
Gross value of produce	30533	29721	29315	29665	22600	21585.3	20277.69	21867.1
Farm business income	19274	18660	18901	19352.68	12217	11719	11975.69	12716.1
Family labour income	13546	13355	13704	14025.52	8433	7879.31	8284.69	8865.9
Net income	10713	11096	12300	12040.12	5775	5848.31	6975.69	7093.05
Benefit: Cost Ratio	1.54	1.59	1.72	1.68	1.34	1.37	1.52	1.48

categories of sample farms increased. This has indicated the economies of scale in operation on sample farms. At the overall level, the per hectare gross returns from paddy was higher by Rs.7797.83 (35.66 per cent) in beneficiary as compared to over non-beneficiary farms. It is also noted that at the overall level, the farm business income, family labour income and net income on beneficiary farms were higher as compared to non-beneficiaries by 52.18, 58.19 and 69.74 per cent respectively.

The above results have indicated that the beneficiary farms were operating at the higher level of income as compared to the non-beneficiary farms under study. This difference in income was largely due to higher level of adoption of modern technologies and partly due to better resource structure on beneficiary farms. The per hectare net income was found to be the highest on beneficiary farms indicating thereby better management of resources.

6.5 Output-Input Ratios and Profitability for Paddy Crop

The input and output ratios for paddy crop production have been worked out for different size classes of sample farms to examine the farm business efficiency. The output-input ratio indicates output per unit to total inputs and is roughly total factor productivity.

It is observed from the Table 6.6 that at the overall level, Benefit: Cost ratio was Rs.1.68 and Rs. 1.48 in the case of beneficiary and non-beneficiary farms respectively. The higher benefit-cost ratio among beneficiary households was mainly due to higher level of input use to obtain the maximum yield.

It is further noted that the productivity of paddy crop across the farm size was observed higher on small farms and showed a decline with an increase in farm size. These results endorsed the findings reported by Sen, A.K. (1962); Bardhan, P.K. (1973) and Bagi (1983).

Among the size classes of beneficiary farms, the output-input ratio was maximum on medium size class (1.93) followed by large (1.72) and small farms (1.54). As regards the non-beneficiary farms, the output-input ratio was maximum on large farms (1.52) followed by medium (1.37) and small farms (1.34). The small sized farms under both the categories had relatively poor performance in returns on per rupee investment made in paddy crop production. Thus, it can be concluded that the net returns from the paddy crop were higher on larger farms. It seems that the small farms are losing their traditional edge of higher returns under the new technological conditions.

6.6 Paddy Production Function and Resource Use Efficiency

6.6.1 Production Function Analysis

The type of analysis presented in the previous section has a weakness that it cannot measure the magnitude of contribution of each specific factor in combination with other factors responsible for changes in out put level. In order to estimate the magnitude of contribution of each input to output, a multivariate analysis of production process has also been undertaken for the beneficiary and non-beneficiary farms separately in this section.

In order to estimate the resource productivities and resource use efficiencies in paddy cultivation on the sample farms, the Cobb-Douglas type of production function was fitted to the data at the farm level. The details regarding specification of model and measurement of variables for crop production function have been given in Chapter 3.

However, in production function analysis based on the cross sectional data there often exist a high correlation between some of the independent variables leading to the problem of multicollinearity. To ascertain the presence and extent multicollinearity in the data, a simple zero order correlation matrix of all explanatory variables was worked out. As suggested by Heady (1946), the correlation coefficient between a pair of explanatory variables is greater than 0.8, it is usually to be considered high multicollinearity. In this connection, Klein (1962) has suggested that multicollinearity should not be considered serious if the simple correlation coefficient between a pair of variables is less than the multiple correlation coefficients. The regression coefficients in the Cobb-Douglas type of production function are the output elasticities and the magnitude of individual coefficients indicate the percentage growth, positive or negative depending upon the sign and statistical significance in output in response to one per cent increase in the input concerned, while having the other factors of production held constant.

The different combinations of the independent variables were taken for the production function analysis and appropriate production function has been taken for the interpretation. The productivities of resources used for paddy production obtained by using Cobb-Douglas production function are presented in Table 6.7.

To take beneficiary paddy production function first, it can be seen that all the regression coefficients have the right sign and are significantly different than zero except the bullock labour. The regression coefficient of bullock labour is – 0.0146, which has turned out to be non-significant indicating no relationship with the output of paddy.

The elasticities of output with respect to nitrogen (X_1), potash (X_3) and FYM (X_4) have turned out to be positive and statistically significant at one per cent level while that of human labour (X_5) is positive and significant at ten per cent probability level. This indicates that the above said economic inputs were important in paddy crop production on the beneficiary farms. Importantly, the coefficient of human labour has turned out to be positive indicating its contribution in raising paddy output on average beneficiary farms. This also rejects the hypothesis of zero marginal productivity of labour on average beneficiary farms. The coefficient of other working capital, which includes expenditure on pesticides, seed, machines, irrigation, incidental charges and repairs of machinery is 0.0172 which has turned out to be non-significant. It seems that nitrogen, potash, manure and human labour are the most important factors of production and when accompanied with matching capital inputs would increase the paddy output on beneficiary farms. The coefficient of multiple determination (R^2) indicated that 71 per cent of the variation in paddy output of beneficiary farms have been jointly explained by the selected seven independent variables under study.

Table 6.7
Results of Cobb-Douglas Type Production Function in Paddy on Sample Farms

Variables		*Beneficiaries (N=116)*		*Non-beneficiaries (N=120)*	
		Elasticities	't' value	Elasticities	't' value
Nitrogen (N)-Kg	X_1	0.2879 * * * (0.0709)	4.060	0.3996*** (0.0853)	4.684
Phosphorus (P)—Kg.	X_2	0.0287 NS (0.0430)	0.667	0.1355*** (0.0384)	3.526
Potash (K)—Kg	X_3	0.0808 * ** (0.0294)	2.748	0.0600 NS (0.0473)	1.267
FYM (Tonnes)	X_4	0.0856 *** (0.0278)	3.079	0.1670*** (0.0446)	3.743
Human Labour (man-days	X_5	0.1949 * (0.1088)	1.791	-0.132 NS (0.1284)	- 1.029
Bullock labour(pair days)	X_6	- 0.0146 NS (0.0494)	- 0.295	-0.003 NS (0.0405)	- 0.079
Other Working Capital	X_7	0.0172 NS (0.0231)	0.744	0.0395 NS (0.0359)	1.1005
Sum of regression coefficients	Σbi's	0.68	-----	0.66	----
R^2	----	0.71	----	0.68	----
'F' test	----	19.14 ***	---	16.19 ***	---

(Figures in parentheses indicate the std errors of their respective elasticities).

***, **, * indicates the significance level at 1, 5 and 10 per cent of probability level.

As regard the crop production function of non–beneficiary farms, it is seen that the elasticities of output with respect to nitrogen (X_1), phosphorus (X_2), FYM (X_4) have turned out to be positive and statistically significant at one per cent level. This means that nitrogen, phosphorous, manures are the factors of economic importance, and their increased use up to an optimum level would have significant positive influence on crop output on non- beneficiaries farms. The elasticity of output with respect to potash (X_3) and other working capital are positive but not significant. However, the coefficient for human labour and bullock labour are negative and non-significant. It is also noted that the selected seven variables jointly explained 68 per cent of the variation in paddy crop output on non-beneficiary farms.

The coefficient of variables viz; manures and fertilisers are found to be positive and significant on both the categories of farms indicating thereby that these variables had the highest influence on output of paddy. In view of this, in the process of modernisation of their traditional agriculture by the sample farms, the optimum use of manures and fertilisers as recommended for paddy crop needs to be intensified.

'Chow test' of equality: The pooled analysis of the entire sample farms is carried out with a view to apply *'Chow test'* of equality. In other words, the significance of difference between the paddy crop production functions of the beneficiary and non-beneficiary farms was tested by using the Chow test. It is seen that the F (8,220) ratio is 3.02 which is significant at a probability level of five per cent indicating that the two regressions are not equal but differed significantly in their overall production relationships. This is also corroborated from the discussion about the difference in resource use, cost and return structure in crop production of these two categories of farms made earlier in this chapter. Since the *Chow's F* test was found significant, the difference between the estimated parameters of the production function for low adopters (non-beneficiaries farms) and high adopters (beneficiaries farms) of technology was significant. Hence, there was a shift in production function of paddy as a result of technological change. It may also be seen that average yield of paddy on high adoption level technology in case of beneficiary farms of the scheme under study was high as compared to that of low adoption level of technology in case of non-beneficiary farms.

The *F ratios* obtained from the analysis of the variance with respect to the production function for paddy crop at the overall level in both the sample farms have turned out to be highly significant indicating thereby overall significance of the estimated production function. The hypothesis of equality of slope coefficients was rejected and it is inferred that neither the intercept nor the slope coefficients were same in the estimated production functions of beneficiary and non-beneficiary sample farms. It can therefore be revealed that there was a structural difference in the parameters of the production function in the two types of sample farms and this difference was not limited to the difference in the intercept.

6.6.2 Nature of Returns to Scale

Production elasticities: The coefficients with respect to each particular input are the elasticity of production. The elasticity of production indicates the change in output relative to the unit change in input, if other inputs are held constant. If the output increases by a greater percentage than input then, the ratio is greater than one; the production is said to be elastic. If the output increases by same rate as input, it is one. For the percentage increase in output is less than the percentage increase in input, the ratio is less than unity, then production is said to be inelastic (Heady & Dillon, 1961).

Sum of the production elasticities indicated the returns to scale in the Cobb-Douglas type of production function. If the summation of these elasticities is greater than 1, shows increasing returns to scale but if less than 1, we have decreasing returns to scale. Constant returns to scale occurs when the summation of the elasticities is equal to 1 (Ayanwale and Isijola,1997).

On examination of the elasticities presented in the Table 6.7, it is seen that the coefficient of each independent variable were less than one, implying thereby decreasing marginal productivity with respect to each explanatory variable. In case of beneficiaries, the elasticity of paddy production was found higher for nitrogen followed by human labour and FYM. In case of non-beneficiaries, the elasticity of paddy production was found higher for nitrogen followed by manures and phosphorous. From the Table 6.7 it is also noted that, in no case, individual elasticity was greater than unity indicating that MPP will increase with an additional use of each of these factors. The sum of the elasticities is 0.68 in case of beneficiary and 0.66 in case of non-beneficiary farms. These $\sum$bis are tested by applying *'Z' test* to know whether they differ significantly from unity and it is noted that there existed a diminishing returns to scale.

6.6.3 Resource Use Efficiency

The estimated production function underlying crop production activities enable us to proceed further in an evaluation of the efficiency of prevalent factors of production in agriculture in the study area. The production function analysis has been generally used to determine the economic efficiency of resources use, which requires estimation of marginal value product of resources. A resource or input is considered to be used most efficiently if marginal value product just offset its cost. Equality of marginal value product to the factor cost is the basic condition that must be satisfied to obtain efficient resource use.

The marginal value product of the resources so obtained at the geometric mean levels from the estimated production functions of the paddy crop production are presented in Table 6.8 along with the per unit acquisition cost of the respective resources. The difference between the marginal value product of the resources and their per unit acquisition cost are tested for their significance with the help of *'t' test.*

At the overall level, It is seen from the Table 6.8 that in case of beneficiary farms, the ratio of MVP to unit cost of factor was higher than unity in case of nitrogen (11.06), potash (12.15), human labour (1.49), Other working capital (1.43), phosphorus (1.35) and FYM (1.31) respectively. This implies the under utilization of these resources and suggests to intensify their use to the optimal level. In case of bullock labour, the ratio of

Table 6.8

Marginal Value Productivities, Factor Costs and Economic Efficiency in Resources Allocation for Paddy Crop on Sample Farm

Variables	*Beneficiaries*				*Non- Beneficiaries*			
	MVP to unit cost of factor	*Unit costs of factor (Rs)*	*Ratio of MVP to unit cost of factor*	*Difference MVP-Factor cost*	*MVP to unit cost of factor*	*Unit costs of factor (Rs)*	*Ratio of MVP to unit cost of factor*	*Differenc MVP-Factor co*
Nitrogen in kg. (X_1)	109.72	9.92	11.06	99.8	134.09	9.92	13.51	124.17
Phosphorus in kg. (X_2)	12.47	8.12	1.35	4.35	14.01	8.12	1.72	5.89
Potash in kg. (X_3)	99.09	8.15	12.15	90.94	73.35	8.15	9.16	65.35
FYM in tonnes (X_4)	656.11	500	1.31	156.11	598.83	500.00	1.19	98.71
Human labour in man-days (X_5)	55.19	36.8	1.49	18.39	- 0.61	36.8	- 0.01	- 37.41
Bullock labour in pair days (X_6)	-21.73	100.14	- 0.21	-121.87	- 160.5	100.14	- 1.60	-260.64
Other working capital in rupees (X_7)	1.43	1	1.43	0.43	1.10	1	1.10	0.1

marginal value product to the unit cost was less than the unity thereby indicating the over utilization of bullock labour.

In the case of non-beneficiary paddy farms, it is observed that the ratio of MVP to unit cost of factor was more than unity in respect of phosphorus (18.22), nitrogen (13.51), potash (9.16), FYM (1.19), and other working capital (1.10) respectively. This indicates the scope for increasing these resources up to optimum level. However, the ratio of MVP to unit cost of factors was less than unity in case of bullock labour (- 1.6029) and human labour (-0.165) thereby indicating over utilization of these resources.

Thus, this led to the conclusion that there is no scope to extend the use of bullock labour on both the sample farms.

To sum up, it can be said that per farm and per hectare resource use was more on beneficiary farms as compared to non-beneficiary farms. The three operations in paddy crop production namely transplanting, weeding and harvesting alone consumed nearly three fourth of female labour on both the categories of sample farms. At the overall level female labour utilization was more as compared to the male labour utilization for paddy crop production on both the sample farms. The per hectare cash expenditure on material inputs and imputed items was higher on beneficiary farms. The beneficiary farms were also operating at the higher level of income as compared to the non-beneficiary farms, which attributed a net gain of Rs. 1.68 on beneficiary and 1.48 on non-beneficiary farms from the each rupee invested in paddy crop production.

The resources like nitrogen, potash, manures and human labour on beneficiary farms and nitrogen, phosphorous and manures on non-beneficiary farms were the factors of economic importance, and their increased use up to an optimum level would have significant and positive influence on paddy crop output on both the sample farms. The marginal value product of the resources obtained at the geometric mean levels from the estimated production function of paddy crop indicated that the ratio of MVP to the unit factor cost was higher than unity in case of nitrogen, phosphorous, potash, manures, human labour and other working capital on the beneficiary farms and nitrogen, phosphorous, potash, manures and other working capital on non-beneficiary farms indicating a further scope to use these resources up to optimum level. It is also seen that there was no scope to extend the use of bullock labour on the beneficiary farms and human labour and bullock labour on non- beneficiary farms as the ratios of marginal value products to the unit costs of these resources were less than unity.

6.7 Farm Business Analysis—Farm as a Whole

The production is said to be efficient if producer does not knowingly waste the resources. If they waste resources but are ignorant of doing so, the loss is attributed to lack of knowledge or information. The increased education both formal and informal may enhance the farmer's ability to acquire and decide about cost and productive characteristics of other inputs. As such, change of education results in change in other inputs including perhaps the use of some 'new' factor that otherwise would not have been used in production. The returns on education have two effects: 'workers effects' and 'allocative effect'. The worker effect of education and exposure to extension refers to the technical efficiency. A more educated farm women has ability to produce more output from given bundle of inputs. The allocative effect of education refers to the allocative efficiency as a part of production. The ability of more educated and trained farm women is enhanced to obtain, analyze and understand economically useful information about inputs, cost of inputs, production and commodity mix for taking optimal decision with regards to input use and optimal product combinations. Under the central sector scheme 'Women in Agriculture', the beneficiary farm women were being regularly trained on various production technologies through village level trainings, exposure visits, result and method demonstrations. Thus, it is hypothesized that beneficiary farm women have better judgement about the efficient use of inputs and their optimisation and significantly would be different than non-beneficiary farms women.

In the preceding discussion, the farm business analysis of

paddy crop was discussed in detail. Resources were used by sample farms for the production of paddy, vegetables viz., chilli and brinjal and horticultural crops viz., sapota and mango which do have influence on entire farm productivity and finally level of income. It would be useful to examine the farm business economy as a whole to find out the difference in resource use pattern, cost and return structure of farm enterprise, profitability and finally the resource use efficiency on sample beneficiary and non-beneficiary farms. The area under the major crops which were grown by the sample farms is shown in Table 6.9 below.

Table 6.9
Area under Vegetables, Fruits and Paddy Crop on Sample Farms

(ha)

Crops	*Beneficiaries (N=120)*			*Non-beneficiaries (N=120)*		
	Number of growers	*Total area under crop*	*Per farm area under crop*	*Number of growers*	*Total area under crop*	*Per farm area under crop*
Paddy	116	98.10 (87.10)	0.84	120	90.70 (92.77)	0.75
Vegetables	28	9.41 (8.35)	0.33	15	4.60 (4.70)	0.30
Fruit crops	7	4.50 (4.00)	0.64	4	2.00 (2.05)	0.50
Other crops	66	0.62 (0.55)	0.51	81	0.47 (0.48)	0.39
Total	----	112.63	0.93	----	97.77	0.81

It is seen from Table 6.9 that the per farm area under paddy, vegetables and fruit crops was comparatively more on the beneficiary farms by 0.12 ha than non-beneficiary farms.

6.7.1 Per Hectare Resources Use

The per hectare resource use for the crops viz; vegetables, fruits and paddy grown by the sample farms was consolidated in order to work out the farm size-wise details as presented in Table 6.10.

Table 6.10
Per Hectare Resource Utilisation on Sample Farms

Resources		*Beneficiaries (N=120)*				*Non-Beneficiaries (N=120)*			
		Small	*Medium*	*Large*	*Overall*	*Small*	*Medium*	*Large*	*Overall*
Family human labour (Man days)	Male	32.62 (30.60)	25.68 (22.70)	14.18 (15.34)	20.86 (21.64)	29.82 (31.89)	22.22 (21.88)	16.57 (19.41)	20.63 (22.47)
	Female	42.20 (49.59)	34.50 (30.50)	25.29 (27.37)	30.55 (31.69)	36.55 (39.09)	35.38 (34.85)	19.88 (23.29)	27.61 (30.07)
Total family labour		74.82 (70.20)	60.18 (53.20)	39.47 (42.72)	51.41 (53.33)	66.37 (70.99)	57.6 (56.74)	36.45 (42.71)	48.24 (52.54)
Hired h. labour	Male	9.55 (8.96)	18.51 (16.36)	18.51 (20.03)	14.65 (15.19)	10.18 (10.89)	13.64 (13.43)	13.28 (15.56)	12.86 (14.00)
	Female	22.20 (20.83)	34.41 (30.42)	34.41 (37.24)	30.33 (31.46)	16.93 (18.11)	30.27 (29.81)	35.60 (41.72)	30.70 (33.44)
Total hired labour (Man days)		31.75 (29.79)	52.92 (46.79)	52.92 (57.27)	44.98 (46.66)	27.11 (29.00)	43.91 (43.25)	48.88 (57.28)	43.56 (33.49)
Total Male labour		42.17 (39.57)	44.19 (39.0)	32.69 (35.88)	35.51 (36.85)	40.00 (42.78)	35.86 (35.32)	29.85 (34.98)	33.49 (36.48)
Total female labour		64.42 (60.42)	68.91 (60.92)	59.70 (64.61)	60.88 (63.16)	53.48 (57.21)	65.65 (64.67)	55.48 (65.01)	58.31 (63.51)
Total Human Labour (Man days)		106.5 (100)	113.1 (100)	92.39 (100)	96.39 (100)	93.48 (100)	101.51 (100)	85.33 (100)	91.8 (100)
Bullock pair days	Family	2.54	8.05	5.90	5.97	4.09	3.82	5.50	4.72
	Hired	17.78	9.6	6.05	9.09	12.46	11.34	6.98	9.50
Total (bullock Pair)		20.32	17.65	11.95	15.06	16.55	15.16	12.48	14.22
Machinery (hrs)		2.96	3.25	5.67	4.16	1.35	1.51	1.88	1.64

(Figures in parentheses indicate percentages to their respective totals)

It is observed from the Table 6.10 that at the overall level, per hectare male labour use was 35.51 man-days, 60.88 man-days of female and 15.06 pair days of bullock labour on beneficiary farms. The corresponding labour use on non-beneficiary farm was 33.49 man-days of male, 58.31 man-days of female and 14.22 pair days of bullock labour. It is also noted that the per hectare total labour use was more by 6.03, 4.40 and 5.90 per cent in case of male, female and bullock labour on beneficiary farms as compared to non-beneficiary farms. The per hectare utilisation of machinery on beneficiary farms was 4.16 hours as compared to 1.64 hours on non-beneficiary farms, which was higher by 2.52 hours on beneficiary farms as compared to non-beneficiary farms. More human, bullock labour and machinery were used on beneficiary farms indicating the intensification of agriculture.

It is also noted that use of bullock power declined with an increase in farm size while use of machinery increased with increase in farm size on both the sample farms.

6.7.1.1 Female Labour

The female labour participation depends on four conditions namely childcare and other domestic duties, nutrition, local customs and other social and economic factors and the family subsistence needs. Other factors influencing the supply of female labour are the extent of mobility allowed to women, the availability of suitable jobs, the desire on the part of women to avail of job opportunities, educational attainments and income level and husband's occupational status.

From the Table 6.10, it is implied that at overall level, female labour share in total human labour utilization was 63.16 per cent on beneficiary farms and 63.51 per cent on non-beneficiary farms. It shows that agriculture in the study area is heavily depends on female work force. In other word it can be said that agriculture in the study area is basically feminine activity.

6.7.1.2 Male Labour

It is seen from the Table 6.10 that the share of male labour in gross human labour utilisation was 36.85 per cent on beneficiary farms and 36.48 per cent on non-beneficiary farms. Male labour utilisation across the farms showed that small and medium size farms used more labour as compared to large size farms which has indicated that small size farms tended to utilise all available family male labour force for crop production.

6.7.1.3 Family Labour

In the farming, family labour is an important input. The quantum of family labour availability depends upon the size of the family and its utilization depends upon size of holding, irrigated area, cropping intensity and subsidiary occupations related to agriculture. It is seen from the Table 6.10 that the utilization of family labour at the overall level for the farm as a whole was 51.41 days (53.33 per cent) on beneficiary farms and 48.24 days (52.54 per cent) on non-beneficiary farms. The gender wise share in total family labour indicated that the family female contribution was more on both the sample households. It is also seen that per hectare use of family labour decreased with an increase in the farm size in both the households.

It is also observed that high family labour utilisation on small farms was either due to adoption of more labour intensive cropping strategies or the availability of family workers on these farms. In the present study, the latter argument holds true. Rao (1986) observed that leisure preference could be higher among the larger farmers, while income itself was an important variable motivating the small farmers to work on land intensively. This finding is similar to the observations made by Bhagwati and Chakravati (1969) and Patnaik (1979).

6.7.1.4 Hired Human Labour

Analysis of data with respect to the hired labour use on the farms (Table 6.10) indicated that at the overall level, the contribution of hired human labour was 44.98 man-days (46.66 per cent) on beneficiary farms and 43.56 man-days (33.49 per cent) on non-beneficiary farms. The use of hired labour increased with an increase in the farm size which indicates that large farms had to depend heavily on hired labour for crop production. Thus, it could be concluded that the hired labour use is directly proportional to the farm size.

The present analysis supports the argument that small farms use comparatively more human labour than large size farms. This higher labour intensity is often attributed to labour market dualism which small farms depend mostly on cheap family labour with low opportunity cost while large farmers depend on hired labour (Reddy, 1993).

6.7.1.5 Fertilisers and Manures

Introduction of chemical fertilizers is partly an offshoot of the progress of science and technology and agro-research. The scarcity of organic manures leads to the adoption of chemical fertilizers. However, organic manure is very important in maintaining soil fertility, but it cannot meet the entire demand of plant nutrients due to its low content of NPK. The per hectare use of chemical fertilisers (NPK), manures on the sample farms as a whole is examined critically and the results are presented in Table 6.11.

It is observed that the per hectare use of manures on beneficiary farms was more by 1.7 tonnes as compared to non-beneficiary farms and it declined with an increase in farm size on both the sample farms. The per hectare average use of fertilisers namely, N, P and K at the overall level was 71.97 kg, 38.94 kg, and 25.61 kg respectively on the beneficiary farms while it was 60.78 kg, 21.91 kg and 17.89 kg respectively on the non-beneficiary farms. At the overall level, the per hectare use of fertilizer use was higher by 35.94 kg (35.73 per cent) on beneficiary farms as compared to non-beneficiary farms. It is further noted that per hectare use of fertilizer increased with an increase in farm size of beneficiary farms. However, on non-beneficiary farms, it was the highest on medium size farm (108.18 kg) followed by large size farms (100 kg) and small size farms (87.80 kg). Comparatively higher use of chemical fertilizers on beneficiary farms was due to higher level of adoption of the crop production technologies and awareness of the beneficiary farm women about the importance of the fertilisers in crop production.

Table 6.11
Per Hectare Resource Use Pattern for Crop Production according to Size Categories of Farms

Resources	*Beneficiaries (N=120)*				*Non-Beneficiaries (N=120)*			
	Small	*Medium*	*Large*	*Over all*	*Small*	*Medium*	*Large*	*Over all*
Manure (Tonnes)	9.62	7.09	6.23	7.64	7.87	7.72	2.23	5.94
Chemical Fertilizers								
N (kg)	77.23	76.45	74.30	71.97	54.60	62.05	62	60.78
P (kg)	37.65	36.72	46.43	38.94	17.50	25.68	21	21.91
K (kg)	26.12	28.13	26.81	25.61	15.70	20.45	17	17.89
Total Fertilizers (kg)	141.00	141.30	147.54	136.52	87.80	108.18	100	100.58
Plant protection (Rs)	460	340	394	371	336	217	370	315

6.7.1.6 Pesticides

If the crops are not protected against various pests and diseases, the realised output could be less than the potential output. Thus, application of plant protection chemicals indirectly contributes in increasing production by preventing crop losses at various stages. Due to implementation of the scheme under study since 1994-95, it was observed in the study area that the beneficiary farm women were trained on control of different pests and diseases on various crops. Thus, it was hypothesized that beneficiary farm women are well aware of the plant protection measures than non-beneficiary farm women which would have led to more use of pesticides.

It is examined from the Table 6.11 that the per hectare average expenditure on plant protection was more on the beneficiary farms by Rs. 56.

6.7.2 Costs and Returns from Crop Production for Farm as a Whole

The crop production activity of paddy, vegetables and horticultural crop (Sapota and Mango) grown by the sample households was evaluated by adopting the usual farm management cost concepts and measures of farm income. The data regarding per hectare costs and returns from the crop production according to the size classes for a farm as a whole is presented in Table 6.12.

Table 6.12
Per Hectare Costs and Returns from Crop Production according to the Size Classes of Sample Farms

(Rs)

Particulars	*Beneficiaries (N=120)*				*Non-beneficiaries (N=120)*			
	Small	*Medium*	*Large*	*Over all*	*Small*	*Medium*	*Large*	*Over all*
Cost A	12618	11341	10752	10858	10850	10790	9963.47	10267
Cost B	19032	17297	16250	16430	14475	15305	14643	14768
Cost C	21815	19533	17703	18334	17125	17430	16002	16560
Gross valu of produce	33821	34161	36981	32232	22996	24899	26568	25177
Farm business income	21203	22820	26229	21374	12146	14109	16604.5	14910
Family labour income	14789	16864	20731	15802	8521	9594	11925	10409
Net income	12006	14628	19278	13898	5871	7469	10566	8617
Benefit: Cost Ratio	1.55	1.74	2.08	1.75	1.34	1.42	1.66	1.52

It is noted from the Table 6.12 that at the overall level, the cost A, cost B and cost C was quite higher on beneficiary farms as compared to non-beneficiary farms. This means that per hectare cost of cultivation of crops at different cost levels was higher on beneficiary farms. This was mainly due to higher input use on the beneficiary farms. It is also seen that net income increased with an increase in the size of holding on both the sample farms. The comparison of various costs, gross value of produce and different income levels on both the sample farms are graphically presented in Fig. 7a and Fig. 7b.

On comparison of various income measures at the overall level, it is observed that the per hectare gross income, farm business income, family labour income and net income of beneficiary farms were higher by Rs.7055 (28.02 per cent), Rs. 6464 (43.35 per cent), Rs. 5393 (51.81 per cent) and Rs. 5281 (61.28 per cent) respectively over non-beneficiary farms. This clearly indicates that the beneficiary farms were operating at the higher levels of income as compared to non-beneficiary farms. These finding are in conformity with the findings of Chandravati *et al* (1999) who examined the impact of ANTWA (Andhra Pradesh Training of Women in Agriculture). In view of the implementation of this scheme, the productivity of paddy had been increased by 7.5 quintals and sugarcane by 60.46 quintals. The total income from all the crop enterprises had increased from Rs. 18235 to Rs. 30359 per hectare. Thus, it was concluded that programme had a positive influence on the farm production.

From the analysis of the results, it is also observed that net returns per hectare increased with an increase in farm size. This indicates that the small farmers were not able to convert their output advantage into higher net profits due to their higher total expenditure on their farms. The low net incomes on small farms calls for development of new farming techniques and extension network has to be strengthened in order to educate farmers so that viability of farming can be improved with the existing technology itself.

To sum up, it shows that in case of beneficiary farms the technical knowledge of farm women had positive effect on farm productivity. The role of agricultural extension is likely to be stronger in modern dynamic set up than in traditional agriculture. These results call for more investment in the scheme 'Women in Agriculture' for larger coverage and thereby to accelerate the agricultural growth.

Fig 7(a) Comparison of various costs and gross value of produce between beneficiary and non-beneficiary farms

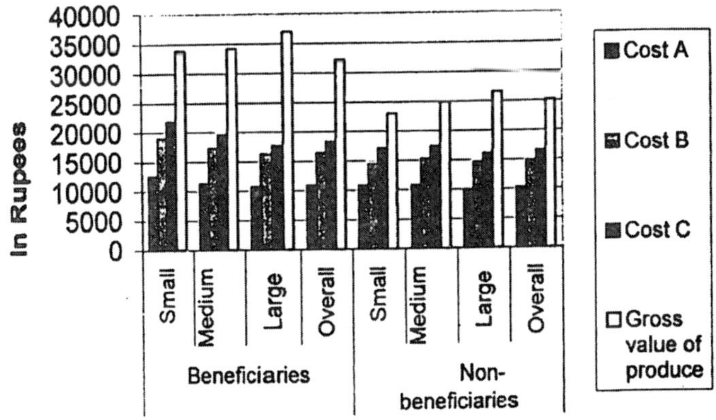

Fig 7(b) Comparision of different of beneficiary and non-beneficiary sample farms

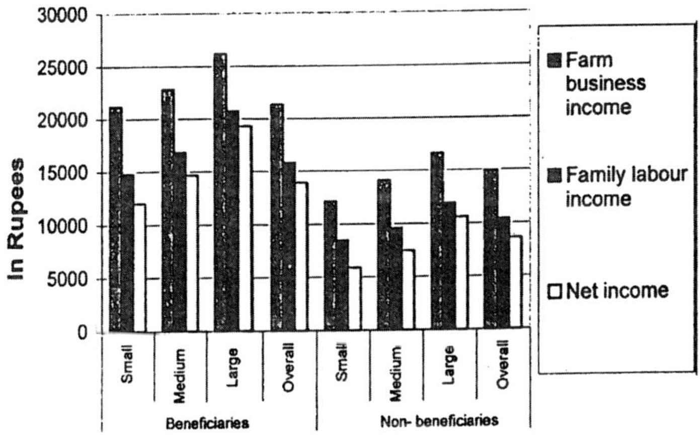

6.7.3 Output-Input Ratio and Profitability

The output-input ratio indicates the magnitude of returns per unit of input in crop production. It indicates the degree of profitability in relation to expenditure. The returns per rupee spent on crop production have importance because it depicts the picture of economies of scale of business. The output-input ratio for the farm as a whole has been worked out on per hectare basis for different size classes of sample farms to examine the farm business efficiency. Details in these regards are presented in Table 6.12.

It is observed that at the overall level (Table 6.12), per hectare output-input ratio in crop production for a farm as a whole was 1.75 in case of beneficiary farms and 1.52 in case of non-beneficiary farms. It is also observed that the output-input ratio increased with an increase in the farm size of the sample households which suggests that the large farms were operating at the higher level of returns from the paddy, vegetable and horticultural crops grown on both the sample households.

6.7.4 Resource Productivities in Crop Production

The agricultural production is considered as a function of different input factors such as land, labour, capital and such other inputs. The variation in the level of these input factors affects the agricultural production. The relationship between input and output as a mathematical expression define the behaviour of dependent variable because of change in one or more independent variables. The functional analysis of the relationship between the output and the level of inputs factor, therefore, serves as a powerful and reliable tool for recommendation of resources both at micro and macro level. Regression coefficients in the Cobb-Douglas type of production function are the output elasticities and the magnitude of individual coefficient indicates the percentage growth, positive or negative depending upon the sign and statistical significance in output in response to one per cent increase in the input concerned, while having the other factors of production constant. The results of the crop production function on the farms of both sample households are presented in Table 6.13.

Table 6.13

Results of Production Function for a Farm as a Whole

Sr. No	Variables		Beneficiaries (N = 120)		Non-Beneficiaries (N = 120)	
			Elasticities	't' value	Elasticities	't' value
1.	Intercept	a	2.87	----	2.46	----
2.	Nitrogen in kg	X_1	0.33 *** (0.07)	4.50	0.64 *** (0.07)	8.28
3.	Phosphorus in kg	X_2	-0.01 NS (0.05)	- 0.20	0.07 ** (0.04)	1.72
4.	Potash in kg	X_3	0.11 *** (0.03)	3.34	0.02 NS (0.04)	0.51
5.	FYM in Tonnes	X_4	0.17 *** (0.02)	5.85	0.12 *** (0.04)	2.95
6.	Human Labour (Man days)	X_5	0.35 *** (0.12)	2.89	0.02 NS (0.09)	0.28
7.	Bullock labour (Pair days)	X_6	- 0.01 NS (0.04)	- 0.24	- 0.04 NS (0.04)	- 0.98
8.	Other working Capital (Pesticides, Seed, Machneries, Irrigation, Incidental charges, Repairs of machineries)	X_7	0.0421* (0.0262)	1.60	0.18 *** (0.04)	4.27
9.	Sum of the regression coefficients	bis	0.998	----	1.04	
10.	R^2	----	0.72	----	0.68	-----
11.	'F' test	----	41.17 ***	-----	34.00 ***	----

(Figures in parentheses indicate the std errors of their respective elasticities).

*** ,**, * indicates the significance level at 1, 5 and 10 per cent of probability level).

To take beneficiaries crop production function first, it is seen from the Table 6.13 that the elasticities of output with respect to nitrogen (X_1), potash (X_3), FYM (X_4), human labour (X_5) have turned out to be positive and significant at one per cent level while the coefficient of other working capital (X_7) is positive and significant at ten per cent probability level. This has indicated that these economic inputs were important to which the crop output on beneficiary farms was highly responsive. Importantly the coefficient of human labour has turned out to be fairly high (0.35) indicating that marginal productivity of labour was high on beneficiary farms. This also rejects the hypothesis of zero marginal productivity of labour on beneficiary farms. It is also observed that nitrogen, potash, FYM, human labour were the most important factors of production and when accompanied with matching capital inputs in terms of expenditure on pesticides, seed, machinery, irrigation, incidental charges and repairs of machinery would increase the output on the beneficiary farms. The coefficient of multiple determination (R^2) has indicated that 72.2 per cent of the total variation in farm output on beneficiary farms has been jointly explained by the selected seven independent variables.

As regards the production function of the non-beneficiary farms, it is seen that the elasticities of output in respect of nitrogen (X_1), phosphorous (X_2), FYM (X_4) and other working capital (X_7) have turned out to be positive and significant. This means that it is economical to extend the use of these inputs in crop production. However, the elasticities of output with respect to potash (X_3) and human labours (X_5) have turned out to be positive but statistically non-significant while that of bullock labour (X_6) has turned out to be negative but statistically non-significant. The coefficient of multiple determination R^2 indicated that the selected seven independent variables have jointly explained 68 per cent of total variation in crop output on non-beneficiary farms. The 'F' statistics has indicated that the regression equations of both the beneficiary and non-beneficiary farms are statistically significant at one per cent level of probability and therefore a good fit.

On comparison of magnitude of elasticities of output between the two categories of farms, it is observed that nitrogen, potash, FYM, human labour and other working capital were important inputs on beneficiary farms while nitrogen, phosphorous, FYM and other working capital were important inputs on non-beneficiary farms. Nitrogen, FYM and other working capital were the common inputs of importance on both the farms. These findings are similar to the findings of Birari *et al* (1999) who observed that human labour, manures, fertilizers and other working capital were the major inputs influencing the crop output in western Maharashtra. The pooled analysis of the entire sample farms was carried out with a view to apply the *'Chow's test'* of equality. In other words, the significance of difference between the crop production function of beneficiary and non-beneficiary farms was tested by using *'Chow's test'*. It is seen that the F (8, 224) ratio is 6.39, which is significant at a probability level of one percent indicating that the two regressions are not equal but differed significantly in their overall production relationships. This is also confirmed from the discussions about resource use, costs and returns structure in crop production of these two categories of farms made earlier in this chapter.

The sum of the production elasticities indicates the returns to scale in Cobb-Douglas type of production function. The sum of the elasticities is 0.99 in case of beneficiary farms and 1.04 in case of non-beneficiaries farms. These Σbis are tested by applying 'Z' test to know whether they differ significantly from unity. It is noted that the sum of the elasticities did not differ significantly from the unity and hence there exists the constant returns to scale in both the cases. This enabled us to say that the magnitude of individual elasticity coefficients indicated the relative shares of different factors of production in the total crop output on both the categories of farms. It appears that the human labour had the largest factor share followed by nitrogen, manures and potash on beneficiary farms and nitrogen followed by other working capital and manures on the non-beneficiary farms.

6.7.5 Resource Use Efficiency on Sample Farms

The marginal value productivity of factor taken at its prevailing market price or opportunity cost indicates the efficiency of resource use. Marginal value products (MVPs) that

efficiency of resource use. Marginal value products (MVPs) that are higher than the opportunity cost or market cost of factors, indicate the scope of raising output profitability through increased use of such resource concerned, whereas those are less than opportunity or factor unit cost depict unprofitable nature of resource use. Any factor is considered to be used most efficiently if its MVP is sufficient to off set its cost. Equality of MVP to factor cost is therefore the basic condition, which should be satisfied to find out the efficient use of resources (Raju and Rao, 1996).

With a view to evaluate the efficiency of resource use on sample farms, the marginal value products of the individual inputs have been estimated at their geometric means. The equality of marginal value to the factor unit cost is the basic condition that must be satisfied to obtain efficient resource use in crop production. The details regarding the marginal value products, factor cost and the ratio of the marginal value product to the factor price for both the sample farms are given in Table 6.14.

It is observed that on beneficiary farms, the ratio of MVP to factor unit cost was higher than unity in case of potash followed by nitrogen, human labour and F.Y.M. This has indicated the scope for increasing the use of these factors to the extent of optimum level for increasing the total farm output on average sample farms. The marginal value product of other working capital is bit lower than factor cost indicating that further use of this input may not be economical under the existing level of technology. The ratio of MVP to the unit cost of factor with respect to phosphorus and bullock labour have turned out to be negative which indicates the over use of these resources and suggested no further use in crop production.

Table 6.14
Marginal Value Productivities, Factor Costs and Economic Efficiency in Resource Allocation on Sample Farms

Variables	Beneficiaries (N=120)			Non-Beneficiaries (N=120)		
	MVP to unit cost of factor	*Unit cost of factor (Rs)*	*Ratio of MVP to unit cost of factor*	*MVP to unit cost of factor*	*Unit cost of factor (Rs)*	*Ratio of MVP to unit cost of factor*
Nitrogen (kg) X_1	143.01	9.79	14.60	262.60	9.82	26.74
Phosphorus (kg)) X_2	-9.68	7.82	-1.23	95.52	7.82	12.21
Potash (kg) X_3	156.47	8.09	19.34	36.26	9.12	3.97
FYM (Tonnes) X_4	785.93	500	1.57	580.32	496.18	1.16
Human labour (Man-days) X_5	108.68	36.76	2.95	6.68	36.3	0.18
Bullock labour (Pair--days) X_6	-212	100	-2.12	-72.45	102.10	-0.70
Other working capital (Rs) X_7	0.759	1	0.75	3.06	1	3.06

Regarding the non-beneficiary farms, it is noted that the ratio of MVP to the unit factor cost was higher than unity in respect of nitrogen followed by phosphorous, potash, other working capital and FYM indicating that there exists a scope for increasing the use of these factors to the extent of optimum level for increasing the total farm output on average non-beneficiary farms. The ratio of MVP to unit cost of factor in case of human labour was quite lower than unity which means that further use of human labour in crop production was not economical. The bullock labour was over used as ratio of MVP to unit cost of factor turned out to be negative. The potash, nitrogen and FYM emerged as common resources on both the sample farms for which ratio of MVP to the factor cost was higher than unity which emphasized to intensify their use in crop production. However, the use of bullock labours has to be curtailed for crop production on both the farms.

To conclude, it can be said that the scheme under study has created a positive impact in the study area and it has resulted into increase in crop productivity on farms as a whole. Higher level of production as well as higher profit was observed mainly through the higher level of technology adoption, which was due to the technical awareness achieved by beneficiary farm women as a result of implementation of the scheme 'Women in Agriculture' in Thane district of Maharashtra.

The input use levels of the non-beneficiary farms suggest that only high use of technical inputs like seeds, manures, chemical fertilisers and plant protection measures per unit of land does not necessarily bring about maximum possible output for a given set of inputs. It is necessary to provide institutional support to the farmers by widening access to the agricultural extension facilities and technical training to the farmers so that farmers may use modern agricultural inputs in order to have maximum possible output.

7

Impact of Scheme on Employment and Income of Sample Households

This chapter deals with the presentation of results of analysis of the data relating to employment and income aspects of beneficiaries and non-beneficiaries sample households. It was hypothesized that the assistance received by sample beneficiaries through the scheme 'Women in Agriculture' helped in increasing the employment and income. Thus, the intention of analysis is to examine the differentials in employment and income due to implementation central sector scheme 'Women in Agriculture' on beneficiary households and to identify the factors influencing these economic indicators in respect of both the sample households. The farm business analysis discussed in Chapter 6 became a useful basis for estimation of employment and income of the sample households. It is now proposed to explain in this chapter the average annual employment of male and female, different sources of employment and the employment function, sources of income and income function of both the categories of households in the discussion that follows.

7.1 Average Annual Employment of Sample Households

The analysis contemplated so far has revealed that the technological changes in agriculture have brought about desirable transformation in the resource use structure and resource productivities in the production of the crops on the sample farms. The cumulative effect could be seen in increased employment and welfare of the farm families. Efforts have therefore been made to study the changes in employment pattern of the sample households during the period 2001-02.

As discussed in the methodology chapter, in the present study, an attempt has been made to calculate the day-to-day work done by children (10-15 years) and adult male and female (15 to 60 years and above) in terms of hours. Eight working hours have been considered equal to one-day work. The women, children working days have been converted into standard man days and 300 man-days in a year have been considered as a full employment norm according to time criteria.

In the study area, the rural population is especially engaged in various economic activities like crop production, wage earning, off farms, non-farms activities and in service sector. The sector-wise employment patterns were analyzed for both the sample households and are presented in Table 7.1.

Table 7.1
Average Annual Employments of the Sample Households

(man-days)

Activities	*Beneficiaries*				*Non-Beneficiaries*			
	Small	*Medium*	*Large*	*Overall*	*Small*	*Medium*	*Large*	*Overall*
On Farm (Crop produ-ction)	30.68 (6.93)	52.48 (12.10)	74.65 (18.38)	49.12 (11.25)	22.81 (6.40)	41.72 (13.76)	62.27 (18.74)	39.12 (11.21)
Other's Farm (Wages)	167.16 (37.78)	91.55 (21.11)	45.79 (11.27)	111.94 (25.64)	166.81 (46.83)	99.39 (32.79)	17.62 (5.30)	106.60 (30.56)
Off-farm Livestock /dairy	36.42 (8.23)	79.02 (18.22)	104.40 (25.70)	68.23 (15.63)	5.10 (1.43)	43.27 (14.28)	69.06 (20.78)	34.24 (9.82)
Goatry	18.95 (4.28)	1.04 (0.24)	----	7.95 (1.82)	---	---	1.37 (0.41)	0.33 (0.09)
Poultry	10.31 (2.33)	26.09 (6.01)	33.27 (8.19)	21.51 (4.93)	5.52 (1.55)	2.79 (0.92)	15.68 (4.72)	9.94 (2.85)
Total off farm	65.68 (14.84)	106.15 (24.47)	137.67 (33.89)	97.69 (22.37)	10.62 (2.98)	46.06 (15.20)	86.11 (25.91)	44.51 (12.76)

(contd. Table 7.1)

Contd/....

Activities	Beneficiaries				Non-Beneficiaries			
	Small	Medium	Large	Overall	Small	Medium	Large	Overall
Non-farm Papad / other activities	31.5 (7.12)	24.06 (5.55)	31.55 (7.77)	28.85 (6.61)	4.06 (1.14)	8.95 (2.95)	8.27 (2.49)	6.83 (1.96)
Mushroom	0.41 (0.09)	1.16 (0.27)	1.37 (0.34)	0.91 (0.21)	---	---	---	---
Honey bees	---	1.97 (0.45)	4.14 (1.02)	1.70 (0.39)	---	1.86 (0.61)	---	0.66 (0.19)
Stiching and bomboo work	30 (6.78)	46.51 (10.72)	16.72 (4.12)	32.70 (7.49)	25.06 (7.03)	25.46 (8.40)	33.96 (10.22)	38.80 (11.12)
Total of Non farm	61.91 (13.99)	73.70 (16.99)	53.78 (13.24)	64.16 (14.70)	29.12 (8.17)	36.27 (11.97)	42.23 (12.71)	46.29 (13.27)
Service	117.08 (26.46)	109.88 (25.33)	94.30 (23.22)	113.7 (26.04)	126.87 (35.61)	79.65 (26.28)	124.13 (37.35)	112.33 (32.20)
Family Gross employ-ment	442.51 (100)	433.76 (100)	406.19 (100)	436.61 (100)	356.23 (100)	303.09 (100)	332.36 (100)	348.85 (100)
Per head Employ-ment	191.15	187.77	161.82	185.00	156.24	132.93	132.41	146.57

(Figures in parentheses indicate the percentage in family gross employment)

It is examined from the Table 7.1 that, at the overall level, the gross family employment was 436.61 man-days in beneficiary and 348.85 man-days in non-beneficiary sample households. Employment pattern of beneficiary household was examined across the farms, which showed that the maximum employment was observed on small farms (442.51 man-days) followed by medium size farms (433.76 man-days) and on large farms (406.19 man-days). In case of non-beneficiaries, the maximum employment was on small size farms (356.23 man-days) followed by large size farms (332.36 man-days) and medium size farms (303.09 man-days). The employment pattern on both the sample households has been depicted with the help of line graph as presented in Fig. 8a and 8b.

The sector wise employment pattern of beneficiary sample households indicated that at the overall level the highest

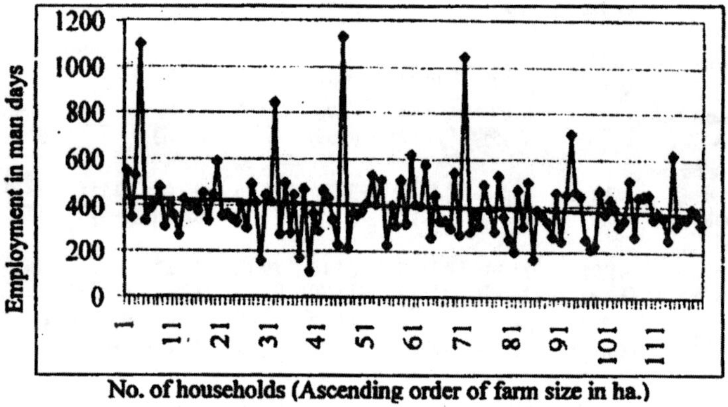

Fig. 8(a) Pattern of annual avarage employment of the beneficiary households

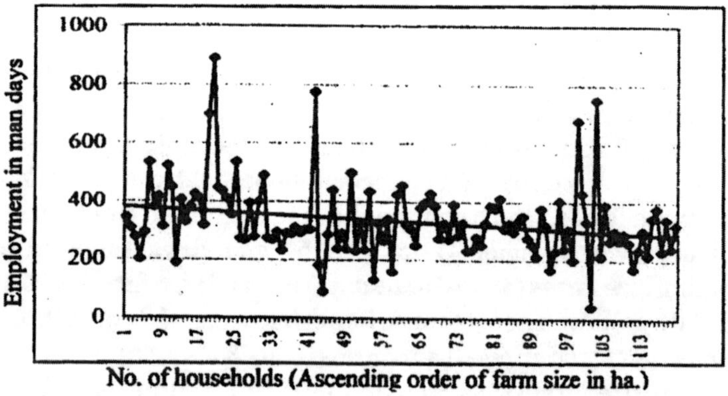

Fig. 8(b) Pattern of annual average employement of the non-beneficiary household

employment was generated through service (26.04 per cent) followed by wages (25.64 per cent), off-farm activities (22.37 per cent), non-farm activities (14.70 per cent) and crop production activities (11.25 per cent).

Similarly, in case of non-beneficiary sample households, the highest employment was generated from the service (32.20 per cent) followed by wages (30.56 per cent), non-farm activities (13.27 per cent), off-farm activities (12.76 per cent) and crop production (11.21 per cent). The service sector emerged as a major employment provider because of the industrial network close to the study area.

The comparison of annual average employment of beneficiary and non-beneficiary is shown in Fig. 9a. The share of different sectors of employment in annual gross employment on the sample households is presented in Fig. 9b.

The analysis of employment across the farms of beneficiary households illustrated that the employment days increased with an increase in farm size in respect of crop production, off-farm activities whereas it decreased with an increase in farm size in case of service and working on others farm. The non-farm activities did not show any linear trend of employment pattern, however the highest employment was accrued on medium farms (73.70 man-days) followed by small farms (61.91 man-days) and on large farms (53.78 man-days). It could be inferred that small and medium size of landholders tend to employ more in service and on others farm due to fragile land base resources and weak economy to support the off-farm and non-farm activities. While in case of non-beneficiaries households, the employment pattern across the farm size showed that employment days increased with an increase in farm size in respect of crop production, off-farm and non-farm activities whereas it decreased with an increase in farm size in case of working on others farm. The employment from service did not show any linear trend of employment pattern, however the highest employment was on small farms followed by large farms and medium farms.

The service and wage earning were emerged as major employment providers especially for the workers of small farms,

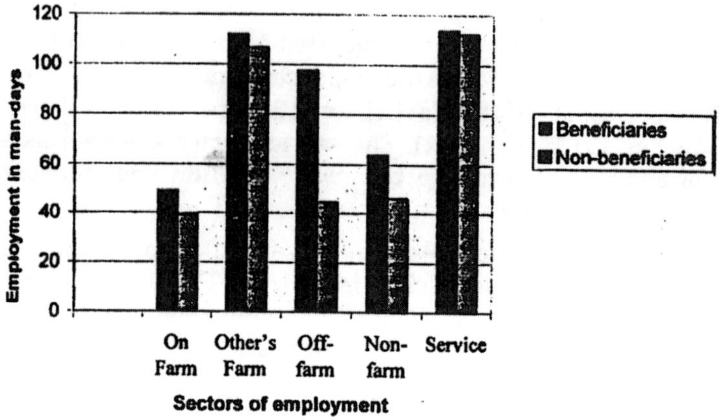

Fig. 9(a) Annual average employment of sample household

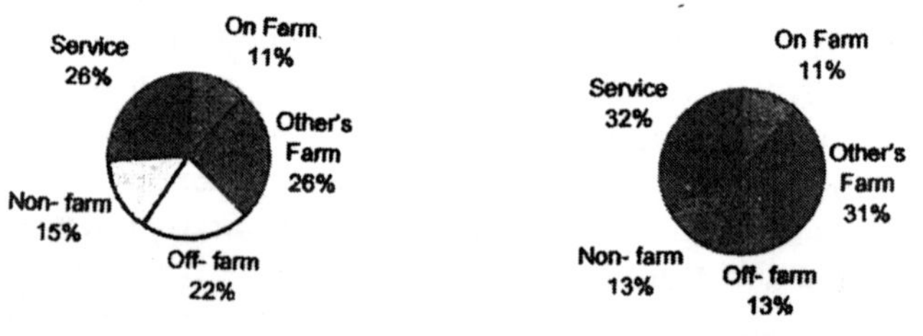

Beneficiary households

Non-beneficiary households

Fig. 9(b) Share of different sectors of employment in annual groos employment cf the sample houehold

which could provide 64.24 per cent employment in beneficiary and 82.44 per cent in non-beneficiary households. On medium size farms, two sectors namely service and off-farm activities provided 49.80 per cent of employment in beneficiary households while service and wage earning activities provided 59.07 per cent of total employment in case of non-beneficiary households. On large sized farms, the two sectors viz. service and off-farm activities jointly provided 57.11 per cent and 63.26 per cent of employment to beneficiary and non-beneficiary households respectively. At the overall level, service and wage earning activities jointly could offered 51.68 per cent and 62.76 per cent employment in beneficiary and in non-beneficiary households respectively. Another largest sectors that could provide maximum employment were the off-farm and non-farm activities, which jointly provided 37.07 per cent employment to the beneficiary households and 26.03 per cent employment to the non-beneficiary households. In the present study, non-farm sector refers to papad making, beekeeping, mushroom, stitching and other business activities. As there is no clear-cut standard definition of the rural non-farm employment. However, some experts argued that the non-farm sector includes the activities that are not closely related with agriculture or agriculture and allied sectors. Elumalai and Sharma (2003) defined non-farm sector as an economic activities except agriculture, livestock and fishing. Muniyandi *et al* (2003) defined farm activity as crop activity, livestock rearing, and agricultural labour and homestead activities, while, in the non-farm activities, services were included like a small-scale village industries, transportation, construction, shop keeping, etc.

It is further revealed that the employment generated through the crop production on both the sample households was more or less equal, i.e., 11.25 per cent in beneficiaries and 11.21 per cent in non-beneficiaries. The crop production activities offered comparatively less employment on both the sample farms because of inadequacy of irrigation vis-à-vis less cropping intensity in the study area.

It is also noted that at the overall level, the off-farm sector that includes livestock and dairy, goat rearing and poultry could generate nearly 97.69 man-days (22.37 per cent) on beneficiary households and 44.51 man-days (12.76 per cent) on non-beneficiary households respectively. When it was examined across the farms, it is observed that the employment through the off-farm sector increased with an increase in farm size. It means, these activities are capital intensive and strong farm based resources are required to undertake livestock, goat keeping and poultry activities. This indicates the positive impact of the scheme on generation of off-farm employment especially during the slack period. The increases in employment through off-farm activities with increase in farm size was be due to the fact that rural households could invest the income generated from other subsidiary activities in agriculture to expand farm output, and in turn farmer produce surplus and invest in off-farm activities in order to generate the additional income.

The off-farm activities like dairy and poultry have been promoted through the scheme under study is shown in Fig. 10.

It can be concluded that the labour absorptive capacity of agriculture is limited. When rural households cannot get adequate employment in agriculture, they spill over the rural off and non-farm sector, which acts as cushion for them. The both off-farm and non-farm activities like poultry, mushroom, honeybees and papad making were promoted through the scheme under study especially by arranging the skill based training classes at village level, exposure visits to the success stories and tie up with the credit agencies which resulted into more employment in case of beneficiaries. It is further noted that, non-beneficiary households also undertook papad making, poultry and goatry which provided gainful employment because of the demonstrative effect, i.e., non-beneficiary farm women could acquire skill from beneficiary farm women and tried to imitate. There is thus a significant impact on employment generation due to intervention of scheme under study on beneficiary households and on non-beneficiary households as well. The diversification in employment as observed on the sample households would help to reduce the vulnerability by smoothing income and spreading the risk across the several activities. The non-farm activities such as basket making and honeybees keeping promoted through the scheme have been depicted in Fig. 11

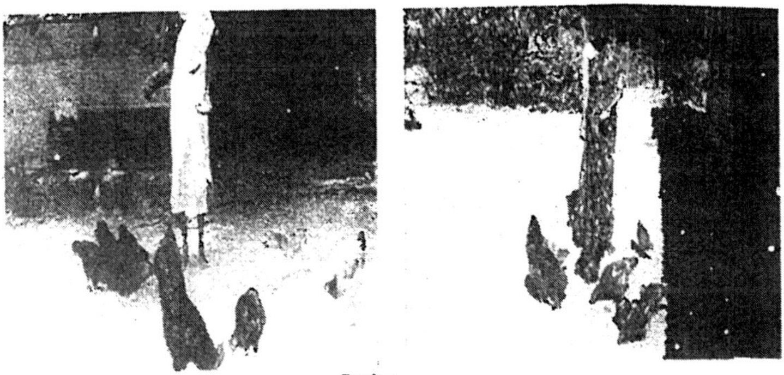

Poultry

Fig. 10 The off farm activities like poultry, diary and goat keeping were promoted through the scheme

Dairy

Goat keeping

Mushroom cultivation

Papad preparation through Self Help Group (SHG)

Bamboo work

Fig. 11 Non-farm activities for the income and employment generation were promoted through the scheme

7.2 Annual Gross Employment Pattern of Male and Female

7.2.1 Average Annual Employment Pattern of a Male Worker

The details regarding average annual employment of a male worker of the sample households are given in Table 7.2. To take beneficiary households first, the total annual employment of an average male worker of beneficiary households during the year 2001-2002, at the overall level, was 245.86 man-days, i.e., 56.31 per cent of the total family employment days in a year. The total annual employment ranged from 214.55 man-days in large size class to 249.52 man-days in small size class. It is also noted that the major employment came from the service sector (46.25 per cent). At the overall level, it is seen that the employment days of beneficiary households decreased with an increase in farm size.

The employment pattern across the farm size indicated that the average male worker on small farms tended to employ more in service to get an additional income for family sustenance. Further, it is observed that the employment days increased with an increase in farm size in respect of crop production, off-farm activities while decreased with an increase in farm size in case of work on others farm and service sector. Regarding employment from non-farm sector, it appeared to be the highest on medium size farms followed by small and large size farms.

The workers of the smaller size classes of households were largely engaged in service and as hired labourers on others farm relatively for more days as compared to those of larger size classes. In other words, the employment of a male worker on others farm declined with an increase in the size class of farms. It is further observed that of the total employment of 245.86 man-days at the overall level, the share of service was 46.25 per cent, off and non-farm activities 27.13 per cent, on other's farm 18.55 per cent and only 8.07 per cent share of crop production activities. It shows that about 73.38 per cent of annual

Table 7.2

Annual Gross Employment Pattern of a Male Worker of Sample Households (2001-2002)

(Man-days)

Activities	Gender	Beneficiaries				Non-Beneficiaries			
		Small	*Medium*	*Large*	*Overall*	*Small*	*Medium*	*Large*	*Overall*
Crop production (On farm)	Male	13.38	22.39	23.58	19.85	10.31	16.09	28.31	16.73
	per cent	5.36	9.06	10.99	8.07	4.73	9.39	12.75	7.82
Work on others farm (Wages)	Male	73.12	32.11	20.1	45.61	65.04	40.95	7.62	42.54
	per cent	29.30	13.00	9.37	18.55	29.81	23.90	3.43	19.87
Off-farms	Male	25.71	46.81	63.65	42.64	4.17	18.97	37.91	18.63
	per cent	10.30	18.95	29.67	17.34	1.91	11.07	17.07	8.70
Non-farm	Male	20.31	35.81	12.92	24.06	11.87	15.69	23.79	23.87
	per cent	8.14	14.50	6.02	9.79	5.44	9.16	10.71	11.15
Service	Male	117.0	109.88	94.3	113.70	126.8	79.65	124.40	112.29
	per cent	46.91	44.49	43.95	46.25	58.11	46.48	56.03	52.46
Overall	Male	249.52	247	214.55	245.86	218.19	171.35	222.03	214.06
	Per cent	100	100	100	100	100	100	100	100
Gross family employment	Total	442.43	433.77	406.19	436.61	356.09	303.09	332.63	348.81
% Share of male in total employment		56.40	56.94	52.82	56.31	61.27	56.53	66.75	61.37

average male employment was generated through three activities namely service, off-farm and non-farm activities. This has clearly indicated that, the off-farm and non-farm activities promoted under the scheme 'Women in Agriculture' provided considerable employment to the male members of the family.

As regards the average employment of a male worker of non-beneficiary households, it is seen that at the overall level the share of male employment in average gross family employment was 214.06 man-days, i.e., 61.37 per cent. The total employment of a male worker ranged from 171.35 man-days on medium to 222.03 man-days on large size farms. It is observed that, the highest employment was generated from service sector which accounted for 112.29 man-days (52.46 per cent) followed by wages 42.54 days (19.87 per cent), non-farm activities 23.87 days (11.15 per cent), off-farms 18.63 days (8.70 per cent) and agriculture 16.73 days (7.82 per cent) respectively. Analysis across the farm size indicated the same trend, as it was observed in beneficiary households except in non-farm activities in which average male employment showed an increase with an increase in farm size. It is also seen that share of service was 52.46 per cent and that of non-service employment was 47.54 per cent.

On comparison of employment position of male workers of beneficiary and non-beneficiary households, at the overall level, it is seen that the average annual male employment of beneficiary households was more by 31.08 man days, i.e., 14.85 per cent than the average male of non-beneficiary sample households. At the overall level, the average annual employment of male worker in all sectors was observed to be higher in case of beneficiary than non-beneficiary households. Largely, there was no significant difference in employment in the case of wage earning, non-farm activities, crop production and service. However, there was a significant difference of 24.01 man-days of employment in the case of off-farm activities because of the supplementary activities like dairy, poultry and goat keeping were promoted through the said scheme.

7.2.2 Average Annual Employment Pattern of a Female Worker

Details regarding the average annual employment of female workers of beneficiary and non-beneficiary are given in Table 7.3.

To take employment pattern of a female worker of beneficiaries first, it was noted that in beneficiary households, the total annual employment at the overall level was 190.75 man-days, i.e., 63.58 per cent of the gross employment of 300 days in a year as mentioned in the methodology chapter. The period of unemployment in a year, as compared to full employment of average 300 days worked out 109.25 man-days, i.e., 36.41 per cent.

At the overall level, the highest employment was through work on others farm (34.77 per cent) followed by off farms (28.86 per cent), non-farm (21.02 per cent), crop production (15.34 per cent) respectively. On examination of employment pattern across the farm size, it is observed that the employment with respect to crop production and off farm activities increased with an increase in farm size while it decreases with an increase in farm size in case of work on others farm. The employment pattern in non-farm activities did not show any specific trend.

In case of non-beneficiary households, it is observed that at the overall level, the average annual employment of a female worker was 134.75 man-days, i.e., 38.63 per cent of the average gross employment in the year. Assuming that 300 days employment in year as full employment, the non-beneficiary farm women were unemployed for 165.25 days, i.e., 55.08 per cent. It is also evident that the employment decreased with an increase in farm size. On the sector wise examination, it is observed that at the over all level, the highest employment was offered through wage earning 64.06 days (47.54 per cent) followed by off-farm activities 25.88 days (19.21 per cent), non-farm 22.42 days (16.64 per cent) and crop production 16.73 days (7.82 per cent) respectively. Across the farm size, it is observed that employment of average female worker increased with an increase in the size class with respect

Table 7.3

Annual Gross Employment Pattern of a Female Worker of Sample Households (2001-2002)

(Man-days)

Activities		*Beneficiaries*				*Non-Beneficiaries*			
	Gender	*Small*	*Medium*	*large*	*Overall*	*Small*	*Medium*	*large*	*Overall*
Crop production (On farm)	Female	17.3	30.09	51.07	29.27	12.5	25.63	33.96	22.39
	per cent	8.97	16.11	26.65	15.34	9.06	19.45	30.71	16.62
Work on others farms (Wages)	Female	94.04	59.44	25.69	66.33	101.7	58.44	10	64.06
	per cent	48.75	31.83	13.41	34.77	73.75	44.36	9.04	47.54
Off-farms	Female	39.97	59.34	74.02	55.05	6.45	27.09	48.2	25.88
	per cent	20.72	31.77	38.62	28.86	4.68	20.56	43.58	19.21
Non-farms	Female	41.6	37.9	40.86	40.1	17.25	20.58	18.44	22.42
	per cent	21.56	20.29	21.32	21.02	12.51	15.62	16.67	16.64
Service	Female	--	--	--	--	--	--	--	--
	per cent	--	--	--		--	--	--	--
Gross female employment	Female	192.91	186.77	191.64	190.75	137.9	131.74	110.6	134.75
	Per cent	100	100	100	100	100	100	100	100
Gross family employment		442.43	433.77	406.19	436.61	356.09	303.09	332.63	348.81
% Share of female in total employment		43.60	43.06	47.18	43.69	38 73	43.47	33.25	38.63

to crop production and off-farms activity, while it decreased with increase in farm size in case of wages. It is quite acceptable since the female worker from smaller farm size class had to secure employment on others farm for family sustenance.

To compare the position of average employment of female worker in both categories, it can be said that at the overall level, the average annual employment in case of beneficiary households was higher by 56 days i.e. 41.55 per cent over non-beneficiaries. It was also seen that total farm employment of female worker from off-farm and non-farm activities was 95.15 days in beneficiaries and 48.30 days in non-beneficiaries which was higher by 46.85 days. This leads us to conclude that the differential of total annual employment of female workers of beneficiary households was mainly due to the promotion of activities like poultry, goatry, dairy, papad making, bamboo work, honey bees and mushroom production through the central sector scheme 'Women in Agriculture' in the study area.

These findings led to the policy implication that the low level of literacy in case of non-beneficiary farm women coupled with their dependence on traditional professions hindered their access to other profession thereby requiring government assistance for training and education to persue more profitable alternatives.

To sum up the whole, it can be said that the annual average employment in case of beneficiary male and female was higher by 14.85 per cent and 41.55 per cent as compared to those of non-beneficiary households under study. The activity wise break up of total farm employment in beneficiaries was significantly higher than that of non-beneficiaries with respect to crop production by 10 days, off farm by 53.18 days, non-farm by 17.87 days. In addition to manifest underemployment in agriculture sector, the potential for employment has been found in activities such as bee-keeping, mushroom, poultry, dairy, papad making and honey bees keeping in the selected areas. These activities will not necessarily lead to greater demand of available land. These findings are similar to the study conducted by Puhazhendhi and Jayaraman (1999) who examined the income generation through the farm women's groups in Chitradurga district of Karnataka. They noted the positive impact on income generation as 172 extra man-days employment was generated through income generation activities. Singh *et al* (1992) also observed that IRDP had increased the level of employment of rural women. The similar observations also noted by Khorate and Hardikar (2003) that DWCRA scheme had brought positive change in the income and employment generation of the beneficiaries.

It is also seen that limited male and female labour were absorbed by the agriculture. When rural worker cannot get adequate employment in agriculture they spill over into the rural non-farm and off-farm sector which act as sponge for the excess labour absorption.

It is seen that significantly higher level of non-farm employment of beneficiary households was mainly due to intensification of agriculture and adoption of non-farm and off-farm activities on a large scale in the area under study.

It is concluded that to generate employment in rural areas it is necessary to think of integrating farm and non-farm sector. Due to lack of skill among both farm men and women, the non-farm sector may face stiff competition from the large-scale industries. Thus, it is necessary to provide the training to the rural masses to enhance their skill. To improve the work participation rate and also to increase non-agricultural employment among women, there is a need to impart the technical education and entrepreneurship development among women. Hidden potential of unemployed educated women can be effectively utilized in organizing the self-help groups and in undertaking micro enterprises in non-agriculture sector with necessary technical and financial support.

7. 3 Gross Family Employment Function

In order to facilitate the comparison of two regressions, the pooled regression of the observations of beneficiary and non-beneficiary households was carried out by introducing a dummy variable not only to examine the differential in intercept but also in slope coefficients of the three independent variables of the employment model. The employment model therefore, involved the annual gross family employment in man-days as a dependent variable (Y) and the independent variables viz. gross cropped area (X_1), working capital investment in agriculture and agro-base activities (X_2), working adult units in the family (X_3)

together with dummy variable D_1 for measuring the shift in intercept, and the variables D_1X_1, D_1X_2, D_1X_3 for measuring the changes in the slopes of three independent variables on account of employment accrued due to the scheme implementation under study. The results of the estimated employment model are presented in Table 7.4.

Table 7.4
Employment Function: Regression Coefficient and Test of their Significance

Independent variables		*Mean*	*Regression Coefficient*	*Standard Error*
1. Gross cropped area in hectares.	X_1	0.87	58.12*	29.80
2. Working capital (agril + agro base) (Rs)	X_2	10342.48	0.036 ***	0.013
3. Working adult units	X_3	2 .31	78.27 ***	22.71
4. Dummy variable (Intercept)	D_1	0.50	122.92 **	58.270
5. Dummy variable (Gross cropped area in hectares.	D_1X_1	0.47	76. 92 ***	21.91
6. Dummy vari-able (Working capital for agril + agro base)	D_1X_2	6094.84	0.054 ***	0.016
7. Dummy variable (Working Adult units)	D_1X_3	1.8	95.46 ***	21.48

N= 240, Y = 362.16, Constant (a) = 66.49, R^2 = 0.72, F ratio = 71.66.

***, **, * Significant at one, five and ten per cent level of probability,

It is seen that the regression coefficient in respect of gross cropped area (X_1), Working capital (X_2), working adult units (X_3) and differential intercept coefficient (D_1) are found to be positive and significant. However, the differential slope coefficients in respect of gross cropped area (D_1X_1) and working adult unit (D_1X_3) have turned out to be significant at one percent level of probability. The coefficients D_1, D_1X_1, D_1X_2 and D_1X_3 have indicated that beneficiaries employment function differed significantly from the coefficient of X_1, X_2 and X_3 of a non-beneficiaries employment function. The coefficient of multiple determination (R^2) suggests that the selected independent variables have jointly expressed 72 per cent of the variation in the annual gross family employment of the sample households. The estimated regression thus gives an excellent fit.

From the result presented in Table 7.4, the individual employment function for beneficiaries and non-beneficiaries easily be derived as under.

7.3.1 Mean Employment Function of the Beneficiaries and Non-beneficiaries

Assuming that E (Ui) =1, then mean employment function of **beneficiaries** would be;

$$E(Yi / D_1=1, X_1, X_2 X_3) = (a + b_4) + (b_1 + b_5)X_1 + (b_2 + b_6)X_2 + (b_3 + b_7)X_3$$

$$Y = (66.49 + 122.92) + (58.12 + 76.92)\ X_1 + (0.036 + 0.054)\ X_2 + (78.27 + 95.46)X_3$$

$$Y = 189.41 + 135.04\ X_1^{***} + 0.090\ X_2^{***} + 173.73X_3^{***}$$

$$(48.94) \qquad (0.016) \qquad (66.81)\ R^2=0.77$$

Similarly, the mean employment function of **non-beneficiaries** would be;

$$E(Yi / D_1 = 0, X_1, X_2 X_3) = a + b_1X_1 + b_2X_2 + b_3X_3.$$

$$Y = 66.49 + 58.12\ X_1^{*} + 0.036\ X_2^{***} + 78.27\ X_3^{***}$$

$$(29.80) \qquad (0.013) \qquad (22.71)\ R^2 = 0.66$$

The estimated parameters of the above two equations were also confirmed by running two regressions separately.

As regards the employment function of the beneficiaries, the regression coefficient of gross cropped area (X_1) is larger in magnitude than that of non-beneficiaries and turned out to be significant at 5 per cent level of probability. The technical backup, high level of resource use and adoption of improved farm high level of resource use and adoption of improved farm technologies in the area under study are the reasons behind the significant contribution of land input in generation of employment. The coefficients of working capital (X_2) and working adult units in the family (X_3) have indicated quite significant positive influence on the gross family employment of the beneficiaries.

The coefficient of gross cropped area would increase family annual employment by 135.04 man-days and found to be significant. This means that increase in one hectare of gross cropped area would increase family annual employment by 135.04 man-days. This means that under the new set of technology and sound resource base on beneficiaries farms, the increase in GCA would have significant contribution to gross family employment on the sample beneficiary households.

The coefficient of working capital (X_2) indicated that the other factors being held constant, the increase in working capital by one hundred rupees, the annual gross employment of an average beneficiary family would increase by nine man-days. This implies that there exists certain scope to increase the gross family employment in the beneficiary households by increasing the working capital. Working expenses especially on the off-farm and non-farm activities have contributed in generating employment which is the reason for having the coefficient of X_2 significant in case of beneficiary households.

The regression coefficient of the working adult unit (X_3) is turned out to be significant at one per cent indicating that other factors being held constant the increase in family size by one adult unit, the annual gross family employment on an average, would increase by 173.73 man-days annually.

In case of the employment function of the non-beneficiaries, the coefficient of gross cropped area (X_1) is 58.12 and found significant at 10 per cent level which means that under the existing level of technology and resource base, the increase in the gross cropped area by one hectare would have positive contribution to the gross family employment by 58.12 man-days of the sample non-beneficiary households. Similarly, the regression coefficient of the working capital investment in crop and agro- based activities (X_2) is 0.036 which is positive and significant at one per cent level indicating the scope for generation of employment of three man days from Rs.100 additional investment of working expenses on the farms of non-beneficiaries. The regression coefficient of the adult working unit (X_3) of the family turned out to be highly significant at one per cent indicating that other factors being held constant, the increase in the family size by one adult unit, the annual gross family employment of an average non-beneficiary household would increase by 78.27 man days annually. This is quite acceptable in the sense that the farm family has to attempt for additional employment for meeting the consumption needs in view of the increased size of family.

To sum up, it can be said that, the employment function of the beneficiaries differed significantly from that of non-beneficiaries since the differential intercept and slope coefficients in respect of all the three variables are found to be statistically significant. This has indicated that the implementation of central sector scheme 'Women in Agriculture' has a significant effect on the annual gross family employment of beneficiary households.

7.4 Impact of Technological Change on Family Income

Income is an important economic measurement, which is applied to measure the standard of living of the people. For the present study, data were collected on the average family income from different sources of both the households. The average family income of sample households from different sources according to their size classes during the year 2001-2002 was analysed and is presented in Table 7.5.

To take the beneficiaries first, at the overall level the average gross family income from different sources was Rs.71309, which increased with an increase in farm size, indicating the direct relationship with the farm size. Among the

Table 7.5
Average Annual Gross Family Incomes from Different Sources on the Sample Households

(Rs)

Activities	*Beneficiaries*				*Non-Beneficiaries*			
	Small	*Medium*	*Large*	*Overall*	*Small*	*Medium*	*Large*	*Overall*
Crop production (At working cost)	21203 (30.14)	22820 (30.56)	26229 (34.96)	21374 (29.97)	12146 (23.67)	14109 (24.62)	16605 (30.84)	14910 (27.14)
Wages	7085 (10.07)	3515 (4.71)	1822 (2.43)	4533 (6.36)	7995 (15.58)	4647 (8.11)	835 (1.55)	5035 (9.16)
Off-Farm	3930 (5.59)	6115 (8.19)	11838 (15.78)	6623 (9.28)	1859 (3.62)	3126 (5.46)	5550 (10.31)	3079 (5.60)
Non-Farm	4978 (7.08)	9202 (12.32)	3007 (4.01)	6015 (8.43)	1020 (1.99)	2730 (4.77)	3345 (6.22)	2428 (4.41)
Service	33156 (47.12)	33016 (44.20)	32120 (42.82)	32764 (45.94)	28291 (55.14)	32674 (57.03)	27500 (51.08)	29488 (53.68)
Gross family income	70352 (100)	74668 (100)	75016 (100)	71309 (100)	51311 (100)	57286 (100)	53835 (100)	54940 (100)
Annual income per adult unit	30455.41	32323.81	29886.8	30215.6	21559	26441.2	21448.2	23084

(Figures in parentheses indicate the percentages to gross family income).

five major sources of family income, the service had the maximum contribution to the extent of Rs. 32764 (45.94 per cent) followed by agriculture Rs.21374 (29.97 per cent), off-farm activities Rs.6623 (9.29 per cent), non-farm activities Rs.6015 (8.44 per cent) and wages Rs. 4533 (6.36 per cent). The study of income across the farm size indicates that income from agriculture, off-farm activities increased with an increase in farm size. Income accrued from the wage earning decreased with an increase in farm size, while income from non-farm activities was maximum in medium size farm followed by small and large farms respectively. Income per adult unit was the highest in medium size class (Rs. 32323.81) followed by small size class (Rs.30455.41) and large size (Rs.29886 .80). At the overall level, the income per adult unit worked out to Rs.30215.60. Further, it is observed that, twin activities namely off-farm (dairy, poultry, goat keeping) and non-farm activities (papad making, bees keeping, mushroom cultivation, basket making and other petty business) have a tremendous potential in rural areas. It is observed that income jointly contributed by off and non-farm activities jointly worked out Rs.15317 (20.52 per cent) in medium size farms followed by 14845 (19.79 per cent) in large size farms and Rs. 8908 (12.67 per cent) in small size farm. It shows that farmers engaged in off- farm and non-farm activities had diverse source of income enabling them to lessen the risk from farming. In fact, income from off-farm is positively related to the agricultural income and established the close relationship between farm and non-farm income in the study area.

In case of non-beneficiary sample farms, the average gross family income was Rs.51311, Rs.57286 and Rs.53835 in small, medium and large farm size classes respectively. At the overall level gross family income was Rs. 54940. It is also noted that out of five major sources of income, the service sector provided Rs.29488 (53.67 per cent) followed by crop production Rs.14910 (27.13 per cent), wages Rs. 5035 (9.16 per cent), off-farms activities Rs.3079 (5.68 per cent) and non-farm activities Rs. 2428 (4.42 per cent) respectively. The average income from agriculture, off-farm and non-farm activities increased with an increase in the farm size while average annual income from wages was the highest in small size class (Rs. 7995) followed by

indicated the inverse relationship with the farm size. The potential areas of income were off- farm and non- farm activities as they jointly contributed income to the family pool to the tune of Rs. 8895 (16.53 per cent) in large size farm followed by medium Rs.5856 (10.23 per cent) and Rs. 2879 (5.61 per cent) in small size farms. Thus, it shows the close linkages with the income from agriculture and farm size. It is concluded that besides service, the major income was derived from the crop production. Thus, in the rural areas, agriculture is still a major income provider to the rural households.

The per cent share of different sources in the gross family income of both the households is graphically shown in Fig. 12.

To sum up the whole, it can be said that the average annual gross income in beneficiary households was higher by Rs 16369 (29.79 per cent), which is supposed to be a substantial difference in income of the two sample households. The per capita annual income of beneficiary households was the higher by Rs.7131.6, i.e., 30.84 per cent over non-beneficiaries. Rural off farm and non-farm sector emerged as the residual source of income to the rural poor who did not have adequate resources to invest in agriculture. It is evident from the analysis that off-farm and non-farm sectors could play a positive role in the removal of the poverty, generation of employment and decentralization of urbanization. These are significant sources of income to the small and medium farmers during the slack season. It also facilitates structural transformation and provides the non-food goods and services to the rural population. This also led to the conclusion that promotion of off-farm and non-farm activities in the rural areas will ease the pressure on agriculture and improve the productivity. Augmenting rural investment in the development of non-farm and off-farm sector will increase the income of rural households.

The farm size-wise changes in the average annual income of the sample households are graphically shown in Fig.13a and 13b.

The findings of the study emphasised that the strategy of rural development should gear not only for agricultural production but also for promoting viable off-farm and non-farm

Fig. 12 Percent share of different source of income in the annual average 12 gross family income

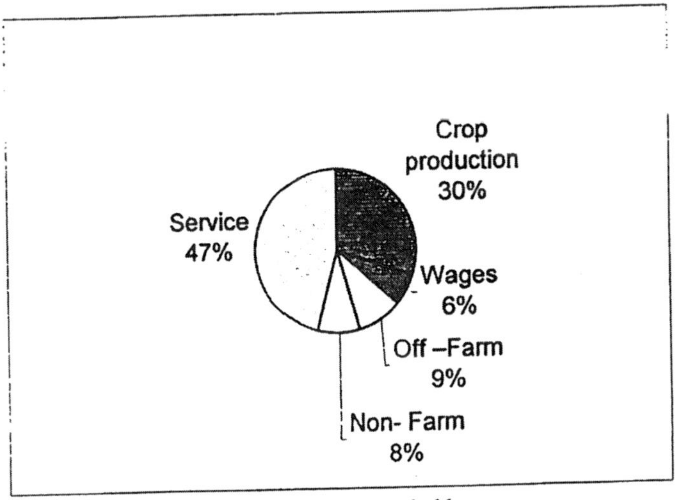

Beneficiary households

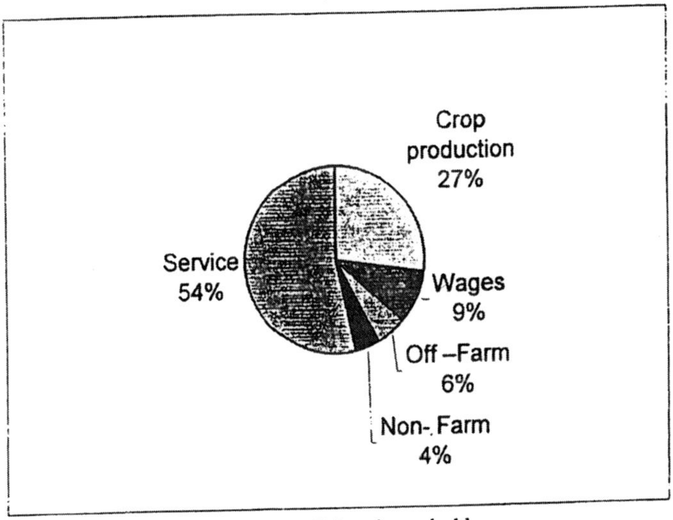

Non-beneficiary households

production but also for promoting viable off-farm and non-farm activities in the rural areas.

7.5 Gross Family Income Function

On the lines of employment model, the gross family income model for the sample households has been estimated. The multiple linear regression equation involving the annual gross income in rupees as a dependent variable (Y) and the three independent variables viz. gross cropped area in hectares (X_1), working capital used in agriculture and agro-based activities in rupees (X_2) and annual employment in off-farm and non-farm activities in man-days (X_3) together with dummy variables. The dummy variables were introduced for knowing the difference in the intercept and slopes of the three independent variables as a result of the implementation of the scheme 'Women in Agriculture' in the study area. The results of the estimated regression equation are given in Table 7.6

Table 7.6
Income Function, Regression Coefficients and Tests of their Significance

Independent variables		*Means*	*Regression coefficient (b)*	*Standard Errors*
Cross cropped area (Ha)	X_1	0.87	12646.76*	6462.40
Working capital (Rs) (Agril+Agro based activities)	X_2	10342.48	1.35*	0.93
Annual employment (off –farms and non-farm activities (man days)	X_3	119.16	74.13***	30.69
Dummy variables	D_1	0.5	21033.02**	10348.02
Dummy variables	D_1X_1	0.47	20533.40***	5992.05
Dummy variables	D_2X_2	6094.84	1.91**	0.87
Dummy variables	D_3X_3	80.94	117.59**	58.23

N=240, Y=44566.76, Constant=37244.46, R^2=0.6820, F ratio=33.50 ***

***, **, * Significant at one, five and ten per cent level of the probability.

Fig. 13(a) Pattern of annual average income of the beneficiary households

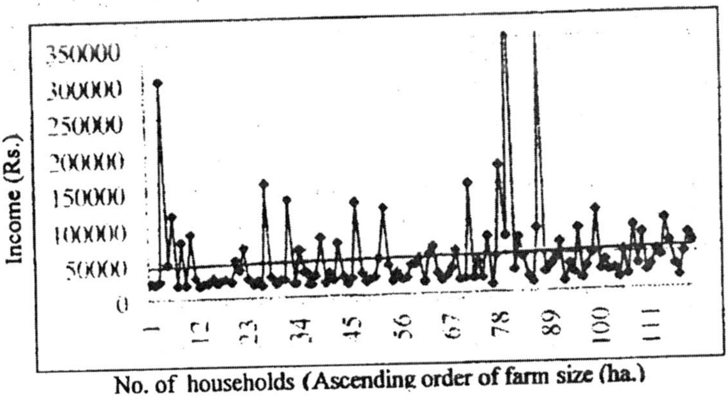

Fig. 13(b) Pattern of annual average income of the non-beneficiary hosehold

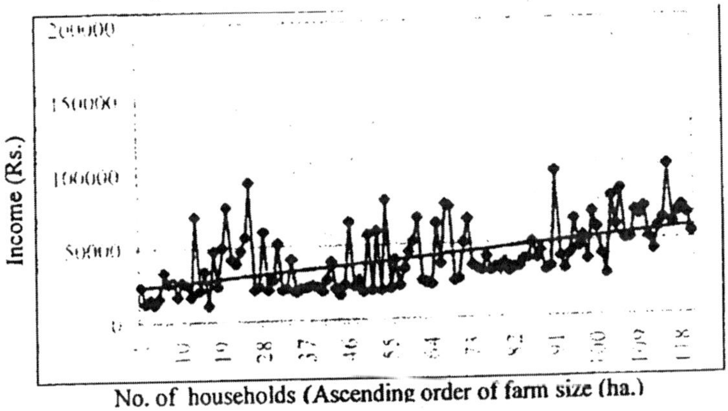

It is seen from the Table 7.6 that coefficient of the variables viz. X_1, X_2 and X_3 are positive and significant. However, the regression coefficient of X_1 and X_2 are observed to be significant at 10 per cent while that of X_3 is found highly significant at one per cent level. The differential intercept coefficient is 21033.02 which indicates that the intercept of the beneficiaries' income function is higher by this much amount as compared to the non-beneficiary households which is found to be statistically significant at 5 per cent level indicating the significant difference in the income between two sample households. Similarly the differential slope in respect of X_1, X_2 and X_3 coefficient is observed to be positive which means that the magnitude of the coefficient of the respective variables of the beneficiaries' income function is more by value of differential coefficients as compared to non-beneficiaries' income function. It has also seen that the selected independent variables have jointly explained 68.20 per cent of the variation in the gross family income of the sample households and the '*F*' ratio indicated the overall significance of the fitted regression equation.

From the result contained in Table 7.6, the individual income functions for beneficiaries and non-beneficiaries can be deduced as under,

(i) Mean income function of **Beneficiaries would be;**

$$E(Yi / D_1 = 1, X_1, X_2, X_3) = (a + b_4) + (b_1 + b_5) X_1 + (b_2 + b_6) X_2 + (b_3 + b_7) X_1$$

$$Y = (37244.46+21033.02)+(12646.76+20533.4)X_1+(1.3554+1.9152) X_2+(74.13+117.59) X_3$$

$$Y = 58277.48 + 33180.16\, X_1{}^{**} + 3.2706\, X_2{}^{**} + 191.72\, X_3{}^{***}$$

(16938) (1.89) (60.33)

$R^2 = 0.7159$ F= 59.57 ***

(ii) Similarly, mean income function of **Non-Beneficiaries** would be;

$$E(Yi / D_1 = 0, X_1, X_2, X_3) = a + b_1 X_1 + b_2 X_2 + b_3 X_3$$

$$Y = 37244.46 + 12646.76\, X_1{}^{**} + 1.35\, X_2{}^{*} + 74.13\, X_3{}^{***}$$

(6462.40) (0.93) (30.69)

$R_2 = 0.6310$ F=38.49**

The estimates of the parameters of these two income functions were also confirmed by running regression for the two categories of households separately.

To take the income function of the beneficiaries first, it is seen that the coefficients of all the variables are positive. The coefficient of the gross cropped area (X_1) and working capital invested in agriculture and agro-based activities (X_2) have turned out to be positive and significant at 5 per cent level while the coefficient of employment in man days from off-farm and non-farm activities (X_3) has turned out to be positive and significant at 1 per cent level. The coefficient of X_1 (Gross Cropped Area) indicates that other factors being held constant, the increase in gross cropped area by one hectare the annual gross income of an average beneficiary household would increase by Rs. 33180.16. Similarly, the variables viz. the working capital (X_2) is positive and significant which indicates that increase in working capital by one rupee in the agriculture and agro-based activities led to increase in income by Rs.3.27. Likewise the coefficient of annual employment in off-farm and non-farm activities (X_3) turned out to be positive and highly significant meaning thereby that by employing one man day in off-farm and non-farm activities could increase the income by Rs. 191.72. This leads us to say that the annual gross family income of the beneficiaries can be significantly increased by the increase in the gross cropped area, working capital and diverting the extra manpower towards the off-farm and non-farm activities.

Income function of the non-beneficiaries, which depicted similar results as described above. The only point of interest is that the magnitude of the intercept and coefficient of the variable X_1, X_2 and X_3 of the income function of non-beneficiaries is observed to be smaller than the beneficiaries income function. It is therefore, appears that the contribution of gross cropped area, investment in agro-based activities and agriculture and employment in off-farm and non-farm activities to the gross family income of beneficiaries was more as compared to the non-beneficiaries households. This was mainly due to the higher per hectare farm business income in crop production on the beneficiary farms and the relatively more employment to the workers in the off- farm and non-farm activities and investment of more working capital in the off- farm and non-farm activities as explained earlier.

It can now be said that the two income functions have the different intercepts and slopes and are therefore heterogeneous since the coefficient of differential intercept and slopes have turned out to be significant. In other words, the income function of the two categories differed significantly from each other. This has been confirmed by testing the significance of difference between the mean of gross family income of beneficiaries and non-beneficiaries by simple ' t ' test (Gupta, 1997). It is noted that 't' calculated worked out to 1.79, which is found to be significant at 5 per cent level of probability.

This leads us to conclude that the implementation of the central sector scheme 'Women in Agriculture' in the Thane district since 1994-95 has made a significant impact on the gross family income of the beneficiary households since the income functions of beneficiaries and non-beneficiaries differed significantly from each other. Further, it can be said that benefits of the scheme under study helped the beneficiary households belonging to all size classes to increase their family employment and thereby income to reach little better position as compared to those of non-beneficiary households under study. From the findings of the study, the hypothesis that the assistance received by sample beneficiaries helped in increasing their additional employment and income is accepted.

8

Problems in Availing the Benefits of the Scheme 'Women in Agriculture' by Beneficiary Farm Women

An attempt is made in this section to understand the problems in availing the benefits of the scheme and the suggestions made by sample beneficiary and non-beneficiary farm women to improve the efficiency of the scheme. Accordingly, the data obtained in this regards were analysed and presented in relation to the points mentioned as below:

1. Problems of the beneficiary farm women.
2. Attitude of beneficiary farm women.
3. Suggestions by the beneficiary farm women for improvement of scheme 'Women in Agriculture'.
4. General problems faced by the beneficiary and non-beneficiary farm women.
5. Suggestions made by non-beneficiary farm women for improving their participation in agriculture and its related projects.

8.1 Problems of Beneficiary Farm Women

The scheme 'Women in Agriculture' basically emphasizes on providing the technical backup to farm women through training, crop demonstrations, study tours, exposure visits, off farm and non-farm activities, promotion of thrift habit by way of organising farm women into Self Help Group (SHGs). The information pertaining to the functioning of the scheme 'Women in Agriculture' was collected from the sample beneficiary respondents during the period from 1994-95 to 2001-2002 and analysed. The results are presented in Table- 8.1.

Table 8.1
Distribution of Beneficiary Farm Women by their Problems While Availing Benefits of the Scheme 'Women in Agriculture'

Particulars	*Frequency*	*No Proble -ms at all.*	*Financi al Proble ms*	*Self health Proble ms*	*Health Problems of family members*	*Lack of Time*
Participation in Training.(village level)	N=120	110 (91.66)	----	3.00 (2.5)	7.00 (5.83)	---
Special skill Training programme	N=120	115 (95.83)	----	----	2.00 (1.66)	3.00 (2.5)
Participation in district level trainings (Mahila Gosthi)	N=120	108 (90)	-----	8.00 (6.66)	--------	4.00 (3.33)
Exposure visits & Study tours	N= 76	76 (100)	----	----	----	----
Participation in Self Help Group (SHG)	N=120	120 (100)	--	---	---	--
Conducting Demonstrations	N=120	120 (100)	---	---	---	---
Adoption of Technology	N=120	118 (98.33)	2 (1.66)	----	-----	----

(Figures in parentheses indicate the percentage to the total frequency)

From the Table 8.1, it is observed that the village level training was attended by about 92 per cent of the beneficiary farm women and few of them could not attend the training due to health problems of their own and of other family members or for some other reasons.

Mahila Gosthi, the one day seminar was generally arranged once in a year at the district level or within the operational area of scheme. The main purpose of mahila gosthi was to give an opportunity to all beneficiary farm women to interact with other farm women outside of their group and listen their successes and failures. Experts from State Agricultural University (BSKKV, Dapoli) and senior officials of the Department of Agriculture and line departments used to address such gathering. Products prepared by the farm women groups were also exhibited in exhibitions. This was a very important event both for the beneficiary farm women and government department for deciding future course of actions. When beneficiary farm women were asked about their participation in this event, it was revealed that, 90 per cent of beneficiary farm women had availed this opportunity while 10 per cent could not attend due to their ill health (6.66 per cent) and lack of time (3.33 per cent).

Exposure visits and study tours were also arranged on get insight of issues and exposure to the success stories within district, State or out of the State. It was observed that 76 beneficiary farm women were selected by the implementing agency for the exposure visits and all the selected beneficiaries could avail this opportunity.

To boost up the off-farm activities, some special skill building training programmes on mushroom cultivation, basket makings, honey bee keeping etc were also arranged by the implementing agency and 95.83 per cent of beneficiary farm women had attended this activity.

The thrift habit was promoted among beneficiary farm women by organizing them into a group of twenty farm women. Certain monthly amount was fixed towards contribution and start-up grants were provided through the scheme under study. It could be noticed that all the beneficiary farm women were associated with these Self Help Groups (SHGs).

The proven farm technologies were generally demonstrated on the farmer's fields for further refinement and adoption of technology on large area. The crop demonstrations were conducted at farmers' field in which all 120-farm women were participated and resulted into the adoption of modern technologies by 98.33 per cent of farm women.

It thus looks that beneficiary farm women had availed maximum benefits of the scheme. Maximum participation of farm women in the scheme was attributed due to cohesiveness in groups, joint working through SHG, and a sense of to-gatherness, regular persuasion by scheme facilitators and interest exhibited in implementation of scheme by the State Department of Agriculture and continuous monitoring by Central Ministry of Agriculture through Directorate of Extension. The problems concerning to finance, self-health, health of other family members and lack of time were noticed to a very limited extent.

8.2 Attitude of the Beneficiary Farm Women

It was presumed that while participating in the scheme, some beneficiaries might have their own ideas about the scheme implementation. Considering this, the data obtained on their views on scheme's implementation were analysed and presented in Table 8.2.

It is observed from the Table 8.2 that about 90 per cent beneficiary farm women reported that the scheme was useful for the up-liftment of socio-economic status of farm women, 8.34 per cent farm women viewed it as less useful and 1.67 per cent farm women reported that the scheme was not at all useful for farm women. The beneficiary farm women were asked about the way of scheme implementation. Out of them, 93.33 per cent responded positively and they were happy about the way of existing pattern of scheme implementation.

Table 8.2
Distribution of Beneficiary Farm Women by Their Attitude about Working of the Scheme 'Women in Agriculture'

Sr. no.	*Attitude shown by beneficiary farm women about utility of scheme (N = 120)*			
	Particulars of views	*Most useful*	*Less useful*	*Not at all*
1.	The scheme is useful for the socio-economic up-liftment of farm women	108 (90.00)	10.00 (8.34)	2.00 (1.67)
2.	The way of scheme implementation	112 (93.33)	8.00 (6.67)	——
3.	The utility of the technology given through the scheme	118 (98.34)	1.00 (0.83)	1.00 (0.84)
4.	The incentives given under scheme are appropriate	105 (87.5)	12.00 (10)	3.00 (2.5)
5.	Visits of the facilitators and extension Personnel to the farm women group were useful	116 (96.66)	4.00 (3.33)	——

(Figures in parentheses indicate the percentages to the total beneficiary women)

Technology back up for farm women was the core objective of the scheme. It is seen that 98.34 per cent of respondents have reported about the high level of utility of the technology imparted through the scheme. Only a few respondents (0.83 per cent) expressed that technology given to them was less useful. Such feelings were due to uneconomic small holding, illiteracy and poor resource base of farm women. Large section of beneficiary respondents (87.5 per cent) reported that the incentives given through the scheme were most useful. The visits of facilitators and extension personnel to the farm women's group were also useful as reported by 96.66 per cent of them.

Largely it could be concluded that beneficiary farm women have expressed their satisfaction on the way of implementation and different provisions made under the scheme.

8.3 Suggestions by Beneficiary Farm Women for Improvement of the scheme 'Women in Agriculture'

The suggestions were also invited from beneficiary farm women for the improvement in the implementation of the scheme. These suggestions have been compiled and presented in Table 8.3

Table 8.3

Distribution of Beneficiary Farm Women by According to their Suggestions for the Effective Functioning of the Scheme

(N= 120)

Sr. no	*Suggestions*	*Agree*	*Do not agree*	*Can not say*
1.	The frequency of the training should be increased.	118 (98.33)	2 (1.66)	----
2.	Master trainers / master craftsmen should be well trained	120 (100)	-----	-----
3.	Raw material should be supplied in adequate quantity and in time.	120 (100)	----	---
4.	Government should facilitate in marketing of the finished products.	120 (100)	----	-----
5.	Quality of training should be improved.	110 (91.66)	9 (7.5)	1 (0.33)
6.	Training should be skilled and practical oriented.	120 (100)	--	---
7.	Stipend of link workers should be increased.	115 95.83)	---	5 (4.16)
8.	Beneficiary farm women must be replaced after every five years.	34 (28.33)	76 (63.33)	----
9.	Agro-based off farm activities must be linked with credit facilities.	120 (100)	---	---
10.	Facilitators must have basic knowledge of agriculture.	120 (100)	---	---

(Figures in parentheses indicate the percentages to the total beneficiary farm women)

It is observed from the Table 8.3 that all respondents (100 per cent) expressed that master trainers or craftsmen should be well trained, raw material should be supplied in adequate quantity and in time as well as government may facilitate in marketing of finished products, training should be based on skill and practical orientated, agro-based off farm activities must be linked with credit. All the beneficiaries expressed that the technical knowledge of the facilitator has facilitated them while selecting the appropriate technology and thereby its adoption, thus facilitator must have sound technical knowledge of agriculture and allied subjects.

Further, it is observed that 98.33 per cent of beneficiary farm women have reported that frequency of training should be increased, quality of training should be improved (91.66 per cent), stipend of link workers should be increased (95.83 per cent) and beneficiary farm women must be replaced every five years (28.33) per cent.

To sum up, majority of the beneficiaries farm women were satisfied with the scheme implementation and different provisions under the said scheme. However, they expressed that there is a scope for improvement in the implementation of the scheme to raise the socio-economic condition and to enhance their ability to improve their situation further.

8.4 General problems Faced by the Beneficiary and Non Beneficiary Farm Women

The data were collected in order to investigate the problems faced by the beneficiary and non-beneficiary farm women while working on their farm. Due to difference in economic status, the farm women of the same village, tahsils may have different problems because of social, situational, economic, organizational and technological constraints. Thus, problems were categorized into four groups namely, situational problems, organizational problems, economic problems and technological problems. The results are presented in Table 8.4.

Table 8.4
Analysis of Problems Faced by the Beneficiary and Non-Beneficiary Farm Women

S. No	Particulars	Beneficiaries (N=120)		Non–Beneficiaries (N=120)	
		No.	Per cent	No.	Per cent
(A)	*Situational Problems*				
1.	lack of irrigation facilities	108	90.00	115	95.83
2.	Lack of marketing facilities	112	93.33	118	98.33
3.	Shortage of agril. labour	96	80.00	107	89.00
4.	Less cultivable land	90	75.00	111	92.50
5.	No suitable place for starting of self-employment	37	30.83	89	74.16
6.	Lack of motivation by family head/members for participation in socio-economic activities	9	7.5	106	88.33
(B)	*Organizational Problems*				
1.	Non- availability of inputs in time	37	30.83	89	74.16
2.	Non –availability of timely information about various schemes	17	14.16	116	96.66
(C)	*Economic Problems.*				
1.	Inadequate finance	113	94.16	119	99.16
2.	Lack of capital	86	71.66	108	90.00
3.	High cost of inputs	116	96.66	120	100
(D)	*Technological*				
1.	Lack of awareness/ understanding about new agricultural technology	16	13.33	117	97.50
2.	Lack of timely technical advice	8	6.66	120	100
3.	Inadequate training facilities	3	2.5	120	100
4.	Cost intensive technical Knowledge	23	19.16	86	71.66

It is revealed from the Table 8.4 that the respondents from both the categories of farm women expressed severity of problems about lack of irrigation facilities, lack of marketing facilities, less cultivable land and no suitable location for starting of self employment. Shortage of labour was a severe problem as 80 per cent beneficiary farm women and 89 per cent of non-beneficiary farm women had reported on this issue. The reason was that most of the labour force was diverted towards nearby industries where they get regular jobs as well as better payment. It was further observed that severity of these issues was more acute in case of non-beneficiary farm women as compared to beneficiary farm women. This was due to more articulation of beneficiary farm women in tapping up of the available resources.

Farm women are not generally motivated by the family members for taking independent decisions and performing an independent farm activities. From these data, it is observed that, 7.5 per cent beneficiary farm women and 88.33 per cent non-beneficiary farm women had never been motivated by their family head or by other family members for participation in socio-economic activities. Comparatively less number of beneficiary farm women had observed this problem which was due to the confidence created in the farm women by the scheme implementation agency i.e. State Department of Agriculture.

Regarding the non- availability of related inputs in time, 30.83 per cent of beneficiary farm women and 74.16 per cent of non-beneficiary farm women had reported about this problem. Timely information about developmental schemes in operation was not available as expressed by 14.16 per cent of beneficiary and 96.66 per cent of non-beneficiary farm women. Majority of non-beneficiary farm women experienced that they lack information on developmental schemes. This was due to their least contacts with the extension agency. This could lead to the conclusion that in the same locality or in the same tahsil, beneficiary farm women were facing relatively less problems as compared to non-beneficiary farm women. These findings are similar to the findings of Arya and Shah (1984) who identified constraints such as lack of labour, lack of inputs, lack of education and extension training to farm women in adoption of technology in dry land agriculture.

In the economic problems, issues namely inadequate finance, lack of capital and high cost of inputs were conspicuous. Majority of the farm women respondents of both the groups expressed serious concern on these issues.

The technological problems faced by the non-beneficiary farm women respondents were lack of technical knowledge (97.5 per cent), and timely advice (100 per cent), inadequate training (100 per cent) and cost intensive technical knowledge (71.66 per cent). Beneficiary farm women were facing less problems in getting technical knowledge.

8.5 Suggestions Made by Non-Beneficiary Farm Women for Improving their Participation in Agriculture and its Related Projects

In general, conventional agricultural extension programs have not been effective in reaching women farmers. Since independence of India, several projects were designed and launched for the rural development. However, little space for farm women was given in these programmes till the launching implementation of scheme 'Women in Agriculture' introduced during 1994-95. Still large section of farm women are deprived of such programmes which are exclusively targeted towards technology dissemination to farm women. Presuming that farm women in general are desirous of such programmes, the views of non-beneficiary farm women were collected to get an idea on improving the extent of participation in the scheme of farm women in developmental process. The prerequisite information was collected and analysed and the results are presented in Table 8.5.

It can be noted from Table 8.5 that, entire respondents (100 per cent) expressed to have a training programme at village level at least once in a year. Further, they expressed that there should be more projects related to agriculture for involvement of farm women, exposure visits for non–beneficiary farm women and further emphasized that the extension agency should reach to farm women. Also, 96.66 per cent of farm women expressed that there is a need to have close linkages between beneficiary farm women and non-beneficiary farm women which would facilitate the information and experience sharing at village level.

Table 8.5

Suggestions Made by the Non-beneficiary Farm Women for Improving the Participation of Farm Women in Agriculture

Sr. No	*Suggestions*	*No. of respondents*	*Percentage*
1.	At every village, the special training programmes must be arranged at least once in a year.	120	100
2.	More agricultural related projects may be designed for involvement of farm women.	120	100
3.	Close linkages between beneficiary farm women and non- beneficiary farm women is essential.	116	96.66
4.	Exposure visits for farm women should be organised on the line of scheme 'Women in Agriculture.'	120	100
5.	Extension agency should reach to non- beneficiary farm women.	120	100

Thus, it can be concluded that the beneficiary farm women felt privileged to have been tapped for the project. In general, there was a sense of achievement on their part and they were satisfied about the benefits from the scheme. According to them, the acquired knowledge has widened their horizon from mere housewives to that of active farm women and they are being consulted by their husbands while making decisions for their farms. The beneficiary respondents perceived less problems as compared to non-beneficiary respondents because their problems were timely solved by the Department of Agriculture, other line departments and personnel of Krishi Vigyan Kendra (KVK).

8.6 Operational Problems Observed by the Researcher During the Collection of Data

While collecting the data, apart from the designed questionnaire, a separate personal diary was maintained to record the observations regarding the implementation process of the scheme. Some operational problems were observed which are enlisted as below:

1. Lack of time with the implementing agencies to follow up activity due to too many assignments and targets of several other programmes being implemented by the State Department of Agriculture.
2. Low honorarium to facilitators, link workers and their contractual term of appointment of facilitators leading to low self-confidence.
3. 'Women in Agriculture' scheme is seen as a separate entity from mainstream of the State Department of Agriculture's operations.
4. Lack of flexibility at the operational level to re-appropriate the funds and to make changes in planned activities to meet the objectives of the programmes thus affecting the ability to respond to the clients quickly.

9

Summary and Conclusions

The various rural and agricultural development programmes have been launched by the Government for increasing the agricultural production and productivity. Yet, full level of impact have not been achieved because, the system has always been biased towards male farmers and the technologies which were generated were not gender sensitive. Despite the strong presence of women in all walk of life, no programmes to support their skill up-gradation in primary, secondary and tertiary sectors of economic activities have been undertaken in a big way exclusively for women except one or two components within a major scheme. Therefore, appropriate institutional supportive measures in the form of separate training, preferential membership in rural co-operatives, access to technology, credit and marketing, inclusion of entrepreneurial and managerial skills needs to be taken up on priority basis for women farmers.

Keeping this in view, the Govt. of India, Ministry of Agriculture had launched a innovative scheme for women farmers. The central sector scheme 'Women in Agriculture' had been formulated and implemented by the Extension Division, Ministry of Agriculture, Govt. of India during Eight Five Year Plan i.e. 1993-94 on pilot basis covering one district each of the seven states of the country and later on it was extended to fifteen states in India.

The present study therefore has been conducted in Thane district of Maharashtra state with the following specific objectives:

(i) To study the impact of the scheme on level of decision making by farm women and their socio-economic empowerment.

(ii) To study the impact of scheme on the farm business economy and resource use productivity of major inputs in crop production on sample households.

(iii) To examine the differentials in employment and income of sample households as a result of implementation of the scheme.

(iv) To identify the factors influencing employment and income of sample households.

(v) To study the problems faced by the beneficiaries while availing the benefits of the scheme.

The hypotheses framed to accomplish the objectives under study were as follows:

1. The continuous training, result demonstrations, exchange visits and mahila gosthies have helped to enhance the knowledge of beneficiary women and have resulted in greater involvement in decision making and family management.
2. The scheme has benefited the farm women beneficiaries in terms of higher input use, productivity and returns besides relatively efficient farm resource use.
3. The assistance received by sample beneficiaries helped in increasing the employment and income.
4. The major problems faced by the beneficiaries of the scheme are redressed regularly.

The central sector scheme 'Women in Agriculture' was being implemented in six villages of Wada tahsil, four villages of Palghar and eight villages of Dahanu tahsil of Thane district of Maharastra since 1994-95. One village from Palghar, two villages from Wada and three villages from Dahanu in proportion to the number of 18 villages covered in three tahsils were randomly selected for the study. Since the scheme was being operated through the group of twenty farm women, it is thus clear that, a total sample of 120 farm women beneficiary of the scheme comprising 40 sample households (two groups) from Wada, 20 (one group) from Palghar and 60 (three groups) from Dahanu tahsil were selected for the present study. In order to assess the impact of the scheme, it was required to have equal number of non-beneficiary farm women households belonging to the same village for study. Therefore, a total sample of 120 non-beneficiary women comprising 40 households from Wada tahsil, 20 households from Palghar and 60 from Dahanu thasil were selected by simple randomisation for the study. Thus, the total sample for the study consists of 240 households comprising 120 beneficiary and 120 non-beneficiary women households spread over six villages of Thane district in Maharashtra.

A pre-tested interview schedule was used to collect the information from the respondents. Data were collected regarding decision-making process in the farm business management, socio-economic empowerment of farm women, farm business economy, employment and income pattern for both beneficiary and non-beneficiary households and problems in availing the benefits of the scheme under study. Field level data were collected for the year 2001-2002 through personal interview keeping in view the objectives of the study. The discussions with the officials of the agricultural department at different levels in Thane district also provided insight into the performance of the scheme under study.

The secondary data regarding features of the Thane district and tahsils under the study were collected from the office of the District Superintending Agricultural Officer (DSAO) and Taluka Agricultural Officer (TAO) of Dahanu, Palghar and Wada. The various statistical reports were also referred for obtaining the requisite information.

The sample households were categorized into three size classes based on operational holdings viz. small (0 to 0.50 ha.), medium (0.51 to 1.0 ha) and large (1.01 ha. and above) for the purpose of analysis of data. To attempt the first objective of the study, the Decision Making Index (DMI) was computed to examine the gaps in the decision making between beneficiary and non-beneficiary farm women. The DMI score was grouped as a low (15 to 30), Medium (31 to 45) and high (46 and above). In computing DMI, 23 major activities for beneficiary farm women and 21 activities for non-beneficiary farm women were selected on which farm women were likely to take decisions. The influence of twelve socio-economic factors on decision-making process was estimated by using the Karl Pearson's correlation coefficient (r-value) and their significance was tested by '*t* ' test. The socio-economic empowerment brought out in farm women as a result of scheme implementation was analysed by simple tabular method.

The second objective concerning to farm business analysis was fulfilled by estimating per hectare resource use for paddy and farm as a whole, per hectare operation-wise labour use and computation of different costs by applying the standard cost concepts. Input–output relationship was studied by *Cobb-Douglas type of production* function and resources use efficiency was estimated by computing the Marginal Value Product (MVP). The *Chow's test* was employed to test whether the two production functions have the same production relations or otherwise.

The third objective of the study regarding impact of scheme on employment and income of the sample households was accomplished by simple tabular method of analysis.

The fourth objective concerning to identify different factors responsible for the employment and income was fulfilled by adopting the multiple regression analysis and the goodness of fit was tested 'F' test. Thc regression equations for employment and income of beneficiary and non-beneficiary households were compared by the use of *dummy variable technique*. The difference in mean income of the beneficiary and non-beneficiary households was tested for its significance by 't' test.

The fifth objective regarding the problems in availing benefits of the scheme at the beneficiary level were studied by simple tabular method. The results of analysis of data are briefly outlined as under.

9.1. Results:

1. As regards the sample households, the average size of family, at the overall level was 4.66 members and 4.61 members in beneficiary and non-beneficiary households. Tribal and Other Backward Caste farmers had the majority in the sample households followed by farmers from SCs and general category. Beneficiaries had possessed more capital assets by Rs.33946.31 over to non-beneficiaries. The average size of holding was 0.89 ha. and 0.81 ha in beneficiary and non-beneficiary households respectively. Due to poor irrigation facilities, cropping intensity was 102.74 and 101.68 per cent on beneficiary and non-beneficiary farms. Paddy was the main crop as it had occupied more than 90 per cent of total cropped area. This crop was followed by the crops such as vegetables, fruits and pulses grown on a small scale.

2. It is noted that 93.33 per cent of beneficiary and 87.49 per cent of non-beneficiary farm women were in the age of between 30-50 years. The beneficiary farm women had a little bit higher literacy level as compared to non-beneficiary farm women. Agriculture was a major source of employment for both the sample households.

3. The beneficiary farm women took independent decisions in grading of produce (68.30 per cent), use of chemical fertilisers (66.70 per cent), and selection of variety (63.40 per cent). In addition, more than 60 per cent of the farm women were involved in joint decision-making process prominently in the activities of use of FYM, sale of produce, choice of market, food processing and selection of crops. The farm women were least involved in the decisions regarding sale and purchase of land, crop harvesting and transport and purchase of agricultural inputs. The reasons for the least involvement of the farm women in these activities could be attributed to involvement of money to carry out these activities.

4. Their counterpart, non-beneficiary farm women were comparatively less involved in decision-making. Less than 25 per cent farm women took independent decisions, where as, about 50 per cent farm women were involved in joint decisions in the activities like use of FYM, intercultural operations, sale of produce and choice of market. Nearly 65 to 75 per cent of farm women were least involved in the decision making process or sometimes they were not allowed to take an independent decision.

5. It is observed that more than 90 per cent beneficiary farm women were highly involved in decision making process (DMI Score 45 and above) while only 50.83 per cent of non-beneficiary farm women were categorized under high DMI score category. It was amply affirmed that beneficiary farm women were either taking decisions independently or were actively involved in joint decisions with her husband / family head.

6. In case of beneficiary farm women, at the overall level, Karl Pearson correlation coefficient ('r') turned out to be positive and significant in respect of six socio-economic parameters namely education of farm women (0.39), extension contacts (0.58), social participation (0.63), technical knowledge of farm women (0.48), farm size (0.16) and occupation of the family head (0.48) which showed a positive and significant impact on decision making of farm women. Six parameters such as age of farm women, status of farm women in family, annual gross family income, caste, family size and educational level of the family head had showed non-significant relationship with decision making of beneficiary farm women.

7. In case of non-beneficiary farm women, at the overall level, Karl Pearson correlation coefficient ('r') turned out to be positive and significant in respect of six attributes namely education of farm women (0.32), status of farm women in family (0.42), annual gross income of family (0.26), caste (0.38), farm size (0.12) and occupation of family head (0.29) which showed a positive and significant impact on decision

making of farm women. The major reasons for low participation of non-beneficiary farm women in decision taking were less extension contacts, low level of technical knowledge, low social participation, large family size, their old age and higher education of family head. High level of decision making by beneficiary farm women as compared to non-beneficiary farm women proved the hypothesis that the continuous training, result demonstrations, exposure visits and mahila gosthis have helped to enhance the knowledge of beneficiary farm women and have resulted in greater involvement in decision making and family management

8. Beneficiary farm women have empowered socio-economically due to implementation of the scheme 'Women in Agriculture' in Thane district of Maharashtra state. It was further observed that beneficiary farm women had better access to the credit facilities and majority of farm women had a ownership of economically important resources like land, house, machinery and milch cow. As beneficiary farm women were more cosmopolite in nature and enhanced social exposure, perhaps, encouraged them to enjoy more liberty in incurring the expenditure. It was further observed that beneficiary farm women had a better access to communication and print media, institutional information sources and continuous up-gradation of technical knowledge through the various training programmes. Since technical knowledge and economic independence are the parameters of women empowerment which could developed self confidence among them and led them to their greater involvement in various farm, economic and social activities.

   In case of non-beneficiary farm women, they had little exposure to extension agencies, lack of access to financial resources, communication media and lack of right to do expenditure etc. They didn't have suitable access to and control over farm technology.

9. It is noted that on the beneficiary farms, comparatively less human labour was used than non-beneficiaries because of the increased use of machinery which was 4.19 hrs and 1.23 hrs per hectare on beneficiary and non-beneficiary farms respectively. Farm machinery especially tractor use was more on beneficiary farms than the non–beneficiary farms indicating relatively more mechanization of operations in paddy cultivation on beneficiary farms. Higher use of bullock labour was also observed on beneficiary farms due to intensification in paddy cultivation.

   The pesticide is one of the most critical inputs for increasing the paddy production. Per farm and per hectare use of pesticide on beneficiary farm was more by Rs. 53.66 and Rs. 32.24 than that of non-beneficiary.

10. The gaps in application of resources indicated that both beneficiaries and non-beneficiaries did not use the recommended level of the resources. However, beneficiaries could utilize more resources as compared to non-beneficiaries. This was because of the adequate finance and technology awareness among the beneficiary farm women.

11. The three operations in paddy crop cultivation viz. transplanting, weeding and harvesting alone consumed nearly three fourth of female labour on both the categories of sample farms. At the overall level female labour utilization was more as compared to male labour utilization for paddy crop production on both the sample farms.
   The small farms engaged more family labour due to inadequate paying capacity for the hired labour indicating their tendency to employ all available family manpower. It is also noted that family male and female labour use showed a decline on both the sample farms with an increase in farm size.

12. As regards the use of hired labour at the overall level, it is observed that the non-beneficiaries could engage more hired labour (45.13 man days) than the beneficiary farms (36.22 man days). The use of hired male and female labour showed

an increase with an increase in farm size on both the sample households. Use of bullock labour was also more on small farms in both the sample households and subsequently decreased with an increase in farm size.

13. Per hectare cost of cultivation of paddy crop at different levels of cost showed decline as the size categories of sample farms increased. This has indicated the economies of scale in operation on sample farms. At the overall level, the per hectare gross returns from paddy was higher by Rs.7797.83 (35.66 per cent) on beneficiary farms as compared to non – beneficiary farm. It is also noted that at the overall level the farm business income, family labour income and net income on beneficiary farms were higher as compared to non- beneficiary by 52.18, 58.19 and 69.74 per cent respectively. It is further noted that the productivity of paddy crop across the farm size was higher on small farms and showed a decline with an increase in farm size. At the overall level, BC ratio was 1.68 and 1.48 in the case of beneficiary and non-beneficiary farms respectively. The higher benefit-cost ratio among beneficiaries households was mainly due to the higher level of input use to obtain the maximum yield.

14. The pooled analysis of the entire sample farms was carried out with a view to apply "Chow's test' of equality. In other words, the significance of difference between the paddy crop production functions of the beneficiary and non-beneficiary farms was tested by using the Chow test. It is seen that the F ratio is (3.02), which is significant at a probability level of five per cent indicating that the two regressions are not equal but differed significantly in their overall production relationships. This is also corroborated from the discussion about the difference in resource use, cost and return structure in crop production of these two categories of farms. Hence, there was a shift in production function of paddy because of technological change.

15. The resources like nitrogen, potash, manures and human labour on beneficiary farms and nitrogen, phosphorous and

manures on non-beneficiary farms were the factors of economic importance and their increased use up to an optimum level would have significant and positive influence on paddy crop output on both the sample farms.

16. The marginal value product of the resources obtained at the geometric mean levels from the estimated production function of paddy crop indicated that the ratio of MVP to the unit factor cost was higher than unity in case of nitrogen, phosphorous, potash, manures, human labour and other working capital on the beneficiary farms and nitrogen, phosphorous, potash, manures and other working capital on non-beneficiary farms indicating a further scope to use these resources up to optimum level. There was no scope to extend the use of bullock labour on the beneficiary farms and human labour and bullock labour on non-beneficiary farms as the ratios of marginal value products to the unit costs of these resources were less than unity.

17. As per the results of farm business analysis of the farm as a whole, at the overall level, the cost A, cost B and cost C were quite higher on beneficiary farms as compared to non-beneficiary farms. This was mainly due to higher input use on the beneficiary farms. The net income showed an increase with an increase in the size of holding on both the sample farms. The per hectare gross income, farm business income, family income and net income on beneficiary farm was higher by Rs.7055 (28.02 per cent), Rs.6464 (43.35 per cent), Rs.5393 (51.81 per cent) and Rs. 5281 (61.28 per cent) respectively over non-beneficiary farms. This clearly indicated that the beneficiary farms were operating at higher level of income as compared to the non-beneficiary farms. At the overall level, per hectare output–input ratio in crops production was 1.75 in case of beneficiary farms and 1.52 in case of non-beneficiary farms. It is also observed that the output–input ratio showed an increase with an increase in the farm size of the sample households which suggests that the large farms were operating at the higher level of returns from the paddy, vegetables and horticultural crops grown on both the sample households.

18. On comparison of magnitude of elasticities of output between the two categories of farms, it is observed that nitrogen, potash, FYM, human labour, and other working capital were the important inputs on beneficiary farms while nitrogen, phosphorous, FYM, and other working capital were the important inputs on non-beneficiary farms. The 'F' ratio of the Chow's test appeared significant at the probability level of one per cent indicating significance difference between the crop production functions of the beneficiary and non-beneficiary farms. The ratio of MVP to factor unit cost was higher than unity in the case of potash followed by nitrogen, human labour and FYM on beneficiary farms while nitrogen, phosphorous, potash, FYM and other working capital on non-beneficiary farm which indicated the scope for increasing the use of these factors to the extent of optimum level for increasing the total farm output on average sample farms.

19. At the overall level, the gross family employment was 436.61 man-days in beneficiary and 348.85 man-days in non-beneficiary sample households. The average annual employment in case of beneficiary male and female was 214.55 man-days and 190.75 man-days and in case of non-beneficiary male and female was 214.06 man-days and 134.75 man-days respectively. The average annual employment in case of beneficiary male and female higher by 14.85 per cent and 41.55 per cent as compared to those of non-beneficiary households under study. The activity wise break up of total farm employment in beneficiaries was significantly higher than that of non-beneficiaries with respect to crop production by 10 days, off farm by 53.18 days, non- farm by 17.87 days. In addition to manifest underemployment in agriculture sector, the potential for employment has been found in sectors such as bee-keeping, mushroom, poultry, dairy, papad making in the study areas. These activities will not necessarily lead to greater demand of available land.

20. The employment function of the beneficiaries differed significantly from that of non-beneficiaries since the

differential intercept and slope coefficients in respect of all three variables i.e. gross cropped area, working capital investment in agriculture and agro-based activities and working adult units in family are found to be statistically significant.

21. The gross annual family income of the beneficiary and non-beneficiary households was Rs. 71,309 and Rs. 54,940 respectively. The average annual income in beneficiary households was higher by Rs. 16369 (29.79 per cent), which showed a substantial difference in the income of the two sample households. The per capita annual income of beneficiary households was higher by Rs.7131.6 over non-beneficiaries. Rural off farm and non-farm sectors emerged as the residual source of income to the rural poor who did not have adequate resources to invest in agriculture. The two-income functions have the different intercepts and slopes and are therefore heterogeneous since the coefficient of differential intercept and slopes have turned out to be significant. In other words, the income functions of the two categories differed significantly from each other. This has been confirmed by testing the significance of difference between the means of gross family income of beneficiaries and non-beneficiaries by simple ' t ' test. It is noted that 't' calculated worked out to 1.79, which is found to be significant at 5 per cent level of probability.

22. Beneficiary farm women had availed maximum benefits of the scheme under study. About 90 per cent beneficiary farm women reported that scheme was very useful to them for the up-liftment of their social status. Higher-level utility of technology was reported by 87.5 per cent farm women and 96.66 per cent respondents reported that incentives given through scheme were most useful. Both the categories of farm women expressed the severity of problems like lack of irrigation, lack of marketing facilities, less cultivable land, no suitable place for starting self employment and shortage of labour.

23. The technological problems faced by the non-beneficiary

farm women respondents were lack of knowledge (97.5 per cent), timely advice (100 per cent), inadequate training (100 per cent), cost intensive technical knowledge (71.66 per cent). On the contrary, beneficiary farm women were facing less problems in getting technical knowledge.

9.2. Conclusions

The forgoing findings led to draw the following specific conclusions from the results of the study:

1. Beneficiary farm women were generally taking decisions regarding the activities requiring technical competency. The technical knowledge, skill, access to various resources and economic independence are the parameters for enhancing decision-making ability of beneficiary farm women.
2. Beneficiary farm women of having age range between 30–50 years, well educated, highly cosmopolite in nature, having good contacts with the extension agencies, belonging to a large farm size and with well remunerative profession of family head were found to be taking independent decisions and were also involved in decision making process in the family.
3. Beneficiary farm women had utilized communication media like radio and television. It is further revealed that farm women of both the households failed to explore these mass media to the full extent.
4. The Department of Agriculture was the major source of information in case of beneficiary farm women. The beneficiaries enjoyed more access to the formal communication media like mass media and institutional extension system than the non-formal media i.e. friends, relatives and village leader.
5. In case of non-beneficiaries farm women, the major sources of information were friends and relatives. The preference of non-institutional source of information over institutional sources and media was due the fact that non-beneficiary farm women usually got the information on agricultural

aspects through their men which tends to be distorted to some extent.

6. Per farm and per hectare utilisation of resources was more on beneficiary farms than the non–beneficiary farms. This was mainly because of the technology awareness among the beneficiary farm women leading to adoption of improved cultural practices.

7. The three operations namely transplanting, weeding, and harvesting of paddy had consumed nearly three fourth female labour on both the sample farms. This emphasized the importance of these operations in paddy crop production from the female point of view to ensure labour availability in the peak period.

8. The beneficiary farms were operating at the higher levels of income as compared to the non-beneficiary farms under study. This difference in income was due to higher level of adoption of modern technologies and also due to better resource use on beneficiary farms. The per hectare net income was found to be higher on beneficiary farms indicating thereby better management of resources.

9. The production relations on both the farms differed significantly from each other in view of the difference in resource use and level of technology adoption. This shows

10. The implementation of central sector scheme 'Women in Agriculture' has a significant effect on the annual gross family employment and income of beneficiary households since income and employment functions of beneficiary and non-beneficiary differed significantly from each other. Further, it can be said that benefits of the scheme under study helped the beneficiary households belonging to all size classes to increase their family income to reach little better position as compared to those of non-beneficiaries households under study.

11. The implementation of central sector scheme 'Women in Agriculture' resulted into more employment in study area. The findings indicated that the sample households spilled over the rural off farm and non- farm sectors as agriculture

has a limited labour absorptive capacity in the study area. The non-farm and off-farm sectors have offered the potential to absorb the rural force and acted as a cushion for them.

12. The beneficiary farm women perceived less constraints intensity as compared to non-beneficiary farm women as their technological problems were solved from time to time by the Department of Agriculture, Scientists of State Agricultural University and Krishi Vigyan Kendra (KVK)
13. Beneficiary farm women were the major source of technical information to non–beneficiary farm women. Thus, beneficiary farm women could play an effective role as a change agent in the diffusion of agricultural technology.
14. As a whole, the farm women felt privileged to have been tapped for the project, a sense of achievement on their part and were satisfied about it. According to them, the knowledge acquired has widened their scope from mere housewives to that of active farm women.

9.3 Policy Implications

9.3.1 Policy Implications for the Beneficiary Farm Women

1. It is recommended that to enhance the role of farm women in decision making, there is need to increase women's access to technical knowledge for which training, support of extension services and development programmes targeted at farm women to address their needs. It is also recommended to consider the constraints observed in the present study while designing developmental programmes especially for rural women.
2. Empowerment of farm women is a complex process which comprises short-term and long-term strategy. To empower the farm women, there is need to increase their access to new information as well as to credit and labour market, furthering their social and political participation at all levels by strengthening educational and training programmes for them. There should be a long drawn strategy for increasing

their access to appropriate technology that affect on reducing work burden.

3. The concerted efforts are needed to develop better technologies for agricultural operations usually perform by the farm women such as transplanting, weeding, harvesting and cleaning of the produce to reduce the physical burden and drudgery of farm women.
4. Manures and fertilizers have positive and significant effect in both the sample farms to influence gross returns. In other words, if farmers have to modernize their traditional agriculture for higher returns, the use of manures and fertilizers needs to be intensified.
5. To generate the employment in rural area, it is necessary to think of integrating farm and non-farm sectors. Thus, it is necessary to provide the training to the rural masses to enhance their skill, technical education and entrepreneurship development.
6. Extension service should be women sensitive, so that women farmers have a full and appropriate access to meetings, demonstrations and exposure visits and other activities that may increase their farm production and income. There should be joint participation of both men and women in common extension activities and farm women should be strongly encouraged to attend them.
7. In case of beneficiaries household, the technical knowledge of the farm women have positive effect on farm productivity. Thus, the role of agricultural extension is likely to be stronger in modern dynamic set-up than in traditional agriculture. The higher productivity and gross returns from the farms call for more investment in the scheme 'Women in Agriculture' as the extension service to accelerate the agricultural growth.
8. The scheme 'Women in Agriculture' in Thane district of Maharashtra, has successfully brought about desirable changes on the beneficiaries farm women. Therefore, this scheme may be expanded on larger area in Maharashtra state and other parts of the country

9. The marketing of the produce is an important aspect of whole programme. May be if local area fails to absorb the produce of self-employed units, the scheme implementing agency i.e Department of Agriculture ought to facilitate beneficiary farm women to establish linkages with the outside marketing outlets.

10. The findings of the study emphasised that strategy of rural development should gear up not only for agricultural production but also for promoting viable off-farm and non-farm activities in the rural area.

9.3.2 Policy Implications for the Non-Beneficiary Farm Women

1. It was observed that participation of the farm women in different social institutions and organization was absolutely nil. It is, therefore, suggested that the farm women should be encouraged and motivated to participate in such institutions. The new women's organization like Self Help Groups should be promoted and be run by them. This will help in developing social contacts and to widen their horizons and to gain self-confidence.

2. It was also found that the farm women had limited contact with extension agencies and these contacts were restricted to local extension workers only and other informal information sources. In order to promote more contacts and acquire know how of different subject matters, the possibilities of employing women extension workers at the village level may be explored.

3. It was observed from the results of the study that non-availability of timely information on different development schemes and their benefits, lack of awareness and understanding of new technology and lack of timely technical advice were the major constraints in respect of non-beneficiary farm women. It is, therefore, necessary that the planners and policy makers may pay attention towards strengthening of agricultural extension agency for diffusion of agricultural technology especially to the farm women.

4. Farm women have a potential in supporting and carrying out agricultural, dairy and family activities. This is evidenced from the present findings that they are capable of taking many decisions and participate actually in doing many of the farm operations. Vocational orientation with confidence building measures, marketing and banking awareness etc. will go a long way in improving the status and the participation of farm women in agriculture, dairy and other related occupations.

Bibliography

Acharya, Sarthi (2002) Measurement of Socio–Economic Status in Social Science – A note, *IASSI Quarterly*, 21 (2): 39-52.

Ahuja, Abha, Neeta Sharma and Shashi Tewari (1999) Women in Hills, Department of Human Development and Family Studies, College of Home Science, G.B. Pant University of Agriculture and Technology, Distt. Udham Singhnagaar, (U.P.), India.

Alagumani, T. (1999) A Study on Decision Behaviour of Rural Women in Madurai District, Tamil Nadu, Indian Journal of *Agricultural Economics*, 54 (3): 300.

Alcober, D.I. and L. S. Parrilla (1989) Gender Roles in Sweet Potato Production Processing and Utilization in Eastern Visayas, the Philippines, International Sweet Potato Symposium. Baybay, Leyte (Philippines), 20-26, May 1987: 227-236.

Anita, Mehta and Sudarshan (2000) Mushroom Cultivation for Income Generation: Changing Attitude of Rural Women in Haryana, *Indian Journal of Social Research*, 40 (4): 257-261.

Anonymous ((2002 a) Background Paper on Technology Dissemination for Women in Agriculture, Ministry of Agriculture, Govt. of India.

Anonymous (2002 b) Proceedings of National Workshop on Women in Agriculture: Farmers to Farmers Extension, 5-6 March, 2002, Organized by Ministry of Agriculture, Govt. of India, New Delhi.

Arya, S.R.S. and S.L. Shah (1984) New Technology of Rain fed Agriculture and Identification of Constraints on its Adoption in Mid Hill of U.P *Agricultural Situation in India*, 39 (7): 487-490.

Atibudhi and J.P. Singh (1994) Impact of Technological Changes on Employment and Production Relationship in Rice Farming in Balasore District of Orissa, Indian Journal of *Agricultural Economics*, 49 (3): 391.

Ayanwale, B. Adeolu and Isijola, C.O. (1997) Farm size , Economic Efficiency: The Case of Some Sectoral Farm in Nigeria, *Indian Journal of Agricultural Economics*, 57:551-564.

Bagi, F.S. (1983) Relationship between Farm size, Productivity and Returns to Scale in Haryana State of India, *Rural System*, 1: 189-212.

Bardhan,P.K.(1973) Farm Size, Productivity and Returns to Scale :An Analysis of Farm Level Data in Indian Agriculture, *Journal of Political Economy*, 81:1370-1386.

Beohar. B.B., A.K.Sarawgi and Choudhari, A.K. (1999) Women's Contribution in Paddy Cultivation – A case Study of a Village of Chattisgarh Region of Madhya Pradesh, Indian *Journal of Agricultural Economics*, 54 (3): 323.

Bhagat R.B. (2003) Towards Measuring Rural Stratification and Agrarian Classes: Socio-Economic and Demographic Variables, *IASSI Quarterly*, 21 (2):25-47.

Bhagwati, J.N and S. Chakravarti (1969) Contribution of Indian Economic Analysis: A Survey, *American Economic Review*, 59(4), Part –2 (Supplement): 1-127.

Bhole, B.D. and S.G. Kharche (1992) Integrated Nutrient Supply System for a Cereal Based Crop Sequence, *Indian Journal of Agricultural Economics*, 47 (3): 524.

Bhuwneshwari, S.and Kavita Kannan (1999) Women in Agriculture and Rural Development, *Indian Journal of Agricultural Economics*, 54 (3): 324.

Bindu, Rani and D.S. Thakur (1996) Pattern of Employment and the Extent of Employment in the Lowhill Zone Agrarian

Economy of Himachal Pradesh, *Manpower Journal*. 31 (4): 23- 46.

Birari, K. S. (1999) Resource use Structure, Resource Productivities and Allocation Efficiency on Farms of Western Maharashtra, Ph. D. Un-published Thesis, M.P. K. V. Rahuri (MS).

Boreth L.S., S.L. Intodia and Solanki Dhiriti (2002) Participation of Women in Decision Making Process Related to Farm Operations, *A Bi-annual Journal of Agricultural Science and Technology*, Allahabad Agricultural Institute– A Deemed University, Allahabad-211007(UP), 56 (1) : 34-37.

Cattle, R.B. (1942) The Concept of Social Status, *Journal of Social Psychology*, 15:293-308.

Chakravarti, Ritu and R. Chakravarti (1996) Comparative Case Studies of Farm Women in the Netherlands and India, *Journal of Dairying Food and Home Science*, 15 (2): 81-87.

Chandravati, C. H., D. V. S Rao and Raju, V. T. (1999) Impact Assessment of Farm Women Training Programme in Andhra Pradesh, *Indian Journal of Agricultural Economics*, 54 (3): 299.

Chapin, F. S. (1928) Quantitative Scale for Rating the Home and Social Environment of Middle Class Families in an Urban Environment: A first Approximation to the Measurement of Socio-Economic Status, *Journal of Educational Psychology*, 19: 19-111.

Chauhan, A. K. and Smita Sirohi (1999) Women Participation in Dairying: Experiences of Intensive Cattle Development Programme in Haryana. *Indian Journal of Indian Economics*, 53 (3): 309.

Chorge, T. L. (1985) A Study of the Impact of 20 Point Economic Programme on the Agricultural Development, Adoption and Socio-Economic Status of the Farmers, Ph. D. Unpublished Thesis Submitted to MPKV Rahuri, Maharashtra.

Chow, C. Gregerry (1960) Test of Equality between Sets of Coefficient in two Linear Regression, *Econometrica*, 28 (3): 591-605

Cohn., Bernard, S. (1979) *Structural Change in Indian Society (1596-1885) in the Land Control and Social Structure in Indian History*, R.E.Frykenberg (ed) Manohar, New Delhi: 53-112.

Deepti (2002) Impact of Dairy Co-operatives on Rural women, M.Sc. Unpublished Thesis, IC College of Home Science, CCS HAU Hisar.

Dhawan, K., and P.K.Bansal (1997) Rationality of the Use of Various Factors of Production on Differential Size Farms in the Punjab, *Indian Journal of Agricultural Economics*, 32 (3): 1-40.

Dhuware, S.R. and A. K. Pande (2003) Constraints in Watershed Management Technology, *Maharashtra Journal of Extension Education*, 22 (1): 133-134.

Dube., S.K. Swarnkar, V.K., Malik and Rasila (1988) Role and Scio-Personal Characteristics of Farm Women in Decision Making Process, Seminar Paper Presented on Role of Farm Women in Agriculture, Organised by Maharashtra Society of Extension Education at PDKV Akola on Oct .7-8, 1988.

Economic Survey (2001) Published by Economic Division, Ministry of Finance, Government of India, New Delhi :245.

Elumalai,K. and R.K.Sharma (2003) Non-Farm Employment for Rural Households in India, *Agricultural Economics Research Review* ,Conference Issue:1-19.

Freeman, C. (1961) *Economic Status and Adoption of New Agricultural and Home Practices, Sociology, Social Research and Social Problems in India*, Asia Publishing House, Bombay.

Gaikwad,V.J and V.P.Dhane (2001) Problems of Tribal Farmers in Obtaining and Utilizing Benefits of Agricultural and Tribal Development Scheme, *Tribal Research Bulletin*, Tribal Research and Training Institute, Maharashtra,Pune, 26 (2):87

Ghose, B. N. (1977) *Disguised Unemployment in Under Developed Countries with Special Reference to India,* Heritage Publisher, New Delhi.

Ghose, D.K. (1993) IRDP and Women Development –A Case Study in West Bengal, *Journal of Rural Development*, NIRD Hyderabad, 12 (6): 659-665.

Gitangali, K and G. H. Kathy (2001) *Strategies for Change: Gender Issues and Poverty Reduction in DANIDA Supported Activities in India*, Published by Royal Danish Embassy, New Delhi.

Gopalan Radha (2001) Sustainable food Production and Consumption : Agenda for Action, *Economic and Political Weekly*, 36(14 &15):1207 –1225.

Gujrathi, Damodhar (1995) *Basic Econometrics*, McGraw- Hill, Inc: 263 and 502.

Gupta, A. K. (1988) *Sociological Implications of Rural-to-Rural Migration*, Ushra Publishers and Distributors, Allahabad: 18-25.

Gupta, S.P. (1997) *Statistical Methods*, Sultan Chand and Sons, New Delhi, 336.

Heady, E. O. (1946) Production Function from a Random Sample of Farms. *Journal of Farm Economics*, 28:998-1004.

Heady, E.O and Dillon (1961) *Agricultural Production Function*, Kalyani Publisher Ludhiana, 134-135

Jayasree, R. (1999) Impact of TANWA Training on Farm Women, ASPEE Agricultural Research Findings, Abstracts from Thesis of ASPEE fellows, Published by ASPEE Agricultural Research & Development Foundation, Mumbai, 1997: 25

Jyoti, K.S., Gracy and Suryaprakash C. P. (1999) Empowerment and Decision Making by Rural Women–An Economic Study Karnataka, *Indian Journal of Agricultural Economics*, 53 (3): 308.

Kadlag, Sangita (1994) Role of Women in Decision Making in Farming in Sangamner Tahsil of Ahmednagar District, Unpublished Thesis of M .Sc Agril. Economics submitted to MPKV Rahuri, Dist Ahmednagar.

Kalaimathi, A. (1988) Labour Force Participation of Women in Agriculture, *Journal of Ravisankar University*, India, 1 (1): 123-135.

Kasar, D. V. (1992) *Economics of Seasonal Migration*, Classical Publishing Company, New Delhi: 31

Kaur, Malkit (1988) *Rural Women and Technological Advancement*, Discovery Publishing House, New Delhi: 89-105.

Kaur, S. and R. K. Punia (1998) Work Participation of Women in Rural Households–An Empirical Study, *Guru Nanak Journal of Sociology*, 9 (92): 51-77.

Khatik, G.L and Pandey M.B. (1997) Participation of Rural Farm Women in Sugarcane Production, *Gujarat Agricultural University Research Journal*, 23 (1): 62-66.

Kazakopoulos, L. and Gidarakou , I. (2001) Young Women Farmers in Greece: Parameters of their Entrance in Farming: Proceedings of an International Conference, Nicosia, Cyperus, 4-6 October 2001, The Agricultural Research Institute, Nicosia-Cyperus : 223-238.

Khorate, V.S. and D.P. Hardikar (2003) Impact of DWCRA Scheme in Terms of Incomes and Employment Generation, *Maharashtra Journal of Extension Education*, 12 (1): 125-126.

Klein, Lawrence (1962) An Introduction to Econometric, Prentice –Hall, England Cliffs N.J :101.

Kofi, A. Annan (2002) Statement on World Telecommunication Day 2002: Empowering people to Cross the Digital Divide, ISNAR Briefing Paper, 55 Sept, 2002: 4.

Korde, P.P., K.D. Kokate and Shirke, V. S. (2003) Study on Impact of Kal Irrigation Project in Raigad District of Konkan Region, *Maharashtra Journal of Extension Education*, 22 (I) : 35-40.

Koutsoyiannis (1988), Theory of Econometrics, Macmilan Publication, London: 84.

Kumavat, S.R. and S. K. Sharma (2000) Major Constraints in Getting the Benefits Under Different Poverty Eradication Programmes, *Indian Journal of Social Research*, .41 (4): 203-207.

Laximidevi (1988) *Rural Women-Management in Farm and House*, Northern Book Center, New Delhi:14.

Lewiss, O. and H. S. Dhillon (1955) *Leadership and Group in South Indian Villages*, Delhi Publications, 9:146-148.

Logamatha, M. (2001) Employment Pattern and Income Generation by Women in Agriculture in Rasipuram Taluk, Namakkal District- An Economic Analysis, Post Graduate Thesis Abstracts –2001 , M Sc Agri . Economics, Unpublished Thesis Submitted to School of Post Graduate studies TNAU Coimbatore: 19-20.

Mahitha, S. and Hemachandrudu (1992) Resource use Efficiency in Paddy Cultivation in Andhra Pradesh, *Indian Journal of Agricultural Economics*, 47 (3): 497

Mali.B.K., Shinde., Kale, C.B. and Pawar P.P.(2003) Employment Pattern of Farm and Non-Farm Families by Gender Groups in Irrigated Area of Western Maharashtra, *Agricultural Economics Research Review, Conference Issue*, 153.

Malviya, Seema. A (1991) *Communication and Rural Women*, Montek Publication (p) Ltd, Delhi- 9:10-14.

Meenakshisundaram, K,S., R. Vijayraghavan and Natraj, M.S. (2001) Influence of Socio-Personal and Psychological Characteristics of Farm Women towards Their Viewing Behaviour, *Mysore Journal of Agricultural Sciences*, 35:176-179.

Mehta, B.C. and Joshi, Pritam (1993) Impact of IRDP on Income of Tribal Beneficiaries, Journal of Rural Development, NIRD, Hyderabad, 12 (2) : 145-164.

Mellor, John (1976) *The New Economics of Growth*, Comell University Press, New York.

Merton, R. K. (1973) *The Sociology of Science*, Chicago Press, Chicago: 115-165.

Mishra, P.K., R.M. Sahu and Agrawal G. P. (1999) Extent and Proportion of Women's Participation in Paddy Cultivation – A Case Study of Kymore Plateau and Satpura Hills of Madhya Pradesh, *Indian Journal of Agricultural Economics*, 54(3) Seminar Issue: 321.

Mohamed, N.K. (1996) *The Impact of Rural Development Programmes on Women* [Sudan], University of Khartoum, Shambat (Sudan), Department of Rural Economy, Khartoum (Sudan): 97.

Muniyandi,B., C Umamaheswari and J.Umamaheswari (2003) Changes in Rural Non-agricultural Employment in India, *Agricultural Economics Research Review*, Conference issue:48-59.

Nand, H., J. P. Sharma and Janardanjee (1994) Contribution and Decision Making among Farm women with Special Reference to Potato, *Journal of the-Indian Potato Association*, 21(1-2): 106-115.

Narayanamoorthy (1999) Farmers' Education and Productivity of the Crops: A new Approach, *Indian Journal of Indian Economics*, 53 (3):.512-515.

Naresh, N.T. and Narayanagowda, K. (1999) Knowledge Behaviour of Improved Sericulture Practices among Trained Farm Women, *Mysore-Journal-of Agricultural Sciences*, 33 (1): 81-84.

Ohki. R. (1983) Proceedings of the Conference on women in Rice System. Held at IRRI,Phillipines, 26-30, 1983: 55-64.

Panghal B.S., Himmat Singh and Luhach, M.S. (1999) A Comparative Study on the Efficiency of Women Labour in Agriculture in Haryana, *Indian Journal of Agricultural Economics*, 54 (3): 325.

Patnaik, U. (1979) Neo Populism and Marxism: The Chayanovan View of the Agrarian question and the Fundamental Fallacy, *Journal of Peasant Studies*, 6(4): 121, 137,375-420.

Patnaik and Sailabala Devi (1986) An Assessment of Women Economic Contribution to the Farm Sector: A Micro Level Study, *Journal of Rural Development*, 5(4): 480-488.

Puhazheendhi, V., Jayaraman, B. (1999) Increasing Women's Participation and Employment Generation Among Rural Poor : An Approach Through Informal Groups, Indian *Journal of Agricultural Economics*, 53 (3):293.

Punia R.K. Kaur Satnam and Punia Deep (1991) *Women in Agricultural Production Process in Haryana*, Northen Book Center, New Delhi:78-96.

Puri, Shashi (1972) Work Role and Decision Making Pattern of Farm Wives and Husband, Ph.D Unpublished Thesis Submitted to the Extension Division of IARI, New Delhi.

Rahane,Suresh (1996) A Study of Some Selected Aspects of Women Engaged in Bidi Making Occupation, Unpublished Thesis of M.Sc. (Agricultural Extension), MPKV Rahuri.

Rai, K.N., A. C. Gangwar and Grover, Indu (1999) Impact of Central Sector Scheme 'Women in Agriculture' on Rural Women in Haryana, *Indian Journal of Agricultural Economics*, 54 (3): 320.

Rajkishor., Gupta, Bhawana., Yadav, S.R and Singh,T.R.(1999) Role of Rural Women in Decision Making Process in Agriculture in District Sitapur (Uttar Pradesh), *Indian Journal of Agricultural Economics*, 54 (3) :282-285.

Raju, V. T. and D.V.S Rao (1996) *Economics of Farm Production and Management*, Oxford and IBH Publishing Co. Pvt. Ltd.: 123-124.

Ramkrishanan K., Reddy, Ramchandra (2002) Problem Express by Trainees Towards ANTWA Training Programme, *Journal of Extension Education*, 13 (4), Published by society of Extension Education, Tamilnadu Agriculture University, Coimbatore –641003

Rathore, O. S. and K. S. K. Gaur (1996) A Comparative Study on Contribution and Time Utilization Pattern of Farm Women in Tribal and Non-Tribal Areas, *Mysore Journal of Agricultural-Sciences*, 30 (1): 87-92.

Rao, C.H. H. (1966) Alternative Explanation of the Inverse Relationship between Farm Size and Output per Acre in India, *Indian Economic Review*, 1 (2),111-112, 117-121.

Rao, Rati (2002) Technology Opportunity for Women–Multi-Dimensional Approach, Proceedings of the National Workshop on Women in Agriculture held at Delhi. March 2002: 19.

Raut, R.C., D. L. Sale and Pawar, P. P. (1995) Employment, Income and Expenditure of Tribal in Igatpuri Tahsil of Nashik District, *Tribal Research Bulletin*. Sept- 1995: 44-45.

Reddy, N. R. V. (1995) Technological Parameters in Paddy Production Function: a Case Study of Cuddapah District of Andhra Pradesh, *Indian Journal of Economics*, 75 (4): 497-503.

Reddy,V.R. (1993) The New Technology in Agriculture and Changing Size Productivity Relationship-A study of Andhra Pradesh, *Indian Journal of Agricultural Economics*, 48 (9):643.

Rimawi, A. S. (1998) The Contribution of the Jordanian Women Farmers in Plant Production Activities and Participation in the Decision Making Process and its Relationship with Selected Socio-Economic Characteristics, University of Jordan, Jordan, 25 (3) : 425-438.

Roy, Bharati and Basu, Arpana (1999) *Farm Independence toward Freedom: Indian Women since 1947*, Oxford University Press, New Delhi: 248.

Sadamate,V.V. and Sinha. B.P. (1977) Farm Education Through Television, *Indian Journal of Extension Education*, (6) :74-76.

Santha, A. M. (1993) A Comparative Analysis of Cost and Returns of Paddy Cultivation for Different Seasons in Trichur, Kerala, *Madras Agriculture Journal*, 80 (2): 41-44.

Sarma, Bina (1991) Education, Employment and Social Status of Women: A Sociological Analysis, *IASSI Quarterly*, 10 (2): 146.

Schultz, T.W. (1964) *Transforming Traditional Agriculture*, Yale University Press, Yale, New Haren.

Seema., Shaiffali and Candy (2000) Participation Pattern of Rural Women in Post Harvest Activities, *Indian Journal of Social Research*, 41 (30) :193- 197.

Sen, A.K. (1962) An Aspect of Indian Agriculture, *Economics and Political Weekly*, 14 (4,5,6) :243-346

Sen, D. (1993) Role Transition of Women in Agriculture: Some Issues, *Journal of Rural Development*, NIRD Hyderabd, 12 (5): 497-513.

Sethi, Rajmohini (1991) Women in Agriculture, Rawat Publication New Delhi:18-25.

Shea (1936) *The Measurement of Urban Home Environment*, Minnesota University Press :134-145.

Sheokand, R.S., Singh, Narindar., Sheoram, O.P., Pannu, R.S. and Singh, N.(1999) Farm Women and Animal Husbandry Practices in Paddy Belt of Haryana, *Journal of Dairying Food and Home Science*, 18 (2) :85-91.

Shirodkar, Vedika Vilas. (1993) A Study of Participation and Decision Making of Farm Women in Dairy Occupation, Unpublished Thesis of M,.Sc (Agricultural Extension) submitted to Mahatma Phule Krishi Vidyapeeth, Rahuri. Dist. Ahmednagar (Maharashtra):140-149.

Shivamurthy M. (1999) Empowering of Rural Women, A Compendium of Lectures–Summer School on Human Resource Development and Management, Organized by Dte. of Extension, University of Agricultural Science, Hebbal, Banglore, July 1-30,1999: 195- 205

Shriram and M.S. Chouhan (2000) Adoption Gaps in Improved Practices of Wheat Cultivation among Tribal and Non-Tribal Farms, *Maharashtra Journal of Extension Education*, 21: 122-123.

Singh, A.K. and G. P. Singh (1999) Female Work participation and Involvement in Decision Making Process: A study in Uttarakhand, *Indian Journal of Agriculture Economics*, (3): 300.

Singh, B.B. and R. B. Prasad (2000) Effect of Integrated Rural Development Programme on Socio-Economic Status of Beneficiaries, *Maharashtra Journal of Extension Education*, 21: 164-165.

Singh, I.P., Verma, Sunita., Gangwar, A.C. (1992) Resource use Efficiency in Haryana Agriculture –A Crop wise Analysis, *Indian Journal of Agricultural Economics*, 47 (3):509

Singh Ram Iqbal., G.N., Singh and Gupta , B.K. (1992) *IRDP for Employment of Women in Agriculture, Education, Training and Development*, Edited by Punia, Northern Book Centre, New Delhi : 200-203.

Singh. R.K., G. N .Singh and Patel, A. (1999) Women's Role in Rice – Wheat Farming in Uttar Pradesh, *Indian Journal of Agricultural Economics*, 54 (3): 316.

Sujatha, R.V., Eswara Prasad, Y and Vasudeo. N. (2003) Impact of DWCRA –A Rural Non Farm Activity in Guntur district of Andhra Pradesh, *Agricultural Economics Research Review*, Conference Issue-2003: 170.

Sobha, I. (2001) Women in Agriculture -- A case study, *Yojana,* July 200 : 40-4

Subhas Chand (2003) Impact Assessment on Socio-Economic Aspects of Watershed Programmes–A Case Study, *Journal of Rural Development*, NIRD Hyderabad, 22 (4) : 437

Sunandini, G.P., Shaik Haffis., Rama Rao, C.A and Reddy, Y.V.R. (1992) Input Use Efficiency on Paddy Farms in West Godawari District of Andhra Pradesh, *Indian Journal of Agricultural Economics*, 47 (3):547.

Suresha .S. V., Jayaramaiah, K. M. (1996) Constraints of Tribal Farmers in Animal Husbandry and Employment Generation Programme, *Rural India*, 59 (4) : 107-109.

Swell,W.H. (1940) Construction and Standardization of Scale for the Measurement of Socio-Economic Status of Oklahoma Farm Families, *Oklahoma Agricultural Experimental Station, Bulletin*, 9:50.

Talathi, M and Veerkar, P.D. (1992) Productivity Response in Rice Cultivation in Konkan Region (Maharastra), *Indian Journal of Agricultural Economics*, 47 (3): 507-508.

Talukdar,R.K.and Anjali, Karmakar (1997) Problems in Decision Making by Women in Agriculture- A study in Golaghat

District of Assam, *Journal of the Agricultural Science Society of North -East India*, 10 (2): 281-282.

Taussing, F.W. (1928) *Principles of Economics*, Macmillan, London.

Trivedi, G. (1963) Measurement and Analysis of Socio-Economic Status of Rural Famililies, Ph. D Thesis, Extension Division, IARI, New Delhi.

Tawade, N.D. and Nalband, S.B. (1993) Impact of IRDP Assistance on Socio-Economic Conditions of Farmers, *Maharashtra Journal of Extension Education*, 12 : 19-24.

Thakor, R. F. (1996) Decision Making in Farm Business by Rural Women, *Rural India*, 59 (3): 79.

Tiwari, R. and D. P. Dheer (1994) Resource Use Efficiency of Ratoon Sugarcane Farms in North Bihar, *Indian Sugar*, 44 (2): 109-111.

Thomas, T.T., K. J. Thomas and Thomas, E. K. (2003) Socio-Economic Constraints of Watershed Development Programmes in Polakad District in Kerala, *Agriculture Research Review*, 16 (1): 50-54.

Thimmaiah, G., R.N. Hadimani and Campbell, M. J. (1990) *New Technology and Rural Development–The Social Impact*, Rautledge, London (UK) : 37-115

Tuteja, Usha (2000) Contribution of Female Agricultural Workers in Family Income and their Status in Haryana, *Indian Journal of Agricultural Economics*, 55 (2): 32-67

Upendra, K., Singh, V. K., Sinha, R.P and Kumar, V. (1998) Resource Use Efficiency in Rice Cultivation under Different Eco-System of Pusa Block of Samstipur (Bihar), *Journal of Applied Biology*, 8 (2): 78-81.

Uta Hoffmann and Altmann wolfgang Vogler (2001) Women in Decision Making Process in Rural Area of Europe, Proceedings of an International Conference, Nicosia, Cyprus, 4-6 October 2001, The Agricultural Research Institute, Nicosia-Cyprus: 36-37.

Vaish, Sarita., Singh, P. and Mishra, B. (2002) Constraints Analysis Regarding Involvement of Rural Women in Decision Making, *Maharashtra Journal of Extension Education*, 21 (2):131.

Vinkare, D.K and Antwal (2002) Television Viewing Behaviour of Rural Women, *Maharashtra Journal of Extension Education*, 21 (2) :81-83.

Wadkar, S.S., D. B. Malve., Pawar, V. N. and Naik V. C. (1999) Impact of Irrigation on Economic Status of Farm families in Konkan Region, *Maharashtra Journal. of Agricultural Economics*, 9 (1&2) : 20.

Wawire, N. W. O., D. W. Norman and Langemeier, M. R. (1996) Rainfed Rice Production in Western Kenya: Productivity and Profitability, Research Report, Deptt. of Agril. Economics. Kansas State University, 22 – 23: 30.

Wimalasena, R.P., P.R. Galgoda., Koppel, B.M. (1989) The Shrilanka Experience in Rural Transformation. Rural Transformation: Issues for Policy, Planning and Project Development Report: 145-166

Yerriswamy J. and Hugar, L. B. (2001) Resource use Efficiency in Paddy Production under Selected Agricultural Systems in Tungabhadra Project Area, Karnataka., *Journal of Agricultural. Science*, 14 (1): 86-89.

Index

E

F

G

H

I